AGREE EARLY, AGREE OFTEN

The Executive Playbook for High-Stakes Acquisitions

ROWLAND CHEN

Framework Foundry
San Jose, California

Published by Framework Foundry, San Jose, California

First edition, 2026.

ISBN: 979-8-9968162-0-0

http://www.frameworkfoundry.ai

To my wife, Vicki Soll.
We agree early and agree often.

Contents

Preface

In 1989, I walked into one of the most expensive misunderstandings in the history of American business. Five years earlier, Texaco had acquired Getty Oil for roughly $10.1 billion. The acquisition should have been a triumph. Instead, it had become a catastrophe because a rival bidder, Pennzoil, believed it had already reached an agreement to buy Getty, having a memorandum of understanding in hand, when Texaco swept in. Pennzoil filed suit against Texaco.

A Texas jury agreed with Pennzoil and returned a judgment of $7.5 billion in compensatory damages plus an additional $3.0 billion in punitive damages, the largest of its kind at the time. By the time the matter was settled, Texaco had paid Pennzoil $3.0 billion and passed through Chapter 11 bankruptcy to do it.

That was the wreckage. My assignment, with the team I helped lead from 1989 to 1991, was to build something out of it. We called the work the New Texaco. Oil prices had collapsed. The combined firm carried billions in debt from the settlement. Roughly 74,000 people on both sides waited to learn whose jobs would survive a reorganization that touched strategy, finances, structure, process, systems, and culture all at once. We sold unprofitable producing properties, re-valued oil reserves, re-engineered the value chain, restructured the organization, streamlined decision-making, rebuilt systems, and over three years delivered a one-time $1 billion cash influx and $75 million in annualized savings. A New Texaco emerged. It was some of the hardest and most instructive work of my career.

Here is what I took from it. The disaster I was hired to repair was not a market accident. It traced to a single failure at the beginning, an agreement that was never truly nailed down. Getty, Pennzoil, and Texaco had left the most consequential question of all, what exactly had been agreed and by whom, unresolved at the moment it mattered most. Everything that followed, the lawsuit, the judgment, the bankruptcy, the years of painful integration, flowed from that one unsettled question. The cost of clarity at the start would have been a difficult conversation. The cost of avoiding it ran into the billions.

I have spent more than forty years in and around deals and other transformation programs like Texaco's. Across two hundred fifty engagements with firms ranging from the Global 1000 to solo-preneurs, I have experienced dozens of acquisitions that looked identical on spreadsheets in triumph or in wreckage. I have come to believe that the difference rarely lies where executives expect to find it. It does not lie in the price. It does not lie in the investment thesis. It does not lie in integration. It lies in the choice the parties make to confront disagreements that every combination of two organizations must eventually resolve. Confront them early, and three things improve together: the risk of missing the deal thesis falls, the value the deal can create rises, and the cost of resolution stays small. Defer them, and all three move the wrong way at once.

This book argues something that runs against the instinct of most dealmakers. The instinct is to preserve momentum, to avoid the friction that might derail a transaction, to save the contentious questions for after the ink dries. The argument of this book runs counter to that. The firms that succeed are the ones that agree early and agree often. They surface the hard questions while the relationship still has the goodwill to absorb them. They reach alignment on the matters that will otherwise fracture them, and they do it before the close rather than after, when alignment is cheap rather than when it is ruinous.

Agreeing early sounds simple. It is not. It requires a discipline that cuts against the emotional current of every deal, the euphoria of the chase, the fear of losing what has been pursued, and the reluctance to introduce conflict into a courtship. The executives who agree early do not do so by temperament. They do so by method. They have a way of structuring the conversations, sequencing the decisions, and aligning the incentives so that early agreement becomes the path of least resistance rather than an act of heroism. This book is that method.

I did not arrive at these conclusions from a lecture hall, though I have taught in several, including the School of Computer Science at Carnegie Mellon University and, more recently, De Anza College in Cupertino, California. I arrived at them from the engagements themselves, from the deals that worked and, more instructively, from the deals that did not. The frameworks in these pages were built in the field, tested under the pressure of real transactions with real consequences, and refined across decades until they became reliable. They are not theory dressed as practice. They are practices, organized and methodical.

What I offer the reader is not a survey of the academic literature on mergers, nor a collection of war stories told for their entertainment. I offer a set of thinking tools that an executive can carry into the next deal and use. Each chapter takes one of the recurring failures of integration, the failure that looks like bad luck but is in fact predictable, and equips you to see it coming and to prevent it. Mergers and acquisitions are the proving ground in this book because they concentrate, into a few intense months, the alignment challenges that every high-stakes strategic decision faces in slower motion. Master alignment under the pressure of a deal, and you will recognize the same pattern and the same remedy everywhere else you lead.

The stakes deserve naming plainly. The majority of acquisitions fail to deliver the value that justified them. The capital is real, the careers are real, and the negative impact of getting it wrong compounds for years. An executive who reads this book and applies it will not eliminate the difficulty of combining two firms. No method can. What the method can do is move the moment of reckoning forward, from the costly aftermath to the inexpensive beginning, where disagreement is still a conversation rather than a casualty.

I have written the following chapters to be read in order because the argument builds. The early chapters establish why alignment fails and how to recognize the failure before it is irreversible. The chapters that follow build the discipline of agreeing early into a repeatable practice, one tool at a time, and then extend it to the deals so distinctive that they demand tools built expressly for them.

The later chapters carry the discipline beyond any single transaction: how a firm turns it into an institutional capability that outlasts the people who learned it, how a leadership team designs the partnership between human judgment and the artificially intelligent machines now entering the deal room, and how the whole of it comes together as a single process, the rhythm of agreeing early and agreeing often, that gives the book its name. By the final pages, the reader who began skeptical of the premise will, I hope, find it difficult to imagine running a transaction any other way.

The Core Thesis

An acquisitive firm whose leadership teams agree early and agree often is more likely to realize its deal thesis than firms that do not.

Between 2019 and 2024, companies invested approximately $29.2 trillion in mergers and acquisitions. Yet despite decades of experience, sophisticated advisors, extensive due diligence, and increasingly mature integration practices, most acquisitions fail to achieve their intended objectives. Industry studies consistently report failure rates of 60% to 70%, implying that roughly $17 trillion to $20 trillion of value was destroyed during those six years alone. Whether overstated or understated, the investment wasted numbers in the trillions of dollars.

Conventional explanations for acquisition failure are well known. Executives point to overpayment, inadequate due diligence, poor integration planning, cultural incompatibility, or execution problems after the close. While each contributes to failure, they are often symptoms rather than root causes.

The deeper problem is executive misalignment. The chief executive officer sees strategic expansion. The chief financial officer sees cost savings. The head of sales sees revenue growth. The chief technology officer sees new capabilities. The head of human resources sees talent retention. Each viewpoint is valid on its own. Yet collectively, the leadership team may lack a shared understanding of the deal thesis, what success looks like, and how value will be created.

What appears to be an integration problem is often an alignment problem that began long before the transaction closed.

This book advances a simple proposition: acquisitions are more likely to succeed when executive teams agree early and agree often. Alignment must begin before a transaction is signed. It starts during growth strategy formulation, continues through target selection, valuation, negotiation, integration planning, Day 1, throughout execution, and operational handoff.

To support this discipline, I present practical methods and frameworks, built from field experience, designed to help executive teams create, maintain, and periodically reassess alignment. Applied through structured workshops, decision-making sessions, and continuous review processes, these frameworks provide a common language for discussing assumptions, priorities, risks, opportunities, and desired outcomes.

The objective is not to eliminate disagreement. Healthy disagreement is essential to sound decision-making. The objective is to surface disagreements early, resolve them constructively, and ensure that leaders move forward with a shared understanding of what matters most. Disciplined executive alignment can materially increase the probability of realizing the deal thesis, capturing intended value, and joining the ranks of successful acquirers.

The goal of this book is simple: increase the probability that your next acquisition joins the 30% to 40% that achieve their intended strategic and financial objectives

Introduction
The $20 Trillion Problem

Figure I.1. The elephant in the boardroom.

Six blindfolded executives stand around an elephant. Each touches a different part.

One grabs the trunk. "It's a snake!" Another feels the tusk. "It's a spear!" The third wraps arms around a leg. "It's a tree!" The fourth presses hands against the side. "It's a wall!" The fifth holds the tail. "It's a rope!" The sixth touches the ear. "It's a fan!"

Each is partially correct. All are completely wrong.

Remove the blindfolds, and the elephant becomes obvious. Keep them on, and disaster follows. Arguments erupt. Resources scatter. The elephant escapes. Value evaporates.

This ancient parable describes most acquisition integrations. The CEO sees market consolidation. The CFO sees cost efficiencies. The head of sales sees revenue growth. The CTO sees technology acquisition. The COO sees operational efficiency. The head of HR sees talent retention challenges. Each executive touches the same deal but sees something different.

The problem is not that they have different perspectives. The problem is that nobody removes the blindfolds. The executives never align on what they are actually buying and why. They proceed with different mental models. Confusion follows. Value evaporates. The acquisition fails.

Scale of the Problem: $20 Trillion Wasted

The numbers tell a brutal story.

Global acquisition volume totaled $29.2 trillion over the six years from 2019 through 2024. That is not a typo. $29 trillion. More than the GDP of every country except the United States and China. More than the combined market capitalization of the NASDAQ-listed companies ($20.6 trillion as of December 2024). An incomprehensible amount of capital is deployed to buy companies.

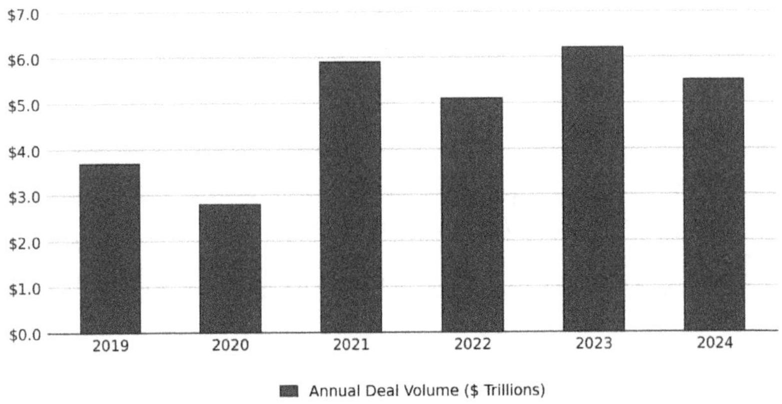

Figure I.2. Global acquisition deal volume totaled $29.2 trillion for the six years 2019 to 2024.

Now consider the failure rate. Every major consulting firm, investment bank, and business school agrees: 60% to 70% of acquisitions fail. McKinsey. Bain. BCG. Goldman Sachs. Alvarez & Marsal. Deloitte. Accenture. PwC. KPMG. M&A Leadership Council. Harvard Business School. They all report similar numbers. The data is consistent across decades, industries, and geographies. Most acquisitions destroy value.

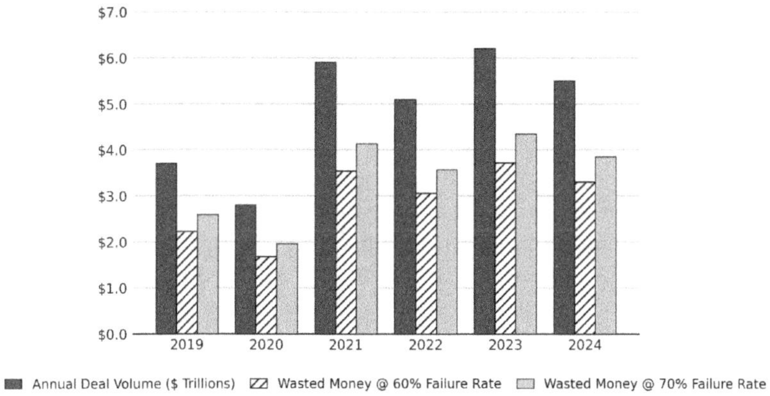

Figure I.3. Cumulatively, $17.5 to $20.4 trillion was wasted in the past 6 years.

Do the "monkey math". 60% to 70% of $29 trillion is $17.5 trillion to $20.4 trillion. That is the amount wasted over six years. Capital deployed. Value destroyed. Shareholder wealth evaporated. Careers damaged. Companies weakened. Employees disrupted. Customers lost.

This is not an acceptable business risk. This is a systematic failure.

The Usual Suspects

Ask why acquisitions fail, and you will hear the standard list:

The acquirer paid too much. Overpaying is real, but rarely the primary cause of failure. Premium multiples can still create value if integration executes well. Reasonable prices can destroy value if integration fails. Price matters. Execution matters more.

Not enough due diligence was performed. Due diligence reveals problems but does not cause failure. You can discover every issue during diligence and still fail integration. You can miss significant problems and still succeed. Diligence informs decisions. Integration creates value.

Adequate integration planning was missing. Planning helps but does not guarantee success. Detailed plans fail if executives are not aligned. Simple plans succeed if everyone knows what matters. Planning is necessary but insufficient.

Integration got off track during execution. Things go wrong in almost every integration. Systems cutovers fail. Customers complain. Employees leave. Competitors attack. Execution problems are symptoms, not causes. The question is why organizations cannot adapt when problems emerge. Usually, because they were not aligned with what mattered in the first place.

Not enough attention was paid to cultural integration. Culture matters enormously. But cultural integration fails when executives hold different views about the target culture. Some want to preserve it. Others want to transform it. Without alignment on a cultural approach, integration fragments. Culture becomes the battleground for unresolved strategic disagreements.

Cost savings were overstated. Revenue gains were never realized. Customers defected. Key employees left prematurely. All these are symptoms of deeper problems. Financial performance improvements fail to materialize because organizations lose focus after the close. Customer and talent attrition happen when integration creates chaos. The root cause is not the specific problem. It is the lack of alignment that prevents smooth execution to reach the investment thesis.

Famous Failures

The graveyard of failed acquisitions is crowded with famous names.

Mattel bought The Learning Company for $3.8 billion in 1998. The acquisition destroyed so much value that Mattel sold the company for pennies a year later. Daimler-Benz merged with Chrysler in 1998 for $36 billion, creating one of history's most studied integration disasters. AOL acquired Netscape for $10 billion in 1999, then bought Time Warner for $162 billion in 2001. Both deals became case studies in value destruction.

Cisco bought Scientific Atlanta for $6.9 billion in 2005. The acquisition never delivered the projected integration gains. Kmart acquired Sears for $11 billion in 2005, combining two struggling retailers into one failed retailer. Google paid $12.5 billion for Motorola in 2012, then sold it at a massive loss. Microsoft spent $7 billion on Nokia in 2013, writing off almost the entire amount within two years.

These were not small companies making amateur mistakes. These were sophisticated acquirers with experienced teams, detailed plans, and significant resources. They had access to top-tier advisors and consultants. They conducted thorough diligence. They paid attention to integration. They failed anyway.

Why? Because having smart people and good processes is not enough. You need those smart people aligned on what matters. Without alignment, expertise fragments. Good processes execute the wrong priorities. Managers deploy resources toward conflicting goals. The organization works hard while going nowhere.

What Failure Means

Acquisition failure has many faces. None is pretty.

The most visible failure is valuation drag. The combined company trades below the sum of the pre-acquisition values. Shareholders lost money. The market punished the acquirer. This shows up in earnings calls, analyst reports, and shareholder lawsuits. It is public. It is quantified. It is painful.

Missed financial goals hurt differently. You projected 20% cost savings. You delivered 8%. You promised a 15% revenue lift. Revenue declined. The business case that justified the premium evaporates. The deal that looked brilliant on paper looks foolish in reality. Credibility suffers. Future M&A becomes harder.

Customer defections compound over time. 5% attrition in year one becomes 10% in year two as service quality degrades and relationships deteriorate. By year three, you have lost significant market share. Competitors that were kind enough not to attack during integration are now taking your customers systematically. Rebuilding takes years.

Revenue disruption shows in the numbers immediately. Sales pipeline collapses because account teams are distracted. Sales cycles extend because customers worry about the acquisition. New business slows because prospects choose competitors who are not in the throes of a merger or acquisition. The revenue hit is immediate. Recovery is slow. Some revenue never comes back.

Cost creep undermines the financial case. The cost of integration exceeds projections. Retention packages balloon. System consolidation costs twice as much as planned. The savings you promised are consumed by the costs you underestimated. Net cost synergy achievement falls short. The CFO struggles to explain the gap.

The loss of key employees creates capability gaps. The acquired company's product leader leaves in month three. The engineering manager who understood the core technology departs in month six. The sales executives with customer relationships exit in month nine. You bought talent. Talent leaves. A major deal driver walked out the door.

These failures do not happen in isolation. They cascade. Customer defections trigger revenue disruption. Revenue shortfalls pressure cost reductions. Cost pressures drive talent loss. Talent loss weakens capabilities. Capability erosion causes customer defections. The death spiral accelerates. Value destruction compounds.

Why Value Realization Is Missed

Even when acquisitions do not fail catastrophically, most fall short of expectations. The deal closes with enthusiasm. Momentum builds. Then value realization stalls. Why?

Early enthusiasm loses steam sixty to ninety days post-close. The initial excitement fades. The adrenaline during the hunt wears off. Deal team members receive tombstones and believe their jobs are done. People realize integration is hard work. Energy dissipates. Progress slows.

Staff driving the deal move on to the next opportunity in the pipeline. The corporate development team that led diligence has another acquisition to manage. The strategy team that developed the thesis has another initiative to support. The champions move on. The integration team loses its advocates.

Other priorities creep in. People's day jobs take precedence over capturing the promised returns. The operations leader has quarterly targets to hit. The sales leader has revenue goals to achieve. The product leader has roadmaps to execute. Integration becomes secondary. Those gains get deferred.

People lose sight of the initial deal rationale. Six months after close, ask integration team members, "Why did the acquisition happen?" You will get different answers. Some remember cost reduction. Others recall revenue growth. A few mention technology innovation. Nobody can articulate the complete thesis. Without a shared understanding of purpose, teams optimize locally. Enterprise value suffers.

30/60/90-day cross-selling plans do not yield desired results. People give up prematurely. The sales team tried to sell the acquired product to existing customers. The response was lukewarm. They conclude it will not work. They stop trying. They never discover that success requires different account strategies, different positioning, and different enablement. They quit prematurely.

Integration is declared completed too early. Day 100 arrives. Systems integration is still in-flight. People and groups are placed on the organization chart, yet responsibilities are unclear. The CEO announces that integration is complete. But value is not realized. Customers are not retained. Capabilities are not transferred. The hard work remains undone. Declaring victory does not create value.

Accountability for value capture gets diffused across the organization. Everyone is responsible. Therefore, nobody is responsible. The finance leader tracks realized gains. The integration leader coordinates workstreams. The business unit leaders execute initiatives. When results fall short, each points to another. Accountability without ownership produces excuses, not results.

The executive team is not in agreement on the integration strategy from the start. This is the root cause of everything else. When executives hold different views about what matters, integration fragments. Different priorities. Different timelines. Different success criteria. Teams receive conflicting guidance. They cannot optimize when they do not know what to optimize for. Misalignment at the top cascades throughout the organization.

A Significant Problem Not to Be Ignored: Blindfolded Executives

Return to the elephant parable. Different perspectives lead to different realities.

The CEO believes the acquisition is about platform expansion. Building scale. Creating market leadership. Establishing a strategic position. This shapes every decision. Resource allocation. Organizational design. Communication priorities. All optimized for platform building.

The CFO believes the acquisition is about cost synergy. Eliminating redundancies. Consolidating functions. Reducing overhead. This shapes different decisions. Headcount targets. Facilities rationalization. System consolidation. All optimized for cost reduction.

The Chief Revenue Officer believes the acquisition is about cross-sell growth. Combining product portfolios. Expanding addressable market. Accelerating revenue. This shapes yet different decisions. Go-to-market strategies. Sales force deployment. Incentive structures. All optimized for revenue growth.

The CTO believes the acquisition is about technology acquisition. Obtaining capabilities. Accelerating product roadmap. Eliminating technical debt. This shapes technical decisions. Technology stack choices. Engineering team structure. Development priorities. All optimized for technology advancement.

Four executives. Four realities. One acquisition. Each is partially correct. All are incomplete. They touch the same elephant but see different things.

The consequences are predictable. Teams receive competing directions. The sales organization hears "drive cross-selling." The operations organization hears "reduce costs." The product organization hears "integrate technology." The strategy organization hears "build a platform." Each pursues its mandate. The mandates conflict. Integration fragments. Value evaporates.

This creates two major risks.

First, falling short of realizing strategic and financial deal theses. When executives optimize for different goals, none are fully achieved. Cost savings fall short because platform building requires investment. Revenue gains disappoint as cost reductions disrupt sales' mindshare. Technology integration stalls because resources focus elsewhere. Every thesis suffers.

Second, a higher probability of confusion, chaos, and churn. Employees do not know which priorities matter. Customers see inconsistent directions and then defect. Key talent leaves. The organization thrashes. Value destruction accelerates.

The Solution: Agree Early, Agree Often

The Chicago way of electing public officials: Vote early, vote often.

Executive alignment is not a one-time event. For maximum effectiveness to increase the probability of acquisition success, alignment is required throughout a deal's ten-stage lifecycle.

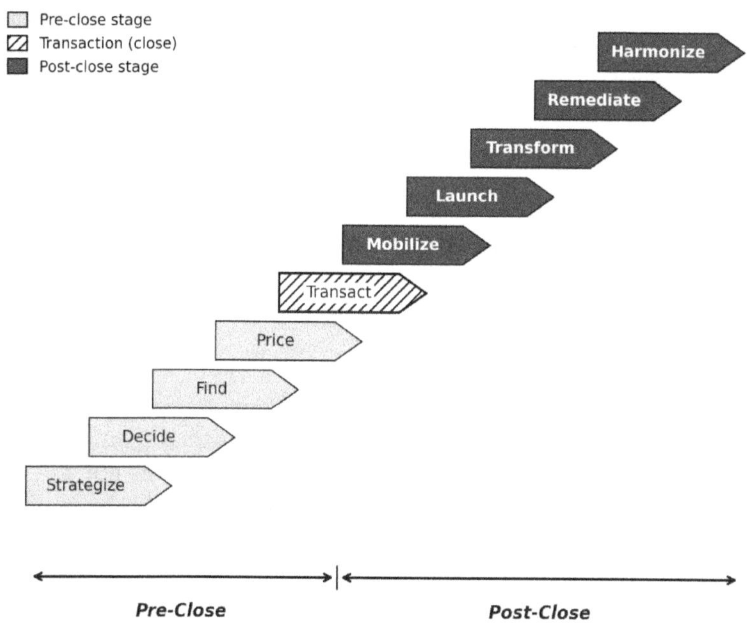

Figure I.4. Ten-stage M&A lifecycle

During the Strategize and Decide stages, align on acquisition criteria. How much and by when do we want to grow? Why? What would make a target attractive? What capabilities are we seeking? What strategic gaps are we filling? Agreements here prevent pursuing deals that do not fit.

During the Find and Price stages, align on the valuation approach. What combined value are we willing to pay for? What risks require proactive mitigation? What integration costs should we model? Agreements here prevent overpaying or walking away from good deals.

During the Transact stage, align on key deal terms. What representations matter most? What indemnifications are essential? What earn-outs make sense? Agreements here prevent post-close disputes.

During the Mobilize stage, the critical window between signing and closing, align on the integration strategy. What is the deal thesis? What does the end-state look like? What is the integration approach? What are the priorities? What are the risks? What assumptions are we making? Agreement here determines integration success or failure.

During the Launch stage, align on days 1 through 10 of strategy execution. What messages do we send? What decisions do we make? What signals do we give? Alignment here sets the tone for the integration and builds confidence. And equally as important as Day 1, the aftermath during Days 2 through 5 can derail teams from all tracks of acquisition integration.

During the Transform, Remediate, and Harmonize stages, align on execution priorities. What initiatives take precedence? What trade-offs are you making? What are you learning? How are you adapting? Are internal and external communications effective? Agreement here maintains momentum and enables course correction.

The principle is simple: achieving agreement early ensures integration starts on the right track. Assessing alignment periodically increases the chances of success. Early and often. Not once. Repeatedly. Alignment is not an event. It is a leadership discipline.

Executive Alignment Workshops

The most effective mechanism for creating and maintaining alignment is through a series of executive workshops. Virtual, in-person, or hybrid. Conduct working sessions to reach agreements on key aspects of an acquisition before you begin.

Ideally, the buyer's senior executives, with occasional attendance by the seller's executives, participate in the workshops. But business-as-usual gets in the way, and mid-managers are often assigned to attend these corporate strategy meetings. Big mistake. Alignment starts at the top and trickles down through an organization.

The objectives are clear. Ensure all executives agree on critical aspects of the acquisition. Not superficial consensus. Real agreement. Tested through discussion. Documented for accountability. Referenced throughout the deal lifecycle.

Provide employees with a consistent vision, guidance on decisions, and credible confidence in leadership. When executives speak with one voice, organizations execute with clarity. When executives speak with different voices, organizations fragment.

Accelerate integration and minimize time to realize multiple deal theses. Aligned teams move faster. They do not waste time resolving conflicting directions. They do not rework decisions. They execute efficiently.

Enable execution with speed, predictability, and control across all organizations. Speed comes from clarity. Predictability comes from alignment. Control comes from a shared understanding of what matters.

Maintain a single voice for internal and external stakeholders. Customers, suppliers, partners, investors, analysts, and employees all hear consistent messages. Consistency builds confidence. Inconsistency breeds doubt.

Secure trust and enthusiasm among customers of pre-acquisition companies. Customers need reassurance. They need to understand what changes and what stays the same. They need to believe the combined company will serve them better. Aligned executives deliver this message credibly.

Identify and provide coaching to executives who might be misaligned. Sometimes misalignment stems from incomplete information. Sometimes from different assumptions. Sometimes from human nature's resistance to change. Workshops surface these issues. Early identification enables intervention. Late identification causes failure. At a minimum, it results in excessive cost of integration.

Executive alignment workshops provide another way to mitigate risks of acquisition failure. They are not silver bullets. They do not guarantee success. But they significantly improve the odds.

What This Book Provides

This book serves four purposes.

First, to help CEOs and their executive teams with the acquisition and integration of firms in the service of growth strategies. The frameworks and tools in this book address real acquisition challenges. They have been devised and tested in actual cases across industries and geographies. They work.

Second, to transfer knowledge about executive alignment frameworks and tools developed on an ongoing basis since 1987. This is not academic theory. This is practitioner knowledge accumulated over nearly four decades. Over two hundred projects. Dozens of acquisitions. Technology companies. Industrial manufacturers. Consumer products. Healthcare. Financial services. The frameworks have been refined through application. The tools have been improved through experience.

Third, to stimulate discussions about acquisitions. Read the frameworks. Debate them with your team. Adapt them to your situation. The conversation they enable matters more than the specific tools. Alignment comes from discussion, not documentation.

Fourth, and importantly, this book is NOT designed to sell you consulting services as other authors do. That is worth stating explicitly because most M&A books are extended sales pitches. They present a framework or two, describe successful engagements, and close with an invitation to hire the author's consulting firm. That is not this book. It gives you the frameworks directly. Use them yourself. Build your own capabilities. If you need help, find good advisors. But you do not need to hire me to benefit from this book. The knowledge is yours. Apply it.

How to Use This Book

Read this book during the formulation or the refresh of your firm's growth strategy. Read it before your next transaction. Read it during a current acquisition integration. Read it after an integration. And then adopt and apply the frameworks presented to you in the book as you determine appropriate.

The frameworks are organized to guide you systematically through executive alignment. Early chapters address the deal thesis and integration strategy. The middle chapters cover specific alignment tools. Later chapters focus on implementation and building institutional capability. Read sequentially or jump to chapters addressing your current severe issues if you do not have the luxury of time.

Use the frameworks in your executive workshops. Do not just read about alignment. Align your team using these tools. The frameworks provide structure for discussions that are hard to have without structure. They surface disagreements that would otherwise remain hidden. They create documented agreements that guide integration.

Adapt the approaches to your situation. Your industry is different. Your organizational culture is different. Your specific deal has unique characteristics. Do not force-fit off-the-rack frameworks to unique situations. Use them as starting points. Modify them as needed. The principle matters more than the specific tool.

Share relevant chapters with your team. Integration is not CEO-only work. Your functional leaders need these frameworks. Your teams need these tools. Your business unit leaders need this perspective. Get the book into the hands of people doing the work. Their success determines your success.

What Comes Next

The following chapters present frameworks, methods, and tools for achieving and maintaining executive alignment. They can be used on their own or in combination with others. Each deal is different, so attention must be paid to selecting the right framework(s) to apply. Selection requires finesse, finesse achieved by experience with multiple deals that have both succeeded and failed.

Chapter 1: Assumptions and Decisions translate strategy into action. Every acquisition operates on assumptions. This framework documents them and converts them into explicit decisions. When assumptions prove false, decisions can be adjusted. When assumptions prove true, confidence builds.

Chapter 2: Deal Thesis Decomposition breaks down vague acquisition rationales into specific, testable value drivers. It prevents the drift that occurs when executives think they agreed but actually assumed different things.

Chapter 3: Strategic Distortions names the nine cognitive shortcuts that quietly bend executive judgment during high-stakes deals. Either-or thinking. Amplifying. Discounting. Each distortion served humans well across millennia, and each now distorts strategy under pressure. The framework introduces business mindfulness (the disciplined practice of recognizing and correcting these distortions before they destroy value) and provides a self-detection guide for spotting them in the room.

Chapter 4: Classes of Integration categorizes acquisitions by integration intensity. Standalone preservation. Synergy capture. Full consumption. Strategic transformation. Each class requires different approaches. Misalignment on class creates chaos and less-than-optimal resource allocation.

Chapter 5: Timing of Multiple Acquisitions aligns executives on speed, sequencing, and realistic probabilities of success. It makes timing assumptions explicit and testable. It prevents disconnects between aggressive timelines and conservative resource commitments.

Chapter 6: Acquisition End-State Vision creates a shared picture of what the combined organization will become. Structure. Capabilities. Market position. Culture. Brand. It answers the question employees always ask: how do we know we are done?

Chapter 7: Adoption of Better Practices challenges the assumption that the buyer always knows best. Sometimes the buyer's practices are superior. Sometimes the seller's practices are better. Sometimes the integration of processes creates something better than either. The framework forces an objective assessment.

Chapter 8: The Organization Heat Map makes organizational risk visible. Which organizations face the greatest challenges? Across which dimensions? The heatmap shows where risk concentrates. The map guides the effective allocation of the cost of integration.

Chapter 9: Tailor-Made Tools addresses what standard frameworks cannot: unique strategic contexts, complex interdependencies, and aspirational visions. When the preceding tools fall short of capturing your situation, custom tools become necessary. The framework enables their creation.

Chapter 10: Building Institutional Capability demonstrates how to build repeatable M&A capability within the organization. Covers knowledge capture, playbook development, training programs, and continuous improvement processes. Particularly relevant for serial acquirers and private equity firms.

Chapter 11: Designing the Human-Machine Deal Team maps artificial intelligence across the ten stages of the acquisition lifecycle. For each stage, it asks how far automation should reach, from manual work to fully agentic A.I. execution, and where human judgment must stay in command. The deal team is a control system: the human owns the setpoint and is accountable for the controller, and the machine processes against them.

Chapter 12: The Process: Agree Early, Agree Often brings the discipline together as a single process. Agreements deferred raise the risk of missing the investment thesis, erode the value the deal can create, and simultaneously run up the cost of resolution. The chapter shows why surfacing disagreement early, while it is still cheap, and returning to it often is the executive discipline that protects the deal.

Conclusion: Remove the Blindfolds brings back the core thesis: executive misalignment is a significant cause of M&A failure, and repeated, systematic alignment is the solution. I provide a roadmap for implementation and a call to action for changing how organizations approach acquisitions.

The Mandate

Remove the blindfolds.

Your executives are touching the same elephant. Some touch a snake. Others touch a wall. Still others touch a rope, a tree, a spear, a fan. Each perspective is correct. All are incomplete. The combination creates chaos. Customers see inconsistent direction. Employees receive conflicting guidance. Integration fragments. Value evaporates. Investment theses are missed.

The solution is purposeful executive alignment. Bring your executives together. Use structured frameworks to surface differing perspectives. Debate differences openly and quickly. Reach a genuine consensus on what matters. Document agreements clearly. Check alignment regularly, typically monthly, as part of acquisition governance. Maintain discipline throughout a deal's lifecycle.

This is not soft work. This is possibly the hardest work in mergers and acquisitions. It requires confronting disagreements you would rather avoid. It demands decisions when ambiguity feels safer. It forces clarity when vagueness is easier. It creates accountability when diffusion of responsibility is more comfortable. Most organizations avoid this work. That is a major reason why most acquisitions fail.

You can be different. You can do the hard work of alignment. You can achieve the clarity that enables success. You can be part of the 30% to 40% that create value rather than the 60% to 70% that destroy it. The frameworks are here. The choice is yours.

$29 trillion has been deployed in acquisitions over six years. $20 trillion has been wasted. That is unacceptable. Change it. Start with your in-flight or next acquisition. Align your team. Execute with discipline. Create value. Prove that mergers and acquisitions can work when done right. Be part of the 30% to 40% of deals that succeed.

The elephant is real. Remove the blindfolds. See it clearly. Then execute the deal successfully.

Chapter 1
Assumptions and Decisions

Figure 1.1. Have these two executives made a decision based on the same assumptions?

The boardroom goes quiet. Ten executives sit around the table, each holding a copy of the integration plan. The acquisition closes in thirty days. The CEO asks the obvious question: 'Are we aligned on what happens next?'

Heads nod. Everyone agrees.

Three months later, the integration is bleeding. The CFO thought they were consolidating plants immediately. The COO thought they had eighteen months. The CMO launched a rebranding initiative that no one authorized. The CTO started an ERP migration that conflicts with the supply chain strategy. Promised returns evaporate. Costs spiral. Key talent walks out the door.

What went wrong? Everyone thought they were aligned. But alignment is not agreement. Alignment is clarity.

This chapter presents a framework that prevents this failure mode. It is built on a simple premise: before you integrate anything, align on everything. Not in broad strokes. In specifics. In decisions. In assumptions that can be validated or invalidated by facts.

Why Assumptions and Decisions Matter

Acquisitions fail for predictable reasons. Leadership assumes different things. Teams work from different playbooks. Value leaks through the cracks between what people think they agreed to and what they actually do.

The solution is not more planning. It is better alignment. Alignment requires three things:

First, explicit assumptions. Not vague hopes. Testable statements about markets, operations, people, and systems. Statements that can be proven right or wrong.

Second, clear decisions. Not intentions. Commitments about what will happen, when it will happen, and who will make it happen.

Third, a shared framework. A common language that spans functions, geographies, and hierarchies. A structure that prevents misalignment before it starts.

The Cost of Misalignment

Consider what happens when executives are not aligned:

Operations builds a plan to consolidate manufacturing within six months. Finance budgets for eighteen months of dual-site costs. The CFO discovers the gap in month four, after the capital has been deployed.

Sales assumes the acquired company's brand will be retired immediately. Marketing assumes it will be maintained for three years. Customers receive conflicting messages. The sales pipeline freezes.

HR designs a retention program for critical talent. Operations identifies who is critical three months too late. Twenty percent of the engineering team has already left.

These failures are not about competence. They are about assumptions. Everyone assumed something different. No one validated what others were assuming. The integration proceeded on divergent paths until the paths collided.

Three Objectives

The assumptions and decisions framework serves three purposes. Each purpose addresses a specific failure mode in acquisition integration.

The first objective: provide guideposts for achieving the deal thesis and value-creation strategies. Acquisitions are bought on a thesis. Revenue gains from cross-selling. Cost savings from shared infrastructure. Geographic expansion. Market share gains. The thesis drives valuation. It justifies the premium. But the path from thesis to value is rarely direct. Markets shift. Competitors respond. Internal resistance emerges. Without clear guideposts, teams drift. They pursue local optimizations that undermine global strategy. The assumptions framework prevents this drift. It translates the thesis into testable assumptions. It makes strategy concrete.

The second objective: provide a starting point for pre- and post-transaction integration planning. Integration planning does not begin on Day 1. It begins before the deal closes. But pre-close planning operates under constraints. Limited access to the target. Confidentiality restrictions. Incomplete information. The assumptions framework gives planning teams a structure to work within these constraints. It allows them to build plans on explicit assumptions rather than perfect information. When information arrives, assumptions can be validated or revised. Plans adjust. But the structure holds.

The third objective: align buy-side executives along key dimensions of integration. This is the hardest objective. It is also the most critical. Executives approach acquisitions with different priorities, different risk tolerances, and different mental models of how integration works. The CFO sees cost savings. The CMO sees revenue lift. The COO sees operational complexity. The CHRO sees retention risk. None of them is wrong. But uncoordinated, they pull in different directions. The assumptions framework forces these differences into the open. It creates a space where executives must reconcile their views before the integration starts. Not by compromise. By clarity.

The Holistic Framework

Successful integrations leverage a holistic approach. This is not theory. It is a method tested across dozens of business transformations at Hewlett-Packard, Apple, Texaco, Hitachi, DuPont, Zeneca Pharmaceuticals, General Motors, and other global firms spanning multiple industries and multiple decades.

The holistic approach recognizes a fundamental truth: acquisitions are complex. Change one component, and you affect all the others. Launch a new product without aligning sales compensation, and the product stalls. Migrate an ERP system without training the workforce, and productivity collapses. Consolidating manufacturing without updating supply chain logistics results in customer delivery interruptions (read "revenue discontinuity").

The framework decomposes integration into seven components. Each component requires its own assumptions and decisions. But the components are interdependent. Decisions in one area constrain choices in others. The framework makes these interdependencies visible.

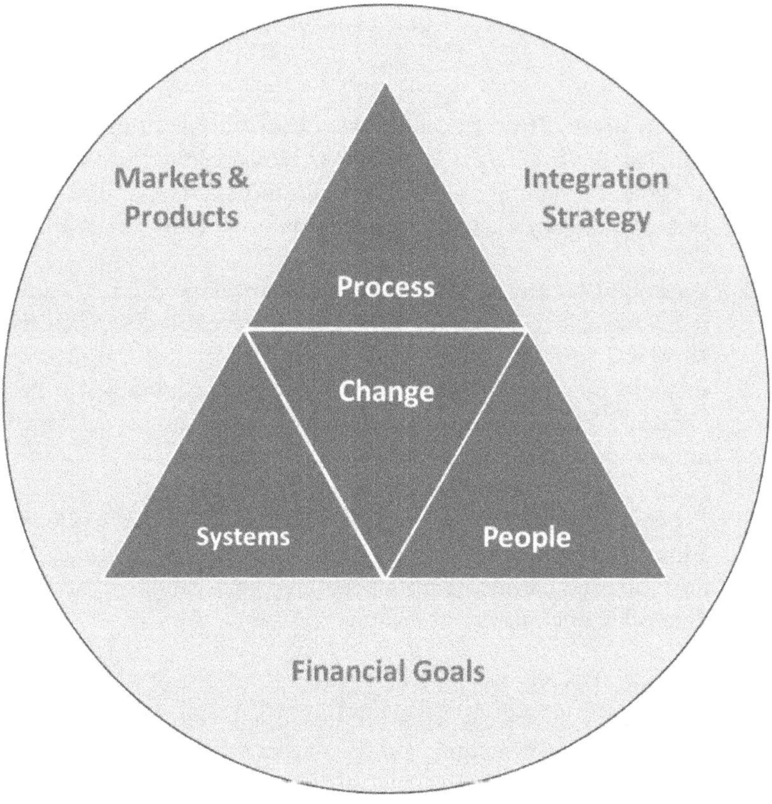

Figure 1.2. Seven components make the approach holistic, inspired by the United Research Company.

The seven components are: Markets and Products, Integration Strategy, Financial Goals, Process, People, Systems, and Change Management. Each component operates at a different level of the organization. Each requires different expertise. But together they form a complete picture of what must happen for the acquisition to succeed.

Why Seven Components

The number seven is not arbitrary. It reflects the core dimensions in which acquisitions create or destroy value. Fewer components and critical elements get overlooked. More components and the framework becomes unwieldy.

1. **Markets and Products** addresses the external dimension. How does the combined entity compete? What does it sell? To whom? At what price? These questions determine whether combined revenue gains materialize.

2. **Integration Strategy** addresses the post-transaction execution dimension. How fast do you move? How deeply do you go? Do you integrate everything or leave some autonomy? These decisions set the pace and scope of acquisition-led transformation.

3. **Financial Goals** addresses the monetary dimension. What are you trying to achieve? What are the targets for revenue, cost, and cash flow? How will you measure it? How much will you need to invest? Is the financial investment thesis sound? Who is accountable for capturing the deal's value? The financials drive behavior and set the tone for the integration environment.

4. **Process** addresses the operational dimension. Whose methods do you adopt? Does the buyer or seller have better policies and practices? How do you standardize without stifling innovation? These choices determine operational efficiency.

5. **People** addresses the human dimension. Who stays? Who goes? How do you retain critical talent? What about culture? Does the buyer impose its own culture on the seller? Is culture change a key component of the value drivers? These factors determine retention strategies for key people in both the seller's and buyer's ranks.

6. **Systems** addresses the technical dimension. Which information technology systems do you keep? Which do you retire? How do you migrate data? When do you consolidate infrastructure? These decisions enable or constrain full implementation of operational strategies.

7. **Change Management** addresses the psychological dimension. How do you communicate? How do you handle resistance? How do you maintain momentum? This component determines whether people can adapt to a changing internal environment, including culture, and how quickly.

The Method

The method is simple. Simplicity is the point. Convoluted approaches confuse situations. Focus is drawn towards debating one theoretical methodology against another, diverting attention from the task, problems, and solutions at hand. Keep it simple, Sam.

Five steps are all that are required. Not to downplay the enormity of the task of agreeing on assumptions and decisions, but the five steps keep moving the executive team forward towards the resolution of any visible and hidden agendas.

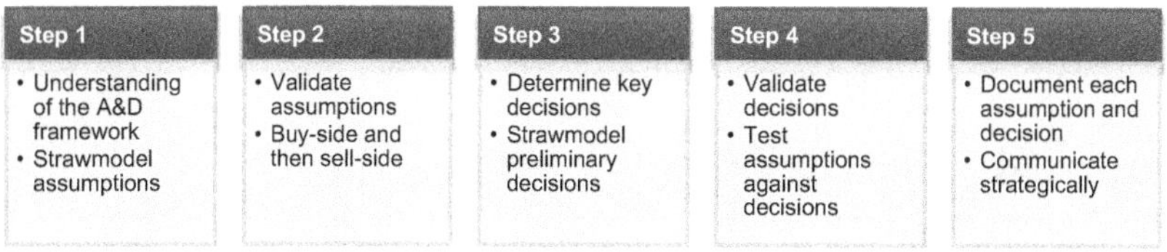

Figure 1.3. Five-step Assumptions and Decisions process.

Step 1: Develop Initial Assumptions

Take each component of the holistic framework. For each component, develop a strawmodel of assumptions. A strawmodel is a starting point. It is wrong. It is supposed to be wrong. The goal is not perfection. The goal is to create something concrete that executives can react to, refine, or reject.

Assumptions must be specific. Not: 'we will achieve synergies.' Instead: 'the acquired company will not cannibalize sales of current products.' Not: 'we will retain key talent.' Instead: 'These key employees in sales, engineering, and operations must be retained.' Not: 'we will integrate systems.' Instead: 'the acquired company's ERP environment is stable and will be migrated in tranches over eighteen months.'

Specificity enables validation. Vague assumptions cannot be tested. Specific assumptions can be proven true or false. When they prove false, plans can adjust. When they prove true, confidence builds.

Step 2: Validate Assumptions

Validation occurs in two directions. First, validate with buy-side executives. Do they agree with the assumptions? Do they see gaps? Do they have information that contradicts the assumptions? Should some assumptions be tested with sell-side executives during due diligence? This validation prevents internal misalignment.

Second, validate with integrationists. These are the people who will execute the plan. Do the assumptions make sense operationally? Are they realistic? What risks do they see? This validation prevents integration strategy failures.

One warning: do not over-analyze. Time is scarce. Pre-close windows are short. Analysis paralysis is a trap. The framework calls these assumptions for a reason. They are not facts. They are educated guesses that will be refined as more information arrives. The goal is good enough to start, not perfect. As a friend in the U.S. Navy once told me, "If the minimum weren't good enough, then it wouldn't be the minimum."

Step 3: Make Initial Decisions

Once assumptions are validated, make a first pass at decisions. Decisions flow from assumptions. If you assume the acquired company's brand has value, decide how to leverage it and for how long. If you assume critical talent is at risk, decide how to retain them. If you assume ERP migration takes eighteen months, decide when to start.

Decisions must be actionable. Not: 'we will address retention.' Instead: 'an employee retention program will be designed and funded before Day 1, and implementation will begin on Day 1.' Not: 'we will integrate manufacturing.' Instead: 'create a Joint Task Force to develop and execute a long-term plant rationalization initiative with no shutdowns or lift-and-shifts in the near term.'

Decisions have owners. Decisions have timelines. Decisions have success criteria. Anything less is an intention, not a decision.

Step 4: Validate Decisions

Validate decisions with the same stakeholders who validated assumptions. This creates a feedback loop. Assumptions inform decisions. Decisions test assumptions. When decisions seem wrong, revisit assumptions. When assumptions change, revisit decisions.

Validation occurs in an executive workshop. In-person is better than virtual. Virtual works if in-person is impossible. The format matters less than the outcome: every executive leaves with the same understanding of what will happen, when it will happen, and who is accountable.

Step 5: Document and Distribute

Write everything down. Assumptions. Decisions. Owners. Timelines. Determine who needs to be in the loop and for what purpose. Distribute the document accordingly. Make certain parts accessible for the sake of change management. Reference it in integration meetings. Update it when assumptions change, or decisions evolve.

Documentation serves two purposes. First, it prevents memory drift. People forget. Details blur. Written records preserve clarity. Second, it creates accountability. When all executives have the same document (and the correct version), no one can claim they thought something different.

Case Example: A Specialty Steel Acquisition

Consider a real case from the specialty steel industry from 2022. The buyer, based in a U.S. midwestern state, acquired a target based in France of similar size in the same industry with complementary products. The key value driver was market share growth, to be achieved through geographic expansion outside the United States. The integration had to preserve the target's European presence while capturing cost savings from shared infrastructure.

This case illustrates how assumptions and decisions translate into action. It also shows the interdependencies between components. A decision in one area triggers assumptions in another. Change propagates through the system.

The following sections walk through each component of the framework. For each component, the buyer developed specific assumptions and made specific decisions. These examples serve as a starting point for any deal, but they must be adapted to the specific context of each acquisition.

Markets and Products

Markets and Products is where value either materializes or evaporates. Combined revenue gains depend on market assumptions holding true. If customers defect, incremental gains vanish. If products cannibalize each other, growth stalls. If channel partners resist, distribution suffers.

The buyer made seven assumptions:

1. The seller will not cannibalize sales of current buyer products. This assumption matters because the two companies had overlapping product lines. If overlap causes internal competition, revenue gains never materialize.

2. The buyer's channel partners' book of business will not suffer due to the presence of a new business-to-consumer capability brought in by the seller. The seller had direct-to-consumer channels. The buyer relied on distributors. Conflict between channels could damage existing relationships.
3. The buyer can leverage the seller's know-how to bring existing buyer products to Europe. This assumption captures the geographic expansion thesis. If it proves false, the acquisition fails to achieve a primary value driver.
4. Customers might defect to competitors for any number of reasons: price, product, service, or relationship. This assumption acknowledges risk. It prevents complacency. It drives retention strategies.
5. Price elasticity: prices of seller and buyer products can be increased. This assumption supports margin expansion. If price increases trigger volume losses, the assumption fails.
6. Any sales force automation initiatives are out of scope for the integration. This assumption creates a boundary. It prevents scope creep. It protects the integration timeline.
7. Seller branding post-close has not yet been determined. This assumption acknowledges uncertainty. It flags a decision that must be made, but does not block integration planning.

From these assumptions, the buyer made five decisions:

1. Key customers of the seller will be embraced by senior leadership. This decision assigns accountability. Senior leaders own customer relationships during the transition.
2. Special sales programs with the buyer are not needed. This decision simplifies execution. It avoids creating parallel incentive structures.
3. Product lines will not be rationalized in the short term. This decision provides stability. It allows the organization to focus on integration rather than portfolio management.
4. Product management functions will be integrated by a specific date. This decision creates a deadline. It forces action.
5. Joint product roadmaps will be developed by a specific date. This decision aligns product innovation and technologists. It ensures the combined company moves in a coordinated direction.

Integration Strategy

Integration Strategy determines how the integration unfolds. Fast or slow. Deep or shallow. Centralized or distributed. These choices affect everything else. They set the rhythm of change.

The buyer made two assumptions:

1. The integration of the seller will be completed in eighteen months or less. This assumption establishes a timeline. It creates urgency. It prevents the integration from becoming permanent.
2. The buyer will have acquisitions of similar complexity and scale in the future. This assumption justifies building reusable integration capabilities rather than one-off processes.

From these assumptions, the buyer made six decisions:

1. The seller integration will adopt a workstream project structure. This decision defines the organizational model. Workstreams create clear boundaries and ownership.
2. Each workstream will be functional in nature. This decision aligns workstreams with the existing organizational structure. It leverages existing expertise.
3. Each workstream will tie to value drivers. This decision ensures focus. Work that does not drive value does not happen.
4. Any integration capability developed will be used for future acquisitions. This decision builds institutional knowledge. It turns integration from a one-time event into a repeatable capability.
5. Develop a global supply chain and manufacturing strategy. This decision addresses operational complexity. It forces the organization to think holistically about physical operations.
6. Create a Joint Task Force to develop and execute a long-term plant rationalization initiative with no shutdowns or lift-and-shifts in the next nine months. This decision balances short-term stability with long-term optimization. It acknowledges that manufacturing consolidation is necessary, but cannot happen immediately.

Financial Goals

Financial Goals translate strategy into numbers. They define a tangible and objective measure of success. They drive accountability. Without clear financial goals, integration becomes an activity without outcomes.

The buyer made two assumptions:

1. Key financial drivers are the valuation of the new combination of two firms, revenue, cost of goods sold, cost of sales, and capital expenditures. This assumption identifies what to measure. It focuses attention on metrics that matter.
2. The preliminary budget for the cost of integration is inadequate. This assumption acknowledges a common failure mode: underestimating integration costs. Integrations typically cost more than initial estimates. Better to acknowledge this reality upfront.

From these assumptions, the buyer made four decisions:

1. $9.2 million will serve as a base case for cost reduction. This decision sets a floor. It establishes minimum expectations. Teams know what they must achieve.
2. Revenue gains will be as important as cost savings for the integration. This decision balances priorities. Many integrations focus exclusively on cost. This buyer recognized that revenue growth mattered equally.
3. A financial scorecard will be used to track the realization of value drivers. This decision creates transparency. Everyone can see progress. Accountability becomes visible.
4. Increase the cost of integration to better practice levels proven effective: 8% to 12% of deal value. This decision allocates resources appropriately. It prevents under-resourcing. It acknowledges that successful integration requires investment.

Process

Process determines how work gets done. Whose methods prevail? Where do better practices reside? I say "better" because no practice is ever truly the best, and improvement should be continuous. How do you standardize without destroying what makes each company effective? These questions have no universal answers. They depend on the specifics of each acquisition.

The buyer made four assumptions:

1. Better practices reside in either the buyer or the seller. This assumption prevents arrogance. It acknowledges that the acquired company has valuable methods worth preserving.

2. A Kaizen approach, as used by the buyer, does not run counter to any existing seller's continuous improvement methodology. This assumption tests compatibility. If the buyer's improvement methods conflict with the seller's culture, adoption will fail if a single process improvement method is not adopted.

3. Plant consolidations are in scope for the integration. This assumption establishes boundaries. It clarifies what can and cannot be changed.

4. Supply chain and manufacturing management will be centralized and integrated. This assumption defines the target operating model. It commits to standardization where it matters most for producing and delivering the right products to the right customers at the right time. "On-time, in-full" is the mantra here.

From these assumptions, the buyer made six decisions:

1. The seller need not adopt the buyer processes in their entirety. This decision preserves autonomy where it makes sense. It prevents forced standardization.

2. The seller will adopt buyer processes selectively. This decision establishes selective integration. Not everything needs to change. It is also a testament to the seller that certain of its processes are world-class, which has enormous positive emotional impacts.

3. The buyer will investigate better practices at the seller. This decision demonstrates respect. It signals that integration is bidirectional.

4. The buyer will adopt seller processes selectively. This decision follows logically from the previous one. If the seller has better methods, adopt them.

5. The buyer's continuous improvement approach will be adopted by the seller. This decision standardizes improvement methodology. It creates a common language for operational excellence.

6. Develop a global supply chain and manufacturing strategy. This decision addresses complexity. It forces strategic thinking about physical operations before tactical execution begins.

People

People make or break integrations. Lose the wrong people, and technical knowledge walks out the door. Lose customer relationships. Lose operational continuity. The people component of integration is where many deals fail silently. The failures do not show up in immediate financial results. They show up six months later when performance deteriorates. No one understands why.

The buyer made five assumptions:

1. There are seller employees who are critical to current and future financial performance in sales, engineering, and operations. This assumption identifies risk. It names the functions where talent loss would hurt most.
2. Achieving investment ROI is at risk, and business continuity is at risk. This assumption escalates the stakes. It frames retention as business-critical, not just HR administrative work.
3. A portion of targeted cost reductions is based on selective downsizing. This assumption acknowledges reality. Some people will lose their jobs. Pretending otherwise creates confusion and ill feelings. Not everyone can work efficiently and effectively with ambiguity
4. Not giving seller employees the buyer's benefits program will have a slight effect on voluntary turnover. This assumption tests sensitivity. If benefits drive retention more than expected, the assumption fails, and the strategy adjusts.
5. Leadership is at risk of flight. This assumption focuses attention on the top of the organization. Executives have options. They will leave if the future looks uncertain.

From these assumptions, the buyer made four decisions:

1. An employee retention program will be designed and funded before Day 1. Implementation will begin on Day 1. This decision creates urgency. Retention programs cannot wait. People make decisions quickly in uncertainty.
2. A severance program will be developed by Day 30 for subsequent implementation. This decision establishes a timeline and enables fairness. People who will lose jobs deserve to know terms quickly.
3. Maintain seller benefits in the interim. This decision reduces immediate disruption. Benefits changes are complex and distracting. Defer them

until core integration work is complete. Timing with open enrollment periods can be advantageous for messaging and for employee satisfaction.

4. A leadership retention program will be designed before close and implemented on Day 1. This decision prioritizes the leadership layer. If leaders leave early, the organization loses direction.

Systems

Systems are infrastructure. They enable everything else. But systems integration is expensive, time-consuming, and risky. Migrate too quickly and operations break. Migrate too slowly, and the organization operates on duplicate infrastructures indefinitely. The systems component requires careful sequencing and clear priorities.

The buyer made four assumptions:

1. Any risks to business continuity are known and will be mitigated. This assumption forces risk identification upfront. It prevents surprises during execution.
2. The seller's ERP environment is stable. This assumption is critical. If the ERP is unstable, migration becomes exponentially more complex. Validation of this assumption is essential.
3. The seller has an active IT project portfolio. This assumption acknowledges ongoing work. The integration must account for projects already in flight.
4. The seller's data centers are optimized. This assumption tests whether infrastructure consolidation makes sense. If the seller's data centers are inefficient, consolidation can create value under the right circumstances. If they are already optimized, leave them alone. Leaders can also determine if and when it makes sense to consolidate data centers.

From these assumptions, the buyer made six decisions:

1. The seller will be migrated to the buyer's infrastructure in tranches, including VPN, email, voice, and network. This decision establishes phased migration. It reduces risk by breaking the work into manageable pieces.

2. Determine sequence and timing. This decision acknowledges that order matters. Some systems must migrate before others. Dependencies must be mapped.

3. Harmonize service-level agreements. This decision standardizes expectations. Users should receive consistent service regardless of which legacy system they came from.

4. Incorporate seller ERP conversion into the existing buyer IT roadmap. This decision integrates rather than separates. The ERP migration is not a standalone project. It is part of the broader IT strategy.

5. Rationalize the seller's portfolio of IT projects, including open tickets. This decision addresses backlog. The integration cannot carry forward every project. Some must be canceled or deferred.

6. Leave seller data centers alone for the interim. This decision defers complexity. Data center consolidation is expensive and risky. It can wait until core integration work is complete. Given today's demand for data, in part driven by the accelerated adoption of artificial intelligence, the safe bet is to follow a philosophy: "If it ain't broke, don't fix it."

Change Management

Change Management is the component most often underestimated and underfunded. Technical integration can be perfect. Financial targets can be met. But if people do not follow, the integration fails. Change management addresses the psychological and cultural dimensions of integration. It is not optional.

The buyer made three assumptions:

1. Change and transition management are critical to the success of the integration. This assumption elevates change management to strategic importance. It is not just a communications exercise. It is a success factor.

2. Rumors about the potential acquisition are already circulating among the seller's people. This assumption acknowledges reality. By the time deals close, rumors have been spreading for months. Silence does not prevent rumors. It makes them worse.

3. A high degree of resistance to change will exist. This assumption prevents complacency among senior leaders. Resistance is normal. Expecting it allows the management to prepare.

From these assumptions, the buyer made three decisions:

1. Establish a dedicated global change management workstream resourced appropriately. This decision commits resources. Change management requires dedicated people with specific expertise. It cannot be an add-on responsibility.
2. Establish a communications channel to address rumors reactively and proactively. This decision creates infrastructure for information flow. Reactive channels address false rumors. Proactive channels shape the narrative. The implementation of this decision was to write and distribute to all employees a weekly email with the subject line "Rumors, Rumors, Rumors", which acknowledged rumors (big and small) and communicated whether or not any particular rumor had validity.
3. Decide on the right change model and apply it immediately. This decision forces methodological choice. Multiple change management frameworks exist. Examples include Elizabeth Kübler-Ross's stages of grief and John Kotter's 8-Stage Change Model. Pick one. Train people on it. Use it consistently.

Putting It into Practice

The framework is not theoretical. It is operational. It works when executives use it to surface disagreements, test assumptions, and make decisions before a transaction is executed. It fails when it becomes a documentation exercise disconnected from real choices and real implementation.

Three principles guide effective implementation:

Principle 1: Start Early

Do not wait until the deal closes to develop assumptions and decisions. Start during due diligence. Information is limited, but that is acceptable. The framework is designed to work with incomplete information. Build assumptions on what you know. Refine them as you learn more.

Early alignment prevents Day 1 chaos. When the deal closes, teams already know what to do. They do not spend the first month debating strategy. They execute

Principle 2: Stay Specific

Vague assumptions are worthless. They sound good, but they tell no one what to do. 'We will achieve synergies' is not an assumption. $9.2 million will serve as a base case for cost reduction, which is an assumption. It can be tested. It can be tracked. It drives action.

Vague decisions are equally worthless. 'We will integrate systems' tells IT nothing. 'The seller will be migrated to buyer infrastructure in tranches over eighteen months, starting with VPN and email,' tells IT exactly what to plan.

Principle 3: Keep Iterating

Assumptions and decisions are not static. They evolve as information improves. An assumption that made sense in due diligence might prove false after close, during deep dives into operational diligence. When that happens, update the assumptions. Revise the decisions. Communicate the changes.

The framework creates a feedback loop. Reality tests assumptions. Assumptions inform decisions. Decisions produce results. Results validate or invalidate assumptions. The cycle continues throughout the integration.

Implications for the CEO

Return to the boardroom. Ten executives around the table. The CEO asks: 'Are we aligned?'

This time, the answer is different. This time, everyone has the same document. The same assumptions. The same decisions. They know what will happen in markets and products. They know the integration strategy. They know the financial goals. They know how processes will be harmonized, how people will be retained, how systems will be migrated, and how change will be managed.

More importantly, they know what they do not know. They have identified assumptions that might prove false. They have flagged decisions that might need revision. They have created a structure for learning as the integration unfolds.

Three months later, the integration is on track. Not perfect. Integrations are never perfect. But the major failure modes have been avoided. Executives are aligned. Teams are executing. When assumptions prove false, the organization adjusts quickly because everyone knows which assumptions matter most.

This is what executive alignment looks like. Not agreement for the sake of agreement. Clarity about what matters. Specificity about what will happen. Transparency about what might change.

The Assumptions and Decisions framework makes this alignment possible. It does not guarantee success, but it eliminates a major cause of failure: executives pulling in different directions because they think they were operating under the same assumptions and decisions when they actually were not.

Use the framework early. Use it specifically. Keep refining it. The investment in alignment before Day 1 pays dividends in achieving a deal's value drivers.

Note: Do Not Get Stuck. Take the First Practical Step.

The Assumptions and Decisions example presented as a case study is ready to use by you and your executive team if you are a manufacturing company. First, start with the assumptions from the specialty steel case, determine which apply to your deal, and which do not. Add, delete, or edit assumptions specific to your transaction. Then, move on to step 2 from Figure 1.3.

Chapter 2
Deal Thesis Decomposition

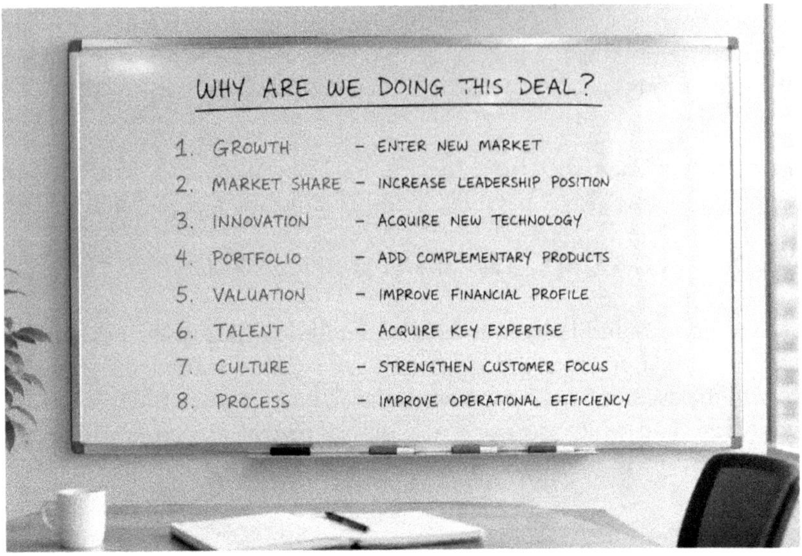

Figure 2.1. The deal.

Here is one question that often kills M&A deals: Why are we doing it?

Simple question. Sometimes hard to answer. In boardrooms across the world, executives fumble it. They point to expected gains. They talk about strategic fit. They wave at market opportunities. But ask them to be specific, ask them what matters most, and the clarity often vanishes.

As we know, 60% to 70% of acquisitions fail. That is not a rounding error. That is a systematic failure to understand what one is buying and why it matters. Many deals die not from bad assets but from confused purposes. When the CEO sees growth, the CFO sees cost savings, and the board sees market consolidation, you do not have a unified strategy. You have three strategies pretending to be one.

Deal Thesis Decomposition (DTD) fixes this. It is a framework, visual, direct, and impossible to hide behind. You take your acquisition rationale and break it into eight value drivers: growth, market share, innovation, portfolio expansion, valuation, talent, culture, and process. Then you do the hard part. You pick the ones that actually matter. Primary drivers get one shade. Secondary drivers get another. No hedging. No saying everything matters equally.

This is not "spray and pray." It is surgical. Think of it as triage in an emergency room. When the patient arrives, doctors do not treat every wound equally. They identify what will kill the patient first and focus on that. When integration teams hit problems, and they will, the DTD tells them what to protect and what to sacrifice. When boards ask tough questions about returns, the decomposition gives you a scorecard. When employees wonder if they still have jobs, the DTD shapes honest answers. Clarity compounds. Confusion kills.

This chapter walks through the framework piece by piece. The chapter examines each value driver, discusses how different industries emphasize different elements, and traces the path from DTD to the realities of integration. The goal is not perfection. It is precision. Know what one is buying. Know why it matters. Know what success looks like. Everything else follows.

Creating Common Ground

The CEO looks at an acquisition target and sees market expansion. The CFO sees operational leverage. The CTO sees a technology platform that solves a three-year roadmap problem. The business unit leader sees competitive threat elimination. Everyone is right. Everyone is also working from different playbooks.

This divergence often does not surface until it is too late. Due diligence proceeds with people nodding in meetings while harboring fundamentally different assumptions about value creation. The deal closes. Integration starts. That is when the fractures open. Sales wants to preserve the target's go-to-market model. Operations wants to consolidate immediately. Finance wants cost cuts. Product wants autonomy for the engineering team. Each group thinks its priority reflects the deal logic. None of them is wrong, exactly. But they cannot all be right.

DTD forces the conversation early. Picture a room full of executives, each carrying a different map to the same destination. Before anyone takes a step, you compare the maps. You gather the stakeholders. You map the value drivers. You debate which ones justify the premium you are paying. Then you commit. This becomes the shared reference point. When trade-offs emerge, and they always do, you do not argue from scratch. You point to the DTD. "We said growth was primary. That means we protect the sales team and accept higher costs in year one." Done. Next problem.

The board benefits too. Directors cannot evaluate deals they do not understand. When management presents a transaction as generically "strategic" without specificity about value creation, directors are forced to trust rather than evaluate. That is not governance. That is faith. A decomposed deal thesis lets directors do their job. They can probe assumptions about growth rates, challenge claims about market position, or question whether talent retention is realistic. The conversation elevates from "do we like this deal?" to "do we believe these specific value drivers will materialize?"

Visual Clarity

Words hide complexity. Pictures expose it.

A ten-page memo about acquisition rationale lets writers bury the key points under qualifications and caveats. A visual diagram does not. You have a central node, the DTD, connected to eight potential value drivers. Each driver is marked to show priority. Primary drivers stand out in solid dark boxes, labeled primary. Secondary drivers sit in light boxes, labeled secondary. That is it. One glance tells you what matters.

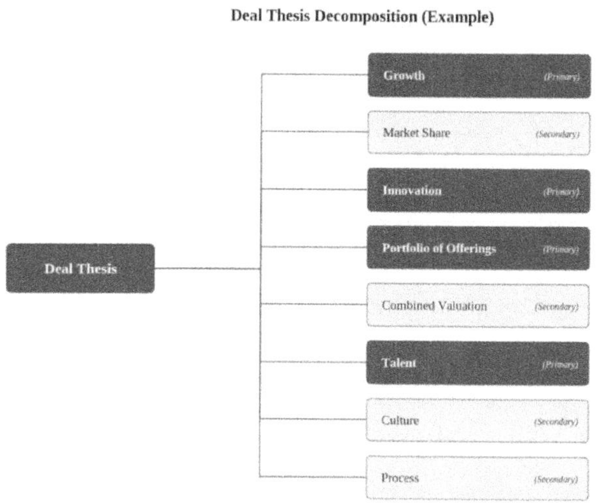

Figure 2.2. A Deal Thesis Decomposition unveils the primary value drivers.

This visual compression forces discipline. You cannot say everything is important when you are limited to a single diagram. You must choose. That choice, that explicit prioritization, is where strategy lives. Not in the comprehensive list of potential benefits. In the short list of financial performance gains that justify the price.

The format also enables comparison. When you are evaluating three acquisition targets, you can place their DTD diagrams side by side. Target A offers strong growth and innovation but weak market share gains. Target B delivers market consolidation and cost savings but limited growth. Target C brings talent and culture but requires significant investment in innovation and the portfolio of offerings. These trade-offs, obscured in prose, become obvious in visual form. The decision criteria crystallize.

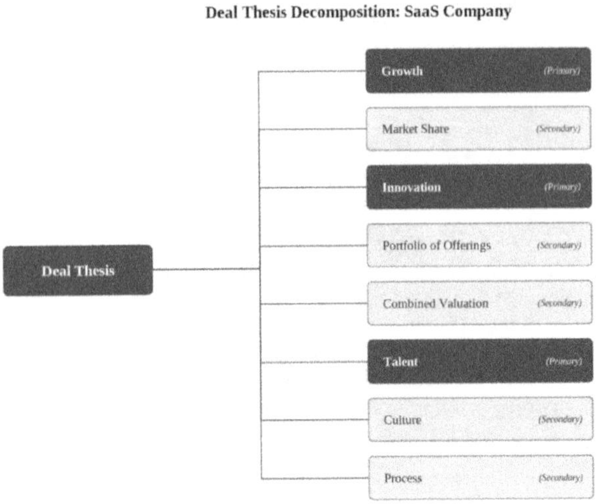

Figure 2.3. Deal Thesis Decomposition for a software-as-a-service (SaaS) company.

Speed matters, also. Executives do not have time to read thirty-page decks before every deal discussion. They do have time to look at a diagram. The visual format respects attention scarcity while maintaining analytical rigor. You can go deep when needed. Each value driver has supporting analysis behind it. But you start with clarity, not detail.

The Bridge to Integration

Strategy without execution is daydreaming. The Deal Thesis Decomposition builds one of several possible bridges.

Integration teams need direction, the way a construction crew needs blueprints. They face a thousand decisions about which systems to keep, which processes to standardize, which people to retain, and which customers to prioritize. Without a clear DTD, they default to what is easiest: impose the acquirer's way of doing things across the board. This organizational imperialism destroys value. It eliminates the very capabilities you acquired while creating resentment and driving talent away.

A Decomposition gives integration teams a filter. Start with the primary value drivers. If innovation is primary, you protect the target's R&D culture and engineering practices even if they differ from corporate standards. If market share is key, you move quickly on cross-selling, even if it disrupts the target's sales motion. If talent is primary, you build retention programs before you worry about process harmonization. Each value driver implies a different integration approach.

This also enables systematic value driver identification. Take each primary value driver and decompose it further. Growth? Map all the ways the combination could accelerate revenue: cross-selling, geographic expansion, product bundling, channel leverage. Market share? Identify all major competitors' vulnerabilities and exploit them. The Decomposition does not give you the answers. It gives you the right questions.

Most importantly, the thesis creates accountability. You said growth was primary. Six months later, revenue is declining. That is a problem. You cannot claim success based on cost savings you never promised to prioritize. The thesis becomes the scorecard. It tells you whether you are winning or losing the game you said you were playing.

Case Example: The Decomposition Behind Figure 2.3

The decomposition in Figure 2.3 began as a fight.

A mid-cap enterprise software firm had agreed to acquire a smaller vertical SaaS provider at a price 40% above its last funding round. The deal cleared the board on a thesis that everyone endorsed, and no one had examined. Then the executive team sat down to build the Deal Thesis Decomposition, and the endorsement came apart.

The CEO marked growth as primary. The target opened a vertical the firm could not reach organically, and the cross-sell opportunity justified the premium. The CFO marked valuation as primary. The target's revenue carried a higher multiple, and the combined entity would re-rate. The chief revenue officer marked the portfolio as primary. Her sales force needed the product to defend accounts under competitive attack. Three executives. Three primary drivers. One diagram with room to emphasize only a few.

The debate took two sessions. The CFO conceded that multiple arbitrage was an outcome, not a driver; the market would re-rate the firm only if revenue actually accelerated. Valuation moved to secondary. Growth and portfolio stayed primary, with talent secondary, because the target's engineers were essential to both. The team documented the reasoning behind each choice.

The decomposition earned its keep six months after close. Integration costs ran over budget, and the CFO proposed reducing the target's customer success team to recover the variance. The integration leader pointed to the diagram. Growth was primary. The customer success team drove improvements in customer lifetime value, which in turn drove growth. The cut would have rescued the quarter and damaged the thesis. The proposal died in one meeting because the argument had already been settled in the first one. That is what the decomposition buys. Not better intentions. Faster decisions when intentions collide with events.

The Value Drivers

Growth

Growth is the most seductive value driver. It is also the hardest to deliver.

When you mark growth as primary, you are making a specific bet: this combination will generate faster revenue expansion than either company could achieve alone. That revenue acceleration will create enough value to justify the acquisition premium plus integration costs plus the opportunity cost of deploying that capital elsewhere. It is a high bar. Most acquirers clear it in their models, but not in reality.

Growth materializes through several mechanisms. Geographic expansion opens new markets where you had no presence. Product extension fills gaps in your offerings. Customer penetration increases the share of wallet with existing accounts. Channel addition provides new routes to market. Each mechanism has different risk profiles and execution requirements. Geographic expansion requires local market knowledge and regulatory navigation. Product extension depends on sales force capability and customer receptiveness. Customer penetration needs deep relationship management. Channel addition can create conflict with existing distribution partners.

The fundamental challenge with revenue gains is that you cannot control them unilaterally. Cost savings? You can force those. Close a facility, lay off redundant staff, and consolidate vendors. The savings appear. Growth requires customers to say yes. Customers are fickle. They resist change. They worry about service quality during integration. They use the acquisition as leverage to renegotiate terms. Your best customers might be your target's competitors. Your target's best customers might be your competitors. Navigation gets complex fast.

Integration creates drag. Think of two rowing crews trying to synchronize mid-race. Your sales team needs to learn the target's products. The target's sales team needs to learn yours. Both teams are distracted by organizational uncertainty and compensation changes. The first six months usually see revenue decline, not grow. You need conviction and patience to weather this valley. Most management teams panic and pivot to cost-cutting, abandoning the growth thesis that justified the deal.

When growth works, though, it works big. Revenue gains compound. A 5% revenue lift in year one becomes 10% in year three as cross-selling deepens and market presence strengthens. This creates a sustainable competitive advantage that pure cost plays cannot match. The math works. The execution is just brutal.

Market Share

Market share grab is growth's tough cousin with regulatory concerns in the foreground.

When market share drives the thesis, you are not expanding the pie. You are grabbing a bigger slice of the existing pie. Think of it as an old-growth forest where no new trees will sprout. The only way to get bigger is to absorb your neighbors. You are buying a competitor, consolidating operations, reducing market competition, and harvesting the benefits of increased scale. This logic dominates mature industries where organic growth remains scarce and competitive dynamics remain stable.

Scale creates real advantages. Your cost per unit drops as you spread fixed costs across a higher volume. Your negotiating power with suppliers strengthens. Your brand becomes harder for customers to ignore. Industry pricing improves as excess capacity exits the market. These benefits are measurable and achievable.

The execution playbook is well-established. You identify overlapping facilities and close the least efficient ones. You consolidate back-office functions, including finance, HR, and IT, into shared services. You rationalize product lines and eliminate redundant SKUs. You merge sales forces and optimize territory coverage. You renegotiate supplier contracts using combined volume. You standardize processes and systems to eliminate waste. Each of these moves has a clear business case and timeline.

Regulators watch these deals closely. Antitrust review can drag on for months. Authorities might require divestitures that gut the strategic logic. They might impose pricing restrictions or market conduct requirements that limit your ability to capitalize on scale. The risk of deal block is not zero, especially in concentrated industries or when you are already a major player.

The human cost is real. Market share deals mean layoffs. Facility closures. Career disruption for people who did nothing wrong except work for the company that got bought. You can execute with dignity and fairness, but you cannot eliminate the pain. This reality tests management character and organizational culture. How you handle these moments defines who you are.

Done right, market share consolidation creates durable value. You emerge as the scale leader in your industry. Your cost position is unassailable. Your market presence is dominant. Competitors struggle to match your economics. That advantage funds future investments and protects profitability across market cycles. It is not flashy. It works.

Innovation

Innovation acquisitions are all about time. You are buying speed.

The logic is straightforward: building this capability internally would take three years and might not work. Buying it takes six months and delivers proven technology, tested products, and experienced teams. The opportunity window might close before internal development finishes. The competitive threat might materialize faster than you can respond. Acquisition becomes the only viable path.

What you are really acquiring varies. Sometimes it is a technology platform, a core system, or an algorithm that enables new capabilities. Sometimes it is intellectual property, such as patents or trade secrets, that creates market barriers. Sometimes it is engineering talent that is impossible to recruit in the open market. Sometimes it is an innovation culture and R&D methodology that could transform your organization. Each requires a different due diligence and integration strategy.

The integration paradox hits hard here. You need to extract value from the acquisition. That means some level of integration, resource sharing, and strategic direction. But heavy-handed integration kills innovation. As with organ transplantation, the body's immune system attacks foreign tissue. The engineers who thrived in a startup environment do not want to follow corporate processes. The product team that moved fast and broke things chafes under risk management and compliance requirements. Push too hard. They leave. Be too hands-off, and you miss the investment thesis.

Valuation

Valuation is guesswork dressed up as analysis.

You are paying for future cash flows from products that might not exist yet, serving markets that might not materialize, using technologies that might get leapfrogged. Comparable company analysis helps, but only goes so far when the target is doing something genuinely novel. You are making a bet on potential, not performance. That bet might pay off spectacularly or fail. Middle outcomes are rare.

Smart acquirers develop specialized integration approaches for innovation deals. They grant acquired teams substantial autonomy. They preserve compensation structures and equity incentives. They provide access to resources, including customer relationships, distribution channels, and operational infrastructure, without imposing processes. They set clear outcome metrics but allow flexibility on methods. They accept that some target practices might be better than corporate standards and deserve to be spread, not eliminated.

When innovation acquisitions work, they reshape your competitive position. You enter new markets, defend existing ones, or leapfrog competitors who are still building capabilities internally. You attract better talent because you are now working on the industry's most interesting problems. You create options for future growth that did not exist before. Value compounds beyond the initial transaction.

Portfolio of Offerings

Portfolio expansion is about wallet share. Get more from each customer.

The thesis is simple: your customers need things you do not sell. Your target sells those things. Combine the companies, and you can sell more to the same customer base without increasing sales costs. This is particularly powerful in business-to-business contexts where customers prefer vendor consolidation and value integrated solutions over point products.

Cross-selling looks easy on paper. Your sales team already has relationships with a thousand customers. Just train them on the target's products and start selling. In practice, it is hard. Your salespeople know their existing products cold. They have spent years building expertise and credibility. Now you are asking them to sell something new while maintaining their core business quota. Learning curves are real. Credibility takes time to build. Early attempts often fail, damaging confidence and momentum.

Solution bundling creates value when customers genuinely prefer integrated offerings. Buying one customer relationship management system, one enterprise resource planning platform, and one data analytics tool from a single vendor simplifies a customer's experience, ensures compatibility, and consolidates support. But forced bundling backfires. If customers see your combined offering as inferior to best-of-breed alternatives, they unbundle despite the ease-of-doing-business promise. You need real product integration, not just packaging.

Channel conflict emerges when you and the target serve overlapping customers through different routes. You might go direct while they use distributors. You might focus on enterprise while they serve mid-market through partners. Combining these channels requires careful orchestration. Distributors worry about disintermediation. Direct sales teams resent sharing accounts. Partners fear they will lose access to products. Managing these tensions demands clear policies, fair treatment, and consistent communication.

Product roadmap prioritization becomes more complex as the portfolio broadens. Engineering resources are finite. You cannot invest equally in all product lines. Some will get more attention and funding. Others will enter maintenance mode. These decisions create winners and losers internally. The target's team worries their products will be deprioritized. Your team worries about resource dilution. Strong product management becomes critical.

When portfolio expansion delivers, it transforms customer economics. You increase revenue per customer without proportional cost increases. Customer lifetime value rises. Churn decreases because switching costs increase with solution breadth. You become more strategic to your customers, making you harder to replace. These dynamics create durable competitive advantages that pure product innovation often cannot match.

Combined Valuation

Financial engineering is typically not strategic. But it is still valuable.

When the combined valuation is the primary driver, the thesis rests on financial mechanics rather than operational improvements. The combined entity will trade at higher multiples, access cheaper capital, or generate better returns through financial optimization. This makes some people uncomfortable. It feels like gimmickry. But creating shareholder value through financial structure is legitimate if done transparently and legally.

Multiple arbitrage is the clearest mechanism. Your company trades at twenty times earnings. The target trades at twelve times. You buy the target, and the market applies your multiple to their earnings. Instant value creation. This works when the market believes the combined earnings are more valuable, perhaps because they are more predictable, faster-growing, or part of a more attractive business model. It stops working when the market sees through the arbitrage and reprices your multiple downward.

Capital structure optimization creates value through better leverage, cheaper debt, or more efficient cash deployment. Larger companies access capital markets on better terms. They can refinance the target's expensive debt with cheaper corporate borrowing. They can optimize capital allocation across a broader asset base, moving cash from mature businesses to growth opportunities. They can use combined cash flows to support higher leverage ratios that boost return on equity. These are not trivial benefits.

Tax efficiency drives many deals. You can utilize net operating losses that the target could not monetize on its own. You can optimize legal entity structure across jurisdictions to minimize tax burden. You can relocate intellectual property to lower-tax domiciles. Regulators scrutinize these moves carefully, but legal tax optimization remains a legitimate source of value.

The problem with financial value creation is sustainability. Market conditions change. Multiple gaps narrow. Tax laws evolve. Interest rates rise. The financial benefits that looked durable at close can evaporate. Smart acquirers layer financial value on top of operational value, not as a substitute for it. Financial engineering is the cherry, not the sundae.

Talent

In knowledge businesses, you are buying people. And today, nearly every business is a knowledge business.

Talent as a primary driver acknowledges a hard truth: certain skills are impossible to recruit at scale in reasonable timeframes. The market for top engineers, data scientists, designers, or domain experts is tight. Building teams from scratch takes years. By the time you are staffed up, the market opportunity might have passed. Acquisition becomes the only path to competitive speed.

What makes "tech and talent" acquisitions distinct is the portability of the asset. Factories do not walk out the door if they are unhappy. Software engineers do. You can own a patent or a customer list, but you cannot own people. This creates unique retention challenges. The very uncertainty of acquisition drives attrition. Key employees leave during due diligence, after close, or during integration when they realize the new environment and culture do not fit them.

Leadership acquisition brings proven executives who can drive transformation, enter new markets, or solve specific operational challenges. But successful entrepreneurs often struggle inside corporate structures. The speed they are used to slows down. The autonomy they enjoyed disappears. The bureaucracy they avoided now constrains them. Many do not last. Those that thrive either adapt to corporate reality or convince the acquirer to preserve the startup's dynamics.

Team acquisition is about preserving working relationships and institutional knowledge. A high-performing team is more than the sum of individual talents. They have developed communication patterns, shared context, and collaborative rhythms. Scatter that team through your organization, and you destroy the very capability you acquired. Smart acquirers keep teams intact, even if it creates organizational awkwardness or duplication.

Retention packages are expensive and create internal equity problems. You are paying the target's employees more than comparable people in your organization. That breeds resentment. But if you do not pay up, the talent leaves and the acquisition value evaporates. There is no clean answer. You balance fairness to existing employees against retention of critical new talent. Someone is always unhappy.

When talent deals work, they transform your capabilities. You suddenly have expertise you could not build internally. You can compete in new markets or technologies. You attract other top talent who want to work with the best. The knowledge and skills diffuse through your organization, raising everyone's game. But getting there requires treating acquired talent with respect, preserving what made them great, and accepting that they will operate differently from your legacy organization.

Culture

Culture as a value driver sounds soft. It is not.

When you mark culture as primary, you are making a specific bet: the target's way of working, thinking, and operating is valuable enough to acquire, preserve, and potentially spread through your organization. This might be innovation culture, customer obsession, operational discipline, speed of execution, or entrepreneurial mindset. The key is recognizing that these attributes are strategic assets, not integration challenges to be managed away.

Culture lives in behaviors, not documents. It is how people make decisions when nobody is watching. It is what they optimize for when trade-offs emerge. It is who gets promoted and who gets sidelined. It is what is celebrated and what is punished. These patterns are rarely explicit. They are encoded in stories, norms, and unwritten rules. Due diligence cannot capture them fully. You have to experience them.

The integration challenge is fundamental: how do you preserve cultural attributes within the current organizations while upending the seller's normal mode of operation? Heavy integration destroys culture. Light integration fails to transfer it to the broader organization. The answer lies in selective preservation. You identify which cultural elements are valuable and build protective barriers around them. You grant autonomy in areas that matter culturally while integrating where it does not.

Culture clash is real. The target values speed, and the acquirer values methodical process. The target accepts risk. The acquirer demands certainty. The target is informal. The acquirer is hierarchical. These differences create friction. People from each side assume their way is obviously correct and the other side is dysfunctional. Without active management, one culture dominates, usually the acquirer's, and you lose what you paid to acquire.

Successful culture integration requires humility from the acquirer. You have to believe the target might do some things better than you do. You have to be willing to learn rather than just dictate. You have to check your organizational ego at the door. This is harder than it sounds. Companies that are successful enough to make acquisitions often develop strong cultures that drive that success. Admitting another culture has merit feels like betraying your own.

When culture acquisitions work, they inject vitality into established organizations. The seller's innovation mindset spreads. The customer-first orientation takes root. The bias for action accelerates decision-making. These changes are hard to measure but easy to feel. The organization becomes more dynamic, more confident, more capable. That is worth real money, even if the accountants cannot put it in a spreadsheet.

Process

Process is where discipline meets value.

When process is primary, you are acquiring superior operating models, proven workflows, or efficiency-generating systems. This matters most in industries where execution excellence drives competitive advantage. Manufacturing, logistics, retail operations, and financial processing all qualify. These businesses win through superior process discipline. Better processes mean lower costs, higher quality, faster cycle times, and improved customer satisfaction.

Better practice transfer is the core mechanism. One organization has figured out how to do something better: reduce defects, accelerate turnaround, optimize inventory, and improve yield. Acquiring that organization gives you access to those practices. But knowledge transfer is hard. Processes are embedded in systems, people, and culture. Extracting them and implementing them elsewhere requires patience, investment, and change management capabilities.

Standardization creates scale economies. When both organizations use different processes for the same function, you are maintaining duplicate infrastructure, split vendor relationships, and fragmented learning. Standardizing on the best approach eliminates waste. But people resist standardization. The target's team thinks their process is superior. Your team does not want to change. Both sides have legitimate concerns. Effective navigation requires data, respect, and a willingness to adopt either approach based on merit, not organizational politics.

Automation opportunities multiply at scale. Process harmonization enables technology investments that were not viable at a smaller scale. You can build or buy systems that automate manual work, reduce errors, and improve consistency. But automation requires standardized inputs and workflows. You cannot automate chaos. Process integration must precede technology integration.

The challenge with process-focused deals is the timeframe. Benefits materialize slowly. You need to assess current processes, design the future state, manage change, train people, and embed new behaviors. This takes quarters, not weeks. Management teams under pressure for quick wins often abandon process improvement for more rapid cost cuts. They hit near-term targets but miss long-term value.

When process acquisitions deliver, they create sustainable advantages. Your cost position improves permanently, not just through one-time headcount reduction. Your quality becomes a differentiator. Your cycle times create competitive separation. These advantages compound over time and resist competitive imitation. They are not glamorous. They are durable.

Industry Patterns

Technology: Speed Above All

Technology acquisitions prioritize growth, innovation, and talent. Market share barely registers.

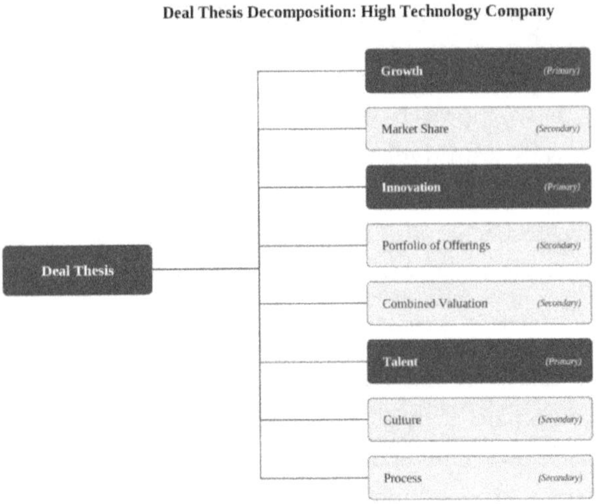

Figure 2.4. Deal Thesis Decomposition for a high-technology company.

This pattern reflects technology market dynamics. Winner-take-all effects dominate. Network effects create exponential advantages for market leaders. First-mover benefits compound. Getting big fast matters more than getting profitable slowly. This shapes acquisition strategy. Firms acquire firms to accelerate growth, add capabilities, or grab talent before competitors do.

Growth is primary because scale creates defensibility in digital markets. Larger user bases attract more developers. More developers create better products. Better products attract more users. This flywheel accelerates with size. Acquisitions that add users, expand geographic reach, or open new market segments feed the flywheel. You pay up for growth because growth compounds.

Innovation drives deals because technology cycles move fast. Last year's advantage becomes this year's table stakes. You either innovate continuously or get disrupted. Building every capability internally is too slow. Acquisition provides speed. You buy the next generation of technology, enter adjacent markets, or acquire defensive capabilities before competitors turn them into offensive weapons.

Talent matters because software development, data science, and product management are scarce skills. The best people have multiple options. They cluster at companies working on interesting problems with strong teams. Acquiring those companies gives you access to talent pools you could not recruit on your own. Many technology acquisitions are talent deals with products attached. The real value walks out the door each night.

Process and culture receive less emphasis because technology businesses prioritize speed and innovation over operational efficiency. Standardization slows things down. Bureaucracy kills creativity. The bias is toward diversity and autonomy rather than integration and control. This creates messy organizations but preserves entrepreneurial energy.

Integration approaches match these priorities. Technology acquirers grant substantial autonomy to preserve innovation velocity. They use earn-outs tied to growth or product milestones. They maintain separate brands and go-to-market motions when appropriate. They accept organizational complexity as the price of preserving what made the target valuable. The integration playbook is light-touch by design.

Consumer Products: Scale and Distribution

Consumer deals emphasize market share, portfolio expansion, and financial optimization. Innovation drops to secondary.

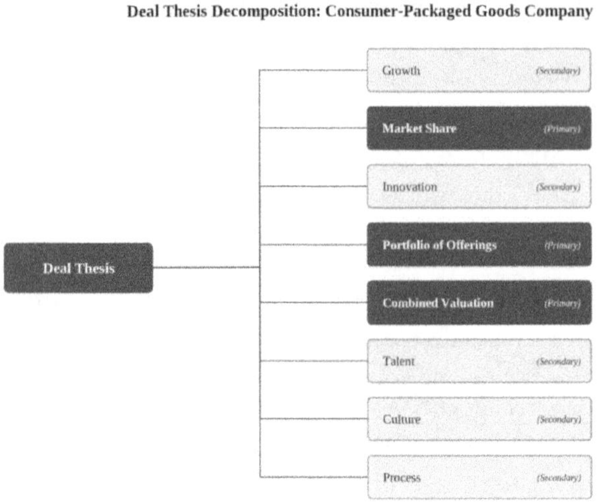

Figure 2.5. Deal Thesis Decomposition for a consumer-packaged goods company.

Consumer markets are mature and consolidated. Organic growth is hard. Category penetration is high. Consumer preferences are established. The path to value creation runs through market consolidation, portfolio management, and operational excellence. You acquire to gain scale, eliminate competition, or fill portfolio gaps.

Market share matters because advantages of scale in consumer businesses are significant. Procurement leverage reduces input costs. Manufacturing efficiency improves with volume. Distribution costs decrease per unit. Marketing investments are spread across a larger revenue base. Shelf space negotiations strengthen with portfolio breadth. These advantages translate directly to margin improvement and cash flow generation.

Portfolio expansion creates value through brand architecture and distribution leverage. Consumers prefer variety. Retailers want to consolidate suppliers. Owning multiple brands at different price points captures more shelf space and appeals to different segments without brand confusion. Your sales team can offer retailers complete category solutions instead of point products. This strengthens relationships and improves terms.

Combined valuation receives emphasis because many consumer acquisitions involve financial buyers or strategic acquirers optimizing returns. Private equity firms use leverage and operational improvement to generate target returns. Strategic acquirers employ multiple arbitrage and tax-optimization improvements. Financial engineering is explicit and central to deal economics.

Innovation matters less because consumer products change slowly. Brand loyalty is high. Distribution relationships are established. Radical innovation is rare and risky. Incremental improvement is safer. Acquisitions focus on proven brands and products, not emerging technologies or unproven concepts. You are buying cash flow, not potential.

Integration is aggressive. Consumer acquirers move fast on cost reductions. They consolidate manufacturing, close facilities, reduce headcount, and integrate supply chains within months. They standardize processes and systems. They optimize the combined portfolio, often discontinuing underperforming products. Speed matters because benefits flow from integration, not autonomy. The playbook is well-established and execution-focused.

Financial Services: Capital and Compliance

Financial services deals prioritize combined valuation and market share. Culture and innovation are afterthoughts.

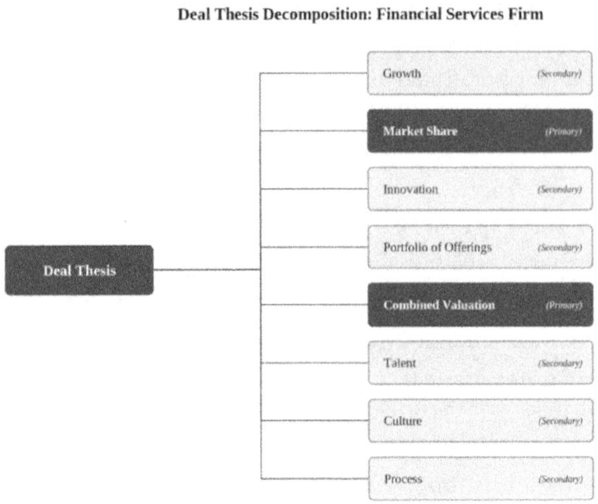

Figure 2.6. Deal Thesis Decomposition for a financial services firm.

Banking, insurance, and investment management are industries operating in regulated environments. Value creation comes from deploying capital efficiently, achieving scale economies, and managing regulatory requirements. Acquisitions follow this logic. You buy to optimize capital structure, consolidate markets, or expand distribution networks.

Combined valuation is primary because financial institutions are fundamentally about capital efficiency and return on equity. Larger institutions access cheaper funding, deploy capital across more opportunities, and maintain better credit ratings. Acquisitions improve capital ratios, enable more efficient balance sheet management, and optimize regulatory capital allocation. Tax benefits from legal-entity structuring add to value.

Market share matters because scale creates durable advantages. Branch networks require years and significant capital to build organically. Acquiring existing networks provides immediate market presence. Larger institutions negotiate better with regulators, spread technology costs across more customers, and achieve back-office efficiencies. Customer acquisition costs decrease with brand recognition.

Innovation receives less emphasis because financial products are largely commoditized. Checking accounts are checking accounts. Mortgages are mortgages. Credit cards are credit cards. Differentiation comes from service quality, distribution convenience, and pricing, not product innovation. Technology matters for operational efficiency but rarely creates a competitive advantage. Customers choose based on relationship and convenience, not features.

Culture is secondary because financial service firms are process-driven and compliance-focused. Regulatory requirements constrain operational flexibility. Risk management frameworks are standardized. The room for cultural differentiation is limited. Execution discipline matters more than entrepreneurial creativity. Integration focuses on process harmonization and system consolidation, not cultural preservation.

Regulatory oversight is intense. Acquisitions require approval from multiple agencies. Review timelines extend for months. Authorities impose conditions around capital ratios, branch divestitures, and competitive behavior. These constraints shape deal structure, integration planning, and post-acquisition operations. Navigating regulation becomes a core competency.

From Thesis to Reality

Integration as Strategy Execution

The Deal Thesis Decomposition is worthless if integration ignores it. Yet this happens constantly.

Integration teams default to standard playbooks regardless of deal thesis. Cost targets get set based on industry benchmarks rather than strategic priorities. System consolidation proceeds on technical convenience rather than business need. Organization design follows corporate templates rather than value drivers. The specific logic that justified this specific acquisition gets lost in a generic integration methodology.

Preventing this requires discipline. Start every integration planning session by reviewing the Decomposition. Make it visual. Put it on the wall. Reference it constantly. When someone proposes an integration decision, ask how it supports the primary value drivers. If it does not, question whether it is necessary. This filter prevents activity trap, doing things because they are possible rather than because they create value.

Governance structures should reflect deal priorities. If growth is the primary focus, establish a value-capture workstream with executive sponsorship and dedicated resources. Give it equal weight to cost reduction work, not leftover attention after the cost work is done. If innovation is primary, create protection mechanisms for R&D teams and product roadmaps. If talent is primary, build retention programs before you worry about organizational charts.

Metrics matter. Track progress against primary value drivers explicitly. Growth deals need revenue metrics, not just cost savings. Innovation deals need product velocity and talent retention, not just P&L impact. Market share deals need scale metrics and competitive position, not just value realization. What gets measured gets managed. If you are measuring the wrong things, you will manage toward the wrong outcomes.

Resist the pressure to declare victory early. Completing the transaction and achieving Day One stability is necessary but insufficient. Real value capture takes time. Revenue gains materialize slowly. Talent retention plays out over years. Cultural integration is never complete. Market position strengthens gradually. Stay focused on long-term value drivers even when short-term pressures mount.

Common Failure Modes

Three traps kill value. Watch for them.

First trap: cost reduction obsession. Cost cuts are easy to identify, quick to implement, and simple to measure. This makes them seductive when you are under pressure to show progress. But when you said growth or innovation was primary, and you delivered only cost savings, you had won the wrong game. You destroyed more value than you created. The target's sales team is demoralized. The innovation engine is broken. Customer relationships are damaged. You hit your cost targets and missed the point.

Second trap: acquirer imperialism. Your processes become the default. Your systems get adopted. Your culture dominates. This happens because it is easier than evaluating alternatives or managing diversity. But organizational narcissism prevents learning. You paid to acquire capabilities, practices, or a culture superior to your own in specific dimensions. Imposing your way across the board eliminates what made the target valuable. You acquire and then destroy. Smart money learns from acquisitions. Dumb money dictates.

Third trap: premature celebration. You close the deal and declare success. The press release goes out. The board applauds. The integration team dissolves. Then reality hits. Revenue growth does not materialize. Talent leaves. Synergies prove elusive. The market does not care that you closed the deal. It cares whether you created value. That takes time to know and discipline to achieve. Maintain focus. Track outcomes. Adjust course. Stay humble.

Value Tracking and Adaptation

The Deal Thesis, and thus its decomposition, should be reviewed regularly.

Market conditions change. Competitive dynamics evolve. Internal capabilities develop differently than expected. The assumptions underlying your DTD might shift. Rigid adherence to an outdated thesis is as dangerous as having no thesis at all. Smart organizations revisit their logic quarterly in year one, semi-annually thereafter. They ask hard questions. Are the primary value drivers still primary? Are we making progress? Do we need to pivot?

These reviews require honest assessment. You need data on value realization, customer retention, talent attrition, product velocity, market share gains, and financial performance. You need qualitative input on cultural integration, organizational health, and competitive response. You need the willingness to acknowledge problems early rather than hope they resolve themselves. Optimism kills when it prevents adaptation.

Adaptation might mean shifting priorities. You planned for growth, but market conditions changed. Pivoting to cost focus might be the right call. You are focused on innovation, but the talent is leaving. Shifting to technology platform consolidation might salvage value. These pivots are hard because they feel like failure. They are not. They are learning. Markets do not care about your original plan. They care about your results.

One industrial software acquirer lived this pivot. The firm bought a European competitor with growth as the primary focus, the thesis resting on selling the target's monitoring platform through the buyer's North American channel. The year-one review told a different story. Channel partners refused to carry the product because it competed with an incumbent line they already sold profitably. Growth through that route was not slow. It was structurally blocked. The leadership team re-ranked the decomposition. Process moved to primary, because the target's implementation methodology was measurably better and transferable across the buyer's service organization. Growth moved to secondary, rebuilt around direct sales in two named verticals. They documented the change and the evidence behind it. The deal did not deliver the thesis it was bought on. It delivered a thesis, on purpose, with the board informed and the organization redirected. That is the difference between a pivot and a drift.

The discipline of value tracking creates organizational learning. You build institutional memory about what works and what does not across different deal types. Pattern recognition improves. Due diligence gets sharper. Integration gets faster. This capability compounds over time. Organizations that do many acquisitions well develop systematic advantages over companies that treat each deal as unique and improvisational.

The Long Game

For mega-deals, value capture is measured in years, not quarters.

The first year after close is chaos. Systems need to be connected, and data migrated. People need reassuring. Customers need to be retained. You are fighting fires daily. Real gains are elusive. Costs temporarily rise. Revenue might decline. This is normal. Panic is counterproductive. Judge year one on whether you avoided disasters, not whether you captured full value.

Year two is when momentum builds. Integration is mostly complete. Teams understand the combined organization. Cross-selling starts working. Innovation velocity recovers. Market position strengthens. The value case you pitched starts to materialize. This is also when competitive response intensifies. Rivals adapt to your new capabilities. Customer defections stabilize but do not fully reverse. You are making progress but fighting headwinds.

Year three reveals whether the thesis was right. Synergies should be realized. Growth should be evident. Innovation should flow. Talent should be stable. Market position should be stronger. Financial returns should exceed the cost of capital. If these are not happening by year three, the deal probably failed. If they are happening, the value compounds from here. This is when successful acquisitions separate from unsuccessful ones.

Patience with urgency is the balance. You need patience to let strategies play out over appropriate timeframes. You need urgency to maintain focus and drive results. Too much patience becomes complacency. Too much urgency becomes panic. The Deal Thesis Decomposition provides the frame. It tells you what matters and on what timeline. Trust the frame. Execute with discipline. Adapt when needed. Measure what matters.

The organizations that master this, the ones that combine clear deal theses with disciplined execution, create substantial value from acquisitions. They use M&A as a strategic tool, not a strategic hope. They make acquisitions that strengthen competitive position, accelerate growth, and generate returns. They build capabilities that compound across deals. This is not luck. It is method.

Implications for the CEO

The question remains: Why are we doing this deal?

If you cannot answer precisely, do not do the deal. If you can answer but your team disagrees, align first. If you are aligned but cannot translate the deal thesis into action, build capabilities. The framework is simple. The execution is hard. The returns justify the effort.

The Deal Thesis Decomposition provides structure for strategic clarity. It breaks acquisition rationale into manageable components. It forces explicit prioritization of value drivers. It creates visual communication that is impossible to misunderstand. It establishes the foundation for integration planning and execution. It is not the full answer to acquisition success. It is the necessary first step.

The eight value drivers, growth, market share, innovation, portfolio, valuation, talent, culture, and process, cover the major mechanisms for value creation. Different industries emphasize different drivers based on their competitive dynamics and strategic priorities. Technology prioritizes growth and innovation. Consumer products emphasize market share and portfolio. Financial services focus on valuation and scale. Understanding these patterns improves decision-making and integration planning.

Success requires more than a good thesis. You need disciplined execution that respects the logic. You need governance that aligns resources to priorities. You need metrics that track the right outcomes. You need patience to let strategies mature and urgency to drive results. You need the willingness to adapt when assumptions prove wrong. These capabilities separate consistent value creators from occasional success stories.

Organizations with M&A capabilities gain competitive advantage. They identify better targets. They move faster through diligence and negotiation. They integrate more effectively. They capture more value. They learn from each transaction and apply lessons to the next. This systematic approach transforms acquisitions from expensive gambles into reliable value creation mechanisms.

Market disruption accelerates. Competitive advantages erode faster. Organic growth becomes harder. In this environment, acquisition capability matters more, not less. Companies that master strategic M&A will outperform competitors who avoid it or execute poorly. The Deal Thesis Decomposition framework provides a proven starting point for building this capability.

The journey from Deal Thesis Decomposition to value realization is long and difficult. Obstacles emerge. Assumptions fail. Markets shift. But clear strategy, disciplined execution, and honest adaptation create paths through complexity. Organizations that embrace these principles turn acquisitions into competitive weapons rather than corporate distractions.

Start with the question: Why are we doing this deal? Answer it precisely. Communicate it clearly. Execute it with discipline. Measure it honestly. Adapt it intelligently. The framework provides the structure. You provide the judgment and commitment. Together they create value. That is the deal.

Chapter 3
Strategic Distortions

Figure 3.1. The Penrose triangle is an impossible figure.

Nine Mind Traps on the Path to Business Mindfulness

When Alan Mulally became CEO of Ford in 2006, the firm had just posted a $12.7 billion loss: the worst in its 103-year history. Ford operated like a collection of feudal kingdoms. Regional divisions ran different strategies, built different products, and kept separate books. Executives hoarded information to protect their turf. Mulally's first act was to align the leadership team around a single strategy he called "One Ford."

Every Thursday, the entire global leadership team gathered for Business Plan Reviews. Every executive reported status using a simple color code: green, yellow, or red. Early on, every project showed green. An obvious lie, given the company's bleeding. Mulally called out the contradiction. The room went quiet.

Eventually, one executive marked a product launch as red. The room went silent again, this time in anticipation of termination. Instead, Mulally thanked him for the visibility and asked the team how they could help fix the problem. That moment broke the culture of concealment. Within weeks, the status reports reflected reality. Mulally knew the turnaround was possible.

Ford reversed $30 billion in losses by 2009 and was the only American automaker to survive the financial crisis without a government bailout. The key was not a great strategy alone. It was a leadership team that finally shared the same information, the same assumptions, and the same definition of success.

Business Mindfulness as Competitive Weaponry

Business mindfulness is not about wellness. It is competitive weaponry. The team that recognizes and corrects strategic distortions outperforms the team that remains trapped. Every framework in this book addresses specific failure modes in decision-making. This one addresses something deeper: how executives think when the stakes are highest.

This framework emerged from an unlikely intersection: the boardroom and the therapist's office. In 1981, psychiatrist David Burns published *Feeling Good: The New Mood Therapy*, introducing the concept of cognitive distortions: systematic errors in thinking that lead individuals toward depression, anxiety, and irrational behavior. Burns identified patterns including all-or-nothing thinking, overgeneralization, and catastrophizing. His work has shaped cognitive behavioral therapy for the past four decades.

In 2007, while working on a stalled cross-border integration, I mapped Burns's clinical framework onto a business strategy context. The mapping led me to develop two new concepts: business mindfulness and strategic distortion (we define "business mindfulness" as the disciplined, ongoing practice of monitoring one's own reasoning for systematic errors). Over the next several years, I tested and refined the framework across dozens of client engagements: different industries, different continents, different high-stakes decisions, different people. Nine distortions emerged as the primary psychological culprits in strategic misalignment. Nine mind traps that derail executive teams with remarkable consistency.

The Nine Strategic Distortions

Strategic distortions are not character flaws. They are not signs of weak leadership. They are cognitive shortcuts that served humans well across millennia. These shortcuts linger in every executive. Almost every leader falls into at least one of these traps during a career. The question is whether the trap is recognized before it closes.

Figure 3.2. Strategic Distortion unpacked.

1. Either-Or Thinking

The world becomes binary. Win or lose. Succeed or fail. Buy or walk away. The rich landscape of strategic options collapses into two stark alternatives, usually positioned as opposites.

Either-or thinking appears most often during crises, when stress narrows cognitive bandwidth. It also surfaces when executives have publicly committed to a position and feel trapped by their own declarations. Be wary of "forced choice" constructions. A board member asks: "Which would you rather be: a smaller firm with great margins or a larger firm with industry-average margins?" Two options. No others offered.

> ***Recognition signal:*** *When you hear "We have no choice" or "It's this or nothing," someone is likely trapped in either-or thinking.*

2. Extrapolation

The future becomes a straight line from the past. If sales grew 12% last year, they will grow 12% this year. If a competitor behaved predictably for the past decade, that competitor will behave predictably in the next. Extrapolation mistakes pattern for certainty.

An extrapolation destroyed a $400 million acquisition. The acquirer had purchased a regional retailer with strong same-store sales growth over the prior five years. The entire deal thesis rested on continuing that trajectory into new markets. No one asked whether the growth reflected a genuine competitive advantage or simply favorable demographics in the retailer's existing footprint. Within eighteen months, the expansion had stalled.

> ***Recognition signal:*** *When someone says "Based on current trends" without examining whether the conditions that created those trends still exist, extrapolation is at work.*

3. Discounting

Strengths shrink. Weaknesses become trivial. Threats appear manageable. Discounting systematically minimizes capabilities, competitors' advantages, people's potential, and the magnitude of challenges ahead.

Discounting operates in all directions. Some executives discount their own strengths, producing overly defensive strategies. Others discount competitors, building strategies on wishful assessments of the competitive landscape. The most dangerous discounting is internal: minimizing the abilities of your own people. This becomes self-fulfilling as talented individuals leave firms that fail to recognize their value.

In due diligence, discounting serves to dismiss identified risks. "Yes, their largest customer is forty percent of revenue, but that relationship is solid." Perhaps. A rigorous analysis would examine what "solid" actually means: contractual protections, switching costs, relationship depth. Waving away the concentration risk is not analysis.

> ***Recognition signal:*** *Phrases like "That's not really a concern" or "They're not that good" without supporting analysis often indicate discounting.*

4. Amplifying

The mirror image of discounting. Amplifying inflates threats, opportunities, capabilities, and risks. Everything becomes superlative. This is the worst market in history. This is the greatest opportunity we have ever seen. This competitor is unstoppable.

Amplifying produces imbalanced resource allocation. When every threat appears insurmountable, organizations cannot prioritize. When every opportunity appears to require total commitment, capital spreads too thinly across too many initiatives. Amplifying exhausts organizations. Teams cannot sustain crisis-level intensity indefinitely. When leaders amplify every challenge into a daily emergency, organizations freeze.

The 2020 pandemic revealed amplifying in full force. Some executives amplified the threat to the point of paralysis, unable to act because every supply chain issue seemed catastrophic. Others amplified the opportunity, launching ambitious transformation programs when their organizations could barely keep the lights on. Both responses reflected the same underlying distortion.

> ***Recognition signal:*** *Superlatives are the tell. "Biggest," "worst," "most important ever": these words often signal amplification rather than accurate assessment.*

5. Presumptive Reasoning

Conclusions arrive before analysis. Presumptive reasoning leaps to outcomes unsupported by facts, borrowing trouble from a future that may never materialize, or assuming success before the work is done.

Fortune-telling is the most common variant. The integration will fail because integrations always fail. The market will reject the new product because customers are conservative. The regulators will block the deal because they blocked the last one. Each statement may contain a grain of truth, but presumptive reasoning elevates pattern to prophecy.

The opposite form is equally dangerous. Executives who presume the deal will close stop preparing for alternatives. Teams that presume the integration will succeed stop monitoring for problems. Presumed success breeds complacency. Presumptive reasoning also shows up as reliance on strategic premises from what I call the "old normal." Executives who presume continuity in discontinuous environments make decisions on foundations that have already crumbled.

> ***Recognition signal:*** *Confident predictions about outcomes without explicit discussion of the assumptions underlying those predictions often indicate presumptive reasoning.*

6. Assumptive Reasoning

"Been there, done that." Assumptive reasoning applies past experiences to present situations without examining whether the situations are actually analogous. The assumptions that worked before will work again. The playbook that succeeded previously will succeed now.

Experienced executives are particularly vulnerable here. Their track records provide evidence that their assumptions have merit. But experience becomes a trap when it blinds leaders to the ways their current situation differs from their past.

I know a CEO who had successfully integrated four acquisitions using a standardized 100-day playbook. His fifth acquisition involved a firm in a different industry with a different culture and different regulatory constraints.

He deployed the same playbook. A fiasco. The assumption that the playbook would transfer without modification was wrong.

> ***Recognition signal:*** *"We've done this before" without explicit examination of what has changed since "before" signals assumptive reasoning.*

7. Normative Reasoning

An ideal world exists. We should be living in it. We are not. We have failed.

Normative reasoning substitutes "should" for "is." It creates guilt for not achieving ideals that may never have been achievable. It establishes failure as the default state because reality never matches the normative vision.

In strategic contexts, normative reasoning shows up as chronic dissatisfaction with performance that is actually strong, obsessive comparison to idealized benchmarks, and the "coulda, woulda, shoulda" syndrome: endless rehashing of past decisions against hypothetical alternatives. When leaders constantly measure reality against unachievable ideals, their organizations learn that nothing is ever good enough. Initiative dies. Risk-taking disappears.

> ***Recognition signal:*** *Heavy use of "should," "ought to," and "needs to be" combined with chronic dissatisfaction despite objective success often indicates normative reasoning.*

8. Mislabeling

Labels replace analysis. Organizations become dysfunctional. People become resistant to change. Minor missteps become failures.

Mislabeling does real damage in integration contexts. Acquiring-firm executives often label the target based on limited information, then treat those labels as fixed attributes rather than malleable conditions. "Their culture is toxic" becomes a self-fulfilling prophecy when every target employee is treated as a carrier of toxins.

The opposite direction carries its own dangers. When organizations label themselves as "innovative," "agile," or "customer-centric," they often stop examining whether those labels reflect reality. They are taken as given. Organizations never forget.

> ***Recognition signal:*** *When labels attach to people or organizations rather than to specific behaviors or outcomes, mislabeling is at work.*

9. Misplaced Accountabilities

Misplaced accountabilities take two primary forms. The first is blaming the organization for externalities: holding teams accountable for outcomes they cannot control. A sales team is blamed for missing targets during an industrywide disruption. An integration team is blamed for culture clash when executive sponsorship evaporates.

The second form is the victim stance. "We are victims of circumstance." "The market moved against us." "The FDA changed the rules." "The competitor cheated." The victim stance absolves leadership of accountability while stripping the organization of agency. If external forces control our fate, why bother trying to shape them?

> ***Recognition signal:*** *When explanations focus primarily on what others did or what circumstances imposed, rather than on decisions within the manager's control, misplaced accountabilities are likely present.*

The Framework in Practice

Cognitive science explains how distortions work. Real decisions show what happens when they go undetected. Two cases follow: one firm that corrected its distortions and won; one that did not and lost

Win Case: Continental Airlines and the Go Forward Plan

When Gordon Bethune became CEO of Continental Airlines in 1994, the firm ranked dead last among major U.S. carriers in on-time arrivals, baggage handling, and customer complaints. Continental was losing $55 million a month and approaching its third bankruptcy. Previous management had created an us-versus-them culture so severe that employees ripped the firm's logo off their uniforms.

Bethune named the distortions rather than managed around them. Misplaced accountabilities had given frontline employees no agency: every decision required supervisor approval, so no one took ownership. Mislabeling had produced a fixed internal story: the airline was broken, and the people in it were the reason. Normative reasoning had led previous executives to measure Continental against idealized benchmarks while ignoring what customers actually needed.

Bethune's response: a turnaround called the Go Forward Plan. He opened the books to all employees, tied bonuses directly to on-time performance, and told frontline workers to use judgment rather than follow rigid manuals. The firm gave every employee a $65 check in the first month Continental finished in the top five for on-time arrivals. People started caring about outcomes they could now influence.

Continental's stock rose from $2 to over $50 per share. *Fortune* named it one of the 100 Best Companies to Work for in America for six consecutive years. Three distortions, named and corrected. One airline, rebuilt.

> **What the Continental case demonstrates**
>
> *Bethune did not diagnose Continental's problems as operational. He diagnosed them as cognitive. Misplaced accountabilities, mislabeling, and normative reasoning had made accurate thinking impossible. Fixing the thinking was what made fixing the operations possible.*

Loss Case: J.C. Penney and the Apple Playbook

In 2012, Ron Johnson arrived as CEO of J.C. Penney fresh from Apple, where he had built the most profitable retail stores in history. His diagnosis: J.C. Penney needed to become a design-led, price-transparent retailer. Everyday low prices. No coupons. No promotions. Clean stores. The Apple model.

The distortion was assumptive reasoning, applied at full force. Johnson transferred a playbook from a context where it had succeeded to a context where the conditions were entirely different. Apple customers were brand loyalists paying premium prices for products they believed were unique. J.C. Penney customers were deal-seekers who derived genuine psychological satisfaction from the feeling of getting a bargain.

Long-serving J.C. Penney executives raised this distinction. The merchant teams warned that eliminating promotions would eliminate traffic. Johnson's leadership group never reconciled the opposing mental models. Mislabeling reinforced the impasse: the existing customer base was labeled as "old J.C. Penney," implying the firm needed to replace rather than serve them. Extrapolation compounded the error: projections assumed that the new positioning would attract a different, higher-value customer at a rate that would offset near-term losses.

In a single year, sales fell $4.3 billion. Same-store traffic evaporated. The firm posted a $985 million loss. Three distortions: assumptive reasoning, mislabeling, and extrapolation. None was named. None was corrected. Johnson was removed eighteen months after his arrival.

> **What the J.C. Penney case demonstrates**
>
> *Review the J.C. Penney case and identify every distortion present. Extrapolation is visible. Assumptive reasoning is visible. Mislabeling is visible. Each fed the*

others. That is how distortions typically operate: not in isolation, but as a cluster that reinforces a single, incorrect premise. The CEO who can name that cluster early can intervene before the losses accumulate.

Diagnostic Tools

Strategic Distortion Self-Detection Guide

Use this table before any high-stakes decision. The giveaways in the right column are observable behaviors, not character judgments. Name the distortion before the decision closes.

Strategic Distortion	Your Giveaways
Either-Or Thinking	You catch yourself saying "We have no choice" or "It's this or nothing." You frame decisions as binary win/lose outcomes with no middle ground. You feel trapped by public commitments and cannot see alternatives.
Extrapolation	You project future performance as a straight line from historical trends. You assume conditions that created past success will persist unchanged. You base valuations on run rates without testing the underlying assumptions.
Discounting	You dismiss identified risks with "That's not really a concern." You minimize competitor strengths or your own team's capabilities. You wave away concentration risks without rigorous analysis.
Amplifying	You use superlatives frequently: "biggest," "worst," "most important ever." Every challenge feels like a crisis requiring immediate response.

Strategic Distortion	Your Giveaways
	You cannot prioritize because all threats seem equally catastrophic.
Presumptive Reasoning	You predict outcomes with confidence before completing the analysis. You assume failure or success based on pattern, not current evidence. You rely on premises from the "old normal" without testing their validity.
Assumptive Reasoning	You say "We've done this before" without examining what has changed. You deploy a past playbook without testing it for the current situation. You fall back on assumptions when overwhelmed by conflicting information.
Normative Reasoning	You frequently use "should," "ought to," and "needs to be." You feel chronic dissatisfaction despite objectively strong performance. You compare reality to idealized benchmarks that may be unachievable.
Mislabeling	You attach labels to people or organizations rather than specific behaviors. Labels like "toxic" or "resistant" end your inquiry rather than begin it. You treat your own firm's self-description as fact rather than a testable claim.
Misplaced Accountabilities	Your explanations focus on what others decided and did. You blame teams for outcomes outside their control. You adopt a victim stance: "The market shifted."

Figure 3.3. Strategic Distortion Self-Detection Guide.

Achieving Business Mindfulness: Eight Practices for Leaders

Identifying distortions is the first step. Correcting them requires business mindfulness: the disciplined practice of monitoring your own reasoning for systematic errors. The organization that builds distortion-detection into its strategic processes will avoid traps that ensnare its competitors. Their distortions create your opportunities.

CEOs can adopt the following eight practices. Each is an observable behavior, not an aspiration.

1. Educate Your Leadership Team

Make sure everyone understands the nine distortions and can recognize them in themselves and others. Shared vocabulary enables shared vigilance. When executives share a common language for cognitive errors, they can challenge one another without making it personal.

> ***Case example: Ray Dalio, Bridgewater Associates***
>
> *When Dalio built Bridgewater into the world's largest hedge fund, he codified more than 210 decision-making principles into a shared framework. Every employee learned the same vocabulary for evaluating ideas. The result was what Dalio calls an "idea meritocracy" where the best arguments win regardless of hierarchy. Bridgewater's consistent outperformance demonstrates that shared cognitive frameworks create measurable competitive advantage.*

2. Practice Daily Self-Reflection

At the end of each day, review your key decisions and the reasoning behind them. Look for distortion patterns. This is not navel-gazing. It is quality control for your thinking.

> ***Case example: Satya Nadella, Microsoft***
>
> *Nadella transformed Microsoft by institutionalizing reflection at every level. Leaders close meetings by asking: "Was that a growth-mindset or fixed-mindset meeting?" Nadella issues monthly videos reviewing his top learnings, prompting groups across the firm to do the same. This practice helped shift Microsoft from a know-it-all to a learn-it-all culture, driving market capitalization from $300 billion to over $2 trillion during his tenure.*

3. Calculate Distortion Risks

When you identify a distortion, assess the risk of allowing it to continue. Some distortions are tolerable in specific contexts. Others demand immediate correction. Not all mind traps carry equal danger. The discipline of risk assessment forces executives to think probabilistically about cognitive errors rather than treating all distortions as equally urgent.

> **_Case example: Andy Grove, Intel_**
>
> *Grove built Intel into the world's largest chipmaker by obsessively calculating the risks of cognitive traps. His philosophy, captured in Only the Paranoid Survive, emphasized that some distortions, particularly extrapolation during strategic inflection points, carry catastrophic risk while others are manageable. When Japanese competitors attacked Intel's memory business, Grove's risk calculation led him to exit memory entirely rather than persist in discounting the threat. The pivot to microprocessors saved the firm.*

4. Engage an External Perspective

Find a coach, advisor, or trusted colleague who can observe your decision-making from the outside. Traps are often invisible from inside. External observers bring fresh pattern recognition, identifying distortions that have become so habitual they function as invisible assumptions.

> **_Case example: Eric Schmidt, Google_**
>
> *Schmidt credits Bill Campbell, the legendary Silicon Valley coach, with helping him navigate Google's explosive growth. Campbell coached Schmidt, Steve Jobs, and dozens of other technology leaders, identifying blind spots and challenging distorted thinking that insiders could not see. Schmidt and colleagues documented Campbell's impact in Trillion Dollar Coach, estimating that his external perspective contributed to over a trillion dollars in market value creation across the firms he advised.*

5. Extend Mindfulness to Customers

Help your customers recognize and correct their own distortions. Customers who think clearly make better purchasing decisions. When you help a customer avoid a cognitive trap, you build trust that goes beyond transactional relationships and positions your firm as a strategic partner.

> **_Case example: Marc Benioff, Salesforce_**
>
> *Benioff built Salesforce on the principle that the firm's success is measured by customer success, not by features sold. When Merrill Lynch threatened to abandon Salesforce due to usability problems, Benioff did not discount the feedback or*

> *blame the customer. He listened, acknowledged the distortions in his own firm's assumptions, and redesigned the product. Customer success as the primary metric helped Salesforce grow to over $30 billion in revenue.*

6. Analyze Competitor Distortions
Study your competitors' public statements and strategic moves for evidence of distorted thinking. A competitor trapped in extrapolation will continue strategies that no longer work. A competitor trapped in either-or thinking will miss creative alternatives. Systematic competitor distortion analysis reveals windows of vulnerability that pure market analysis cannot detect.

> ***Case example: Akio Toyoda, Toyota***
>
> *While competitors fell into the trap of extrapolation, assuming semiconductor supplies would remain stable because they always had, Toyota's team analyzed the auto industry's collective blind spot. After the 2011 Fukushima disaster crippled Toyota's supply chain for six months, the firm required suppliers to stockpile two to six months of chips. When the 2020-2021 pandemic chip shortage devastated rivals, Toyota's North American plants ran at 90% capacity while GM, Ford, and Volkswagen shut down production lines. Toyota seized the #1 sales position in North America for the first time since 1998: not through luck, but through deliberate distortion analysis.*

7. Refuse the Victim Stance
Leaders do not have the luxury of victimhood. Certain external circumstances are beyond a CEO's control. Lead and manage what is in your sphere of influence. Reject explanations that position your firm as helpless. The victim stance is seductive because it absolves accountability.

> ***Case example: Howard Schultz, Starbucks***
>
> *When Schultz returned to Starbucks in 2008, the previous leadership had blamed the economy and rising commodity prices for the decline in performance. Schultz rejected the victim stance entirely. "The company shouldn't just blame the economy," he told employees. "Starbucks's heavy spending to accommodate its expansion has created a bureaucracy that masked its problems." By owning the self-induced mistakes rather than hiding behind external circumstances, Schultz led one of the most studied turnarounds in retail history.*

8. Communicate Constantly
During periods of change, communicate daily with your people. Silence breeds distortion, and distortions breed rumors. In the absence of information, people

construct narratives that amplify threats, discount opportunities, and misalign priorities in ways that undermine execution.

> ***Case example: Indra Nooyi, PepsiCo***
>
> *When Nooyi led PepsiCo through the 2008 financial crisis, she prioritized transparent, constant communication. She held town hall meetings regularly to keep employees informed and engaged. Her transparency prevented the information vacuum where distortions flourish. PepsiCo weathered the crisis with employee engagement intact: a direct result of filling silence with facts rather than allowing speculation to fill it with fear.*

Business Mindfulness Practices at-a-Glance

Do more than hear your people. Listen to each one actively. For true business mindfulness, do not forget to listen to your undistorted self.

Practice	Actions, Behaviors, Words
1: Educate your leadership team	Conduct a half-day workshop on the nine distortions with your executive team. Create a one-page distortion reference card for meeting rooms. Open strategy sessions with: "Which distortions might affect our thinking today?" Normalize the phrase: "I think I am falling into [distortion name]."
2: Practice daily self-reflection	Block fifteen minutes at day's end to review your three biggest decisions. Ask yourself: "What assumptions did I not question?" Keep a decision journal, noting the reasoning behind major calls. Review the journal monthly for recurring distortion patterns.
3: Calculate Distortion Risks	Rate each identified distortion: low, medium, or high impact if uncorrected. Ask: "What is the cost of being wrong here?"

Practice	Actions, Behaviors, Words
	Prioritize correction effort on high-impact distortions first. Accept that some low-impact distortions do not warrant intervention.
4: Engage an external perspective	Hire an executive coach with no stake in your decisions. Schedule monthly sessions focused on decision review, not therapy. Ask your coach: "What patterns do you see that I cannot?" Create a trusted advisor relationship outside your reporting chain.
5: Extend mindfulness to customers	When a customer resists your recommendation, diagnose the distortion. Say: "I wonder if we are both assuming X without testing it." Help customers see how their distortions may limit their own success. Position your firm as a thinking partner, not just a vendor.
6: Analyze competitor distortions	Review competitor earnings calls for evidence of cognitive traps. Ask: "What are they assuming that may no longer be true?" Identify strategic moves that suggest extrapolation or either-or thinking. Time your competitive initiatives to exploit their blind spots.
7: Refuse the victim stance	Ban the phrase "There is nothing we can do" from your vocabulary. When citing external factors, immediately follow with: "And here is what we control." Reframe setbacks as leadership tests, not unfair circumstances.

Practice	Actions, Behaviors, Words
	Hold your team accountable for agency, not just effort.
8: Communicate constantly	During change periods, communicate daily even when there is no news. Say: "Here is what we know, what we do not know, and when we will know more." Fill silence with facts before speculation fills it with fear. Make yourself visible and accessible when uncertainty is highest.

Figure 3.4. Business Mindfulness Practices at-a-Glance

Implications for the CEO

The nine distortions thrive on two conditions: unexamined assumptions and insufficient communication. Remove those conditions and distortions lose most of their power. That is within a CEO's direct control.

I have worked with leadership teams on four continents spanning five decades, from 1986 through today. The executives who make better decisions are not the ones with better information. Competitors often have access to the same data, the same analysts, and the same advisory firms. The executives who decide well are the ones who have built the habit of examining how they think, not just what they know.

Business mindfulness is not a soft skill. It is a competitive position. The firm whose leadership team can name distortions in real time: calling out amplifying in a board presentation, recognizing extrapolation in a valuation model, flagging misplaced accountabilities in a post-mortem: that firm makes fewer catastrophic errors. Over time, fewer catastrophic errors compound into a durable advantage.

The practices in this chapter are not aspirational. They are operational. A half-day workshop on the nine distortions costs one afternoon. A fifteen-minute daily reflection costs seven minutes less than the average executive spends re-reading emails. An external advisor relationship costs far less than one uncorrected distortion in a nine-figure transaction.

The investment is small. The returns are asymmetric. Name the distortions. Build the practices. Drive your competitors into the traps they cannot see.

Chapter 4

Classes of Integration

Figure 4.1. One size seldom fits all, except for baseball caps.

The integration kickoff meeting begins at eight in the morning. Forty people fill the room. Twelve workstream leaders. Six functional sponsors. Three executive committee members. An integration management office armed with status templates, risk registers, and a thirty-eight-page integration charter. The acquired firm has thirty-one employees and $7 million in revenue.

Three weeks later, the founder of the acquired firm resigns, leaving money "on the table". The two engineers she brought with her followed within the month. The technology that justified the acquisition sits idle on a shared drive because no one in the integration steering committee has the authority to deploy it. The deal that was supposed to close in ninety days is still open at month nine. The team that bought a sprinter put it through a triathlon.

Across town, a different scenario unfolds. A regional bank acquires a competitor twice the size of its previous deal. The acquired firm operates in two new states, runs on a different core banking platform, and serves customer segments the buyer has never touched. Leadership treats it like the last three acquisitions: a single integration manager, a quarterly steering committee, and a one-page value tracker. By month six, the chief operating officer is asking why customer attrition is running at 15%. By month nine, the answer becomes clear. The team that bought a triathlon entered it as a sprinter.

Both failures share a single cause: the integration approach was decoupled from the deal at hand. The first firm over-engineered. The second firm under-resourced. Neither asked the prior question. What kind of deal is this, and what kind of integration does it require?

This chapter presents the framework that answers that question. We sort acquisitions into four classes along two dimensions, scale and complexity. Each class demands a distinct integration response. The framework does not promise success. It eliminates a category of failure that destroys value before the integration even begins.

Why Classification Matters

Most firms integrate every acquisition the same way. Same governance. Same workstreams. Same cadence. Same templates. The pattern is comforting because it feels like discipline. The pattern destroys value by ignoring the parameters of individual deals.

Two failure modes recur. The first is over-engineering. A corporate development team that just integrated a billion-dollar acquisition applies the same playbook to a $50 million tuck-in. Steering committees. Functional workstreams. Weekly status reports. Detailed integration plans. Synergy tracking by initiative. The overhead consumes more value than the deal creates. The business unit that should be running the integration spends its days reporting upward.

The second failure is under-resourcing. Leadership sees a small target and assumes the integration will be small. They delegate to a single business unit without central coordination. Then they discover, during detailed operational due diligence, that the target operates in three countries, sells through five channels, and runs on a technology stack that no one in the firm understands.

Business units cannot coordinate with themselves. Functions cannot align priorities. The integration fragments. Value evaporates.

Classification fixes both failures. We right-size the integration response to the deal characteristics. Class 1 deals receive business unit ownership with light corporate oversight. Class 4 deals receive a centralized Integration Management Office, dedicated cross-functional workstreams, and weekly executive attention. The match between deal complexity and organizational response determines integration outcomes as much as strategic logic or purchase price.

Classification also creates a shared language. When leadership says, "This is a Class 3 deal," every executive in the room understands what the integration will require. Resources. Timeline. Governance. Reporting. The conversation moves from negotiation to execution. We have seen firms that adopt this vocabulary cut integration planning time in half. Not because the framework is sophisticated. Because the alternative is endless debate about what kind of attention each deal deserves.

The Classification Framework

The framework uses two axes. Scale on the vertical. Complexity on the horizontal. Four quadrants. Clear boundaries. Nothing more.

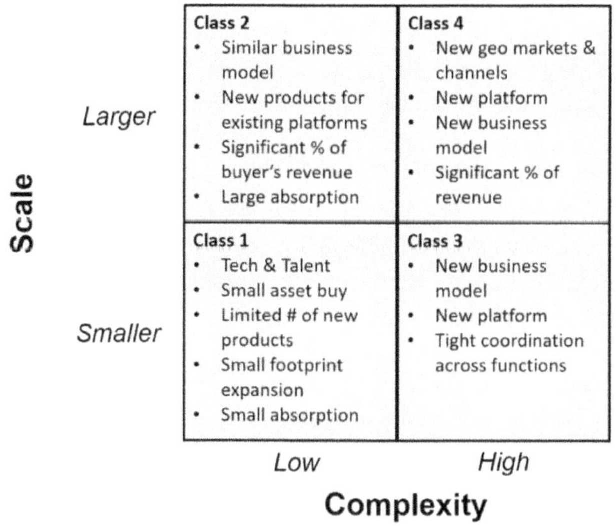

Figure 4.2. Two dimensions, four classes.

Scale measures the size of the target relative to the acquirer (we use revenue as the default proxy, with judgment applied for strategic weight). Targets representing under 10% of acquirer revenue fall in the lower half of the axis. Targets representing 20% or more fall on the upper half. The cutoff is not precise. A 5% target may sit high if it is strategically critical or operationally entangled. A 15% target may sit low if it operates independently. Start with the ratio. Adjust with judgment.

Complexity measures the difficulty of integration. Low complexity means the target operates in known markets with familiar business models on platforms the acquirer already understands. We have done this before. High complexity introduces novelty: new geographic markets, new distribution channels, new business models, new technology platforms, new regulatory regimes. Dependencies multiply across functions, business units, and geographies. Unknowns proliferate. Execution difficulty rises non-linearly with the number of novel elements.

These two dimensions produce four classes. Class 1: smaller scale, low complexity. Class 2: larger scale, low complexity. Class 3: smaller scale, high complexity. Class 4: larger scale, high complexity. Each combination creates distinct integration challenges and demands a different organizational response.

Class 1: Small and Simple

The Tuck-In

Class 1 deals are tuck-ins. Small. Familiar. Business as usual.

The target represents less than 5% of the acquirer's revenue. It operates in the buyer's core market with familiar products and recognizable customers. Integration is straightforward absorption into an existing business unit. The firm is buying technology, talent, or a customer base that plugs into current operations. The deal adds capacity, not novelty.

These deals occur frequently in serial acquirers. Technology firms buy small startups for features or engineering teams. Healthcare systems acquire physician practices. Regional banks absorb community banks. The playbook is well-established. Execution risk is low if the firm has done this before.

The integration approach is decentralized. The receiving business unit owns execution. They know the market, understand the products, and hold the customer relationships. Corporate provides governance oversight, financial controls, and functional support. The business unit makes decisions and owns results. This division works because the business unit has both the knowledge and the capacity to absorb the target without central coordination.

Integration Approach

Keep it simple. Do not create complexity where none exists.

Governance is light. No steering committee. No cross-functional workstreams. A business unit leader accountable for results. A corporate development sponsor who checks in monthly. Two roles. That is sufficient. More governance adds overhead without adding outcomes.

Integration planning focuses on three questions. Which customers need personal contact from leadership? Which employees need retention packages? Which systems need immediate connection? A simple checklist captures the answers. The receiving business unit executes against it. We move on.

Reporting is minimal. Monthly updates to corporate on financials and key milestones. No detailed status reports. No issue logs. No risk registers. If problems emerge, the business unit escalates. Otherwise, we assume progress and trust the leaders we put in place. Micromanagement kills speed and demotivates capable people.

The timeline is short. Most Class 1 integrations are complete within ninety days. Customer transitions occur in the first month. Employee decisions are finalized in the second. System connections finish in the third. Any longer timeline suggests either that the integration is moving too slowly or that the deal is not actually Class 1.

Where Class 1 Deals Fail

The first failure mode is neglect. Because these deals are small, they do not receive executive attention. The business unit leader is already running a full plate. Integration becomes one more item on an impossible to-do list. Customer calls do not happen. Retention packages arrive late. System connections wait for available IT capacity. The target drifts. Talent leaves. Customers defect. The small deal that should have been easy becomes a small disaster.

The second failure mode is over-engineering. Corporate development applies the standard playbook regardless of deal size. Workstreams are created. Plans are demanded. Status meetings are scheduled. The business unit spends more time managing the process than executing the integration. Bureaucracy is bureaucracy for its own sake. It does not improve outcomes. It frustrates the people who could have delivered them.

Class 1 succeeds when attention matches importance. Not too little. Not too much. Clear ownership. Simple plans. Trust. That is the formula.

Case Example: A Technology Tuck-In

A mid-cap software firm acquires a six-person startup for its analytics engine. Purchase price: $17 million. Annual revenue at acquisition: $2 million. The buyer's analytics business unit owns integration. A single product manager from the buyer is assigned as the integration lead. She is given a one-page checklist.

Customer contact. Three customer accounts. Personal call from the business unit head within the first week. Engineering integration. The acquired team moves into the buyer's product team but maintains its own cadence for six months. Retention. Equity grants and one-year retention bonuses for the founder and two key engineers were executed before the announcement. Email, single sign-on, and source control migration within thirty days.

Integration completes in seventy-five days. All six employees are retained. All three customers renew. The analytics engine ships inside the buyer's flagship product within eight months. Total cost of integration: less than 2% of deal value. The reason the integration worked is that no one tried to make it bigger than it was.

Class 2: Large but Familiar

Scale Without Novelty

Class 2 deals are large but not novel. Substantial absorption plays in the firm's core business.

The target represents 20% or more of the acquirer's revenue. The business model is similar. The customers are similar. The platforms are familiar. The firm is scaling its existing business, not entering new territory. Think competitor acquisition, market consolidation, and geographic expansion within known markets. The challenge is scale, not strangeness.

These deals generate substantial cost reduction and revenue growth opportunities. Overlapping operations. Duplicate functions. Redundant infrastructure. Cost reduction is real and achievable. Revenue synergies exist through cross-selling and a combined market position. The value case is straightforward. The execution is large.

Integration follows established playbooks because the firm has done this before. We know how to combine sales forces, consolidate manufacturing, merge back offices, and rationalize product portfolios. The processes are documented. Better practices (we say "better" because no practice is ever truly best, and improvement is continuous) are known. The firm just needs to execute at scale without making mistakes that become proportionally expensive.

Integration Machinery
Class 2 demands coordination without over-complication.

Governance includes a steering committee with functional and business unit representation. The committee meets bi-weekly to review progress, resolve issues, and make decisions. This level of oversight is necessary because the deal is large enough that small problems compound quickly. Early detection and rapid resolution prevent issues from becoming crises.

Functional workstreams handle integration by domain. Sales integration. Operations consolidation. IT rationalization. HR alignment. Each workstream has a leader, a clear charter, and specific deliverables. The workstreams operate semi-independently because the functions understand their own domains. Central coordination ensures sequencing and dependency management without micromanaging execution.

Program management is moderate. The firm needs someone to track milestones, manage status reporting, and coordinate across workstreams. This is not a full Integration Management Office. It is a program manager with administrative support. The role keeps the trains running on time. It does not design the railroad. Business and functional leaders make the integration decisions. The program manager ensures those decisions get implemented and tracked.

Timeline extends to six to nine months. The firm needs time to plan properly, sequence activities logically, and execute without breaking things. Rushing Class 2 integration creates expensive mistakes. Stretching beyond nine months suggests indecision. Six to nine months is the sweet spot for most large, familiar integrations.

Three Execution Priorities

First, value realization must be systematic. These deals justify themselves through cost savings and revenue gains. The firm needs rigorous tracking of every such initiative. Who owns it? What is the value? When does it hit the P&L? Where is the work in execution? This discipline determines whether promised value actually arrives. Without it, those gains remain aspirational.

Second, customer and talent retention requires constant attention. Large deals create uncertainty. Customers worry about service disruption. Employees worry about job security. Competitors attack both. Proactive communication, retention programs, and rapid problem resolution become operational priorities. The cost of losing key customers or critical talent in a large deal is substantial. We protect the base while we integrate.

Third, decision-making must be crisp. Large integrations generate hundreds of decisions. Which products survive? Which facilities close? Which systems win? These decisions cannot linger. Clear decision rights. Empowered leaders. Commitment to choices once made. Indecision creates drift. Drift destroys momentum. We keep things moving.

Case Example: A Consumer Products Consolidation

A mid-cap consumer products firm acquires a direct competitor that accounts for roughly 30% of its revenue. Same categories. Same retail customers. Same distribution model. The deal is large but contains nothing the buyer has not seen before. A textbook Class 2.

The integration machinery matches the class. A steering committee with six functional leaders meets every two weeks. Five workstreams run the work: sales, supply chain, finance, IT, and HR. A single program manager with one analyst keeps the milestones and the value tracker. No Integration Management Office. None is needed.

The discipline shows in the value tracking. The deal case promised $31 million in cost savings. Every initiative has an owner, a value, and a date by which it reaches the P&L. The steering committee reviews the tracker first on the agenda. When the plant consolidation slips by a quarter, the gap becomes visible within two weeks, and procurement accelerates vendor consolidation to cover the shortfall.

The retail customers receive the other half of the attention. The top ten accounts get joint top-to-top meetings within thirty days of close, led by the CEO, with a single message: one supplier, one order system by month six, no disruption to promotions already planned. Nine of the ten accounts hold their volumes through the transition.

Integration completes in eight months. Synergies reach 92% of the announced case by month eighteen. Nothing about the integration was clever. Everything about it was sized correctly. Class 2 rewards exactly that: established machinery, executed at scale, without improvisation and without excess.

Class 3: Small but Complex

The Dangerous Middle

Class 3 is the dangerous middle. Small enough to underestimate. Complex enough to fail.

The target is small, often under 10% of acquirer revenue. The target introduces new business models, operates on new platforms, or requires tight coordination across multiple functions. The deal looks manageable in size. It is not. The complexity creates integration challenges that small teams cannot handle without functional support.

These deals often involve strategic bets. The firm is acquiring capabilities it lacks, entering markets it does not understand, or adopting technologies that are not part of its current stack. The learning curve is steep. The dependencies are intricate. Success requires coordination across functions that typically do not work closely together.

The classification trap closes here. Leadership sees a small deal and assigns Class 1 resources. Business unit ownership. Light oversight. Minimal coordination. Then integration starts. Dependencies emerge. Functions cannot align. The business unit is overwhelmed. By the time anyone realizes the deal needs more support, the integration is already in trouble. Recovery is harder than doing it right from the beginning.

The Right Response

Class 3 needs cross-functional coordination without heavy program management.

We create a lightweight integration team with representatives from the functions that matter most. Product. Engineering. Sales. Marketing. Operations. The team meets weekly to align priorities, resolve dependencies, and make decisions. The group is small enough to move quickly and broad enough to cover the functional span the integration requires.

The business unit still owns execution but receives functional support. Product teams help with roadmap integration. Engineering assists with platform decisions. Sales enables go-to-market coordination. The functions provide expertise and resources. The business unit maintains accountability. The division works because no one is overloaded. Everybody understands the role they play.

Program management is tactical. Track the key dependencies. Flag integration risks early. Coordinate decision-making. The firm does not need elaborate governance or comprehensive reporting. It needs someone making sure the right people are talking to each other at the right times about the right issues. Simple coordination prevents complex problems.

The timeline is moderate, four to six months. The deal is small enough that year-long integration is unnecessary. The complexity makes a ninety-day timeline unrealistic. Allow time for learning, coordination, and adaptation. Class 3 often surfaces unexpected challenges. We build a buffer for addressing them without derailing the whole integration.

Three Success Factors

First, recognize complexity early. The mistake is assuming small size means simple integration. It does not. Complexity is independent of scale. A $50 million target operating in three countries, selling through five channels, and introducing a new business model is objectively complex. Treat it that way. Provide the coordination resources the deal actually requires.

Second, keep functions engaged. Functions cannot delegate to business units and disappear. They need to stay present, provide expertise, and help solve problems as they emerge. This is not a full-time commitment. It is an active partnership. The business unit owns the target. The functions own their domains. Together, they make integration work.

Third, exercise patience with learning. Class 3 deals introduce novelty. The firm does not have all the answers at the start. Integration plans evolve as the team learns. This is normal. We build flexibility into the approach. We expect surprises. We adapt quickly. The firms that succeed with Class 3 are the ones that learn fast and adjust course smoothly.

Case Example: An International Software-as-a-Service Acquisition
A North American enterprise software firm acquires an Australian competitor for $90 million. The target represents 7% of the buyer's revenue. By scale, it looks like a Class 1 tuck-in.

The complexity tells a different story. The target operates in three countries that the buyer does not serve. It runs on a different cloud architecture. It sells through a partner channel that the buyer has never used. Its customer base skews toward mid-market accounts that the buyer's enterprise sales force is not built to serve. Four novel elements stacked on a small base.

Leadership initially treats the deal as Class 1. A single integration manager. A monthly steering call. Three months in, customer churn in Australia is at 12%. The buyer's enterprise sales team is uninterested in mid-market accounts. The cloud platforms cannot share customer data. The partner channel is in revolt over compensation changes.

The chief operating officer reclassifies the deal as Class 3 in month four. A cross-functional integration team forms within two weeks. Product, engineering, sales, and channel leaders meet weekly. A regional general manager is appointed for Australia. The cloud platforms are bridged rather than merged. Mid-market customers receive a dedicated inside sales team. Partners receive transition support.

Integration completes in month nine. Customer churn stabilizes at 4%. The mid-market segment, properly served, grows by 22% in the following year. The deal pays back. The lesson lands: scale and complexity are not on the same axis. Treating them as one costs the firm five months and a portion of its customer base.

Class 4: Large and Complex

Maximum Difficulty

Class 4 is the hardest. Large scale. High complexity. Every dimension matters.

The target is substantial, often 20% or more of the acquirer's revenue. The deal introduces new geographic markets, new channels, new platforms, or a new business model. Integration requires coordination across functions, business units, and geographies. Dependencies are everywhere. Moving parts number in the thousands. Execution risk is high, and the consequences of failure are existential.

These are bet-the-firm deals. Cisco buys Scientific Atlanta. HP acquires EDS. Texaco purchases Getty Oil. Symantec absorbs Blue Coat. AT&T merges with Time Warner. The strategic logic in each case was clear. The execution challenge was enormous. Some succeeded. Some destroyed shareholder value at a scale that took years to rebuild. There is no middle outcome in Class 4. The firm transforms, or the firm pays.

Class 4 demands the full integration apparatus. Centralized program management. Cross-functional workstreams. Executive oversight. Comprehensive tracking. This is not bureaucracy for its own sake. It is the minimum machinery required by the deal. Without structure, Class 4 integrations fragment. With it, the firm has a higher chance of success.

The Integration Management Office

Class 4 requires a dedicated Integration Management Office (IMO, a centralized program management function with its own leader, staff, and operating model). Not optional. Required.

The IMO provides centralized program management to deliver synchronicity, consistency, speed, transparency, predictability, and control. The office establishes workstream structures that span functions, business units, geographies, and platforms. It creates a single source of truth for project status, issues, risks, and decisions. It enforces a common integration language and methodology across all teams. The IMO functions as the central nervous system of the integration.

Workstreams organize integration by domain. Sales and marketing. Product and engineering. Operations and supply chain. IT and systems. Finance and HR. Change management. Each workstream has executive sponsorship, dedicated leadership, and cross-functional membership. Workstreams operate with some autonomy but constantly coordinate. The IMO tracks dependencies, sequences decisions, and escalates conflicts to the steering committee.

The IMO achieves scale economies for critical integration expertise. Project management, change management, financial tracking, and metrics analysis are centralized. Individual workstreams do not need to build these capabilities. The IMO provides them as shared services. The result: less duplication, more consistency, and specialized expertise that improves with each deal the firm completes.

Governance is tight. An executive steering committee meets weekly in the first six months, then bi-weekly through month twelve. Workstream leaders report status, surface issues, and seek decisions. The steering committee resolves cross-workstream conflicts, allocates resources, and maintains momentum. This level of oversight is not heavy-handed. It is the only level that works. Class 4 deals generate too many dependencies and complexities for distributed decision-making.

Six Critical Success Factors

First, top talent runs integration. The firm's best program managers, change leaders, and functional experts. Not the people who happen to be available. The best people. Class 4 failures often trace to under-resourcing the integration team. The firm is investing billions in the acquisition. Do not handicap the investment by staffing the integration with B players.

Second, executive commitment is unwavering. Class 4 integrations last twelve to eighteen months. They consume enormous leadership attention. They generate ongoing problems requiring senior decisions. Executives cannot check out after close. They stay engaged, make decisions quickly, and provide air cover for the integration team. Without sustained executive commitment, Class 4 integrations stall.

Third, a common language and methodology prevent chaos. When teams across functions, geographies, and business units use different terminology, different planning templates, and different status metrics, coordination becomes impossible. The IMO establishes standards and enforces them. Everyone uses the same project plans, reports status the same way, and escalates issues through the same process. The discipline looks bureaucratic from the outside. From the inside, it is what keeps the integration from collapsing under its own weight.

Fourth, transparency is absolute. A single source of truth for everything. One system tracking all workstreams, all issues, all risks, all decisions. No shadow spreadsheets. No offline status. If it matters, it is in the system. This transparency enables coordination and accountability. It prevents problems from hiding until they become crises. Real-time visibility into integration health lets leaders intervene early, when intervention is cheap.

Fifth, decision velocity is high. Class 4 generates thousands of integration decisions. Product directions. System choices. Facility closures. Organizational structure. Each decision has dependencies. Each delay cascades. Clear decision rights. Empowered leaders. A commitment to move fast. Indecision is the enemy. The firm makes the call and moves forward, then adjusts if it learns it was wrong.

Sixth, change management is exceptional. The firm is asking thousands of people to work differently. New systems. New processes. New reporting structures. New locations. New colleagues. Without professional change management, people resist, productivity drops, and talent leaves. Class 4 demands dedicated change management resources, comprehensive communication, and sustained leadership engagement. This is not soft work. It is integration infrastructure.

Case Example: The Specialty Steel Acquisition Revisited

Chapter 1 introduced a specialty steel acquisition: a U.S. midwestern buyer acquiring a French target of similar size. The deal qualifies as Class 4 across all dimensions. Scale: the target represented roughly 40% of the buyer's revenue. Complexity: a new country, a new regulatory regime, a new language, a new customer base, a new manufacturing footprint, a new ERP environment.

The buyer's leadership recognized the classification early. An Integration Management Office was stood up before close. Seven workstreams are aligned to the holistic framework introduced in Chapter 1: markets and products, integration strategy, financial goals, process, people, systems, and change management. Each workstream had executive sponsorship and dedicated leadership. The IMO held weekly steering reviews for the first six months.

The result was not perfection. Class 4 integrations never produce perfection. The result was the absence of the failure modes that destroy bet-the-firm deals. Annualized cost reductions of $9.2 million realized within eighteen months. Critical talent retained at 94%. Customer churn in France held under 3%. ERP migration completed in tranches without business interruption. A weekly "Rumors, Rumors, Rumors" communication that stopped speculation before it could harden into resistance.

The deal worked because the integration approach matched the deal class. Forty workstream members. Six functional sponsors. A dedicated change management team. A weekly executive review. Machinery sized to the difficulty of what was being attempted. The same machinery applied to a Class 1 tuck-in would have been absurd. Applied to a Class 4 cross-border consolidation, it was the minimum work required.

Classification in Practice

Where Classification Happens

Classification happens early. Before close. Ideally, during due diligence when the firm still has time to size the integration team and secure the resources the deal will demand.

We start with scale. Target revenue as a percentage of acquirer revenue. Under 5% typically signals Class 1 or Class 3. Over 20% typically signals Class 2 or Class 4. The middle range requires judgment about strategic importance and operational entanglement. A 10% deal can be large if it is strategically critical or small if it is a clean tuck-in.

We assess complexity through specific questions. Does the target operate in markets where the firm has no presence? Does it use distribution channels that the firm does not understand? Does it run on platforms the firm does not have? Does integration require coordination across multiple functions? Does it involve a new business model? Each affirmative answer increases complexity. Three or more affirmatives signal Class 3 or Class 4.

We plot the deal on the two-by-two matrix. The classification tells us the appropriate integration approach. Class 1 receives business unit ownership. Class 2 receives functional workstreams with moderate program management. Class 3 receives cross-functional coordination. Class 4 receives the full IMO.

The machinery matches the class. The class is determined by the deal, not by what the firm wishes the deal to be.

Classification can evolve during integration. A deal that begins as Class 2 may reveal Class 4 complexity once execution starts. Complexity hidden during due diligence often surfaces during deep dives into operational reality. This is normal. We reclassify and adjust. Staying with the wrong approach because the firm planned otherwise is a failure of discipline. The cost of reclassifying late is high. The cost of refusing to reclassify is higher.

Three Misclassifications That Recur

First, underestimating complexity because the target is small. A $50 million target that introduces new business models and operates globally is Class 3, not Class 1. Treating it like a clean tuck-in guarantees the integration will struggle. We look at complexity independent of scale. Size bias is one of the most reliable predictors of integration failure.

Second, overestimating familiarity because the target is in the same industry. The firm acquires a competitor and assumes the deal is Class 2 because both firms are in the same business. Then the firm discovers the competitor serves different customer segments, uses different sales models, and operates different systems. The business model similarity was surface-deep. The integration complexity is real. What looked like Class 2 turns out to be Class 4. We dig deeper during diligence.

Third, wishful thinking about scope. Leadership wants to treat a Class 4 deal like a Class 2 because Class 4 is expensive and time-consuming. The team convinces itself that certain complexities do not matter or can be handled separately. This is self-delusion. Class 4 deals are Class 4 precisely because multiple complexities interact. The firm cannot ignore geography, platform, and business model novelty and pretend that the integration is simple. We face the deal as it is, not as we want it to be.

Putting Classification to Work

The framework is operational, not theoretical. It works when the firm uses it as a forcing function during deal evaluation and integration planning. It fails when it becomes a slide in a deck that no one revisits after close.

Three practices make classification real.

Practice 1: Classify Before You Close

Add classification to the deal approval process. Every transaction memorandum to the board or investment committee includes a classification slide. Two axes. One placement. A short paragraph explaining why. The discipline forces leadership to consider the cost of integration when deciding whether to do the deal.

The classification matrix also forces honesty. It is easy to write generic integration language. It is harder to defend a Class 1 classification when the target operates in three countries and runs on an unfamiliar platform. The framework surfaces the conversation early, when the firm can still adjust price, structure, or resourcing.

Practice 2: Resource to the Class, Not to the Calendar

Integration budgets and staffing should follow the classification rather than the project plan. Class 1 receives minimal resources. Class 4 receives substantial dedicated capacity. The firm does not staff every integration the same way and then wonder why some succeed and some fail.

Better practice (we say "better" because no practice is ever truly best, and improvement is continuous) is to publish a resourcing standard tied to classification. Class 1: a single integration lead, 1% to 2% of deal value in integration cost. Class 2: a program manager and functional workstreams, 2% to 5%. Class 3: a cross-functional team and tactical program management, 3% to 6%. Class 4: a dedicated IMO and executive steering, 8% to 12%. The numbers are guides, not gospel. The principle is invariant.

Practice 3: Reclassify When the Evidence Demands It

Build a reclassification trigger into the integration governance. At the thirty-day, sixty-day, and ninety-day reviews, the integration leader is asked one question: "Is this still the deal we thought we bought?" If the answer is no, the classification may need to change.

Reclassification feels like failure. It is not. It is learning made operational. The firms that improve their M&A capability are the ones that treat each integration as evidence for the next. The firms that decline as acquirers are the ones that refuse to update their model when the evidence arrives.

Implications for the CEO

Return to the two scenes that opened this chapter.

In the first, a buyer applied Class 4 processes to a Class 1 deal. The integration was drowned in process. The founder left. The technology sat idle. The deal failed not on strategy but on response. Too much machinery for the work at hand.

In the second, a buyer applied Class 2 processes to a Class 4 deal. The integration fragmented. Customers defected. The integration manager could not see the dependencies that mattered. The deal failed not on strategy but on response. Too little machinery for the work at hand.

Both failures shared a single cause and a single remedy. The cause: integration was decoupled from the deal. The remedy: classification, applied early, with discipline.

The framework is simple by design. Two axes. Four classes. Four integration responses. The simplicity is the point. Complex frameworks for choosing simple frameworks defeat themselves. A leadership team should be able to classify a deal in a one-hour meeting and emerge with a shared view of what the integration will require.

The four responses scale predictably. Class 1: business unit ownership with light oversight. Class 2: functional workstreams with moderate program management. Class 3: cross-functional coordination with tactical program management. Class 4: a full Integration Management Office with executive steering. Each response is sized to the difficulty of the work, not to the integration team's preferences.

We have applied this framework across acquisition deals, measured in the dozens, spanning four decades. The firms that classify well outperform the firms that do not. They do not waste resources on small deals. They do not under-resource complex ones. They build the organizational muscle to execute each class effectively. The capability compounds. Each deal teaches the firm something about classification. The next deal applies what was learned.

Start with classification. Look at scale and complexity honestly. Place the deal in the right class. Match the integration response to that class. Adjust the classification if the evidence demands it. The framework is the map. Judgment determines the route. Both are required. The class is step one.

Do Not Get Stuck. Take the First Practical Step.

The classification framework is ready for you and your executive team to apply to the next acquisition the firm considers. Start with the two questions. What is the target's revenue as a percentage of yours? How many novel elements does the acquisition introduce? Plot the answer on the matrix. Discuss the placement until the leadership team agrees.

Next, match the integration approach to the class. For Class 1, identify the business unit owner and a corporate sponsor. For Class 2, name the workstream leaders and the program manager. For Class 3, convene a cross-functional team and set the weekly cadence. For Class 4, stand up the Integration Management Office and appoint its leader before the deal closes.

It is acceptable to revisit the classification at the thirty-day mark. The first weeks of integration always surface information that was invisible during diligence. The framework is robust to mid-course correction. The framework is not robust to leadership that refuses to look at the deal in front of them and adjust accordingly.

Remember, one size does not fit all.

Classify early. Allocate resources for the class. Reclassify when the evidence demands a different approach. That is the discipline. The rest is execution.

Chapter 5
The Timing of Multiple Acquisition Integrations

Figure 5.1. Timing is everything. Well, almost everything.

The chief executive of a distribution platform called with a problem most acquirers never face. His firm, backed by a private equity sponsor, had signed letters of intent with five targets, and all five would close within the same four months. The corporate development team wanted to integrate everything at once and reach the end state within a year. The operating executives wanted to integrate one target at a time and protect the base business. Both sides were certain. Both sides were guessing. The question on the call is the one this chapter answers. When the deals arrive together, how do you sequence the integrations without destroying everything you are trying to build?

This is not theoretical. It happens. Roll-up strategies, market consolidation plays, and transformation deals create situations where you are integrating multiple acquisitions simultaneously. The question is not whether to integrate them. It is when and how.

Most companies default to parallel integration. Close all the deals, integrate all the targets, and hope it works. This maximizes speed. It also maximizes chaos. Your integration team is stretched across five deals. Your business units are absorbing five cultures. Your systems are connecting to five platforms. Your customers are watching five acquisitions unfold. The complexity is overwhelming.

The alternative is serial integration. Integrate one target fully, then move to the next. This maximizes control and minimizes risk. It also maximizes time. By the time you finish integrating the fifth target, eighteen months have passed.

Your competitive window might have closed. Your talent might have left. Your strategic thesis might be obsolete.

There is a third path. Semi-parallel integration sequences the deals deliberately, integrating some simultaneously while staging others. This balances speed against complexity, moving fast where you can while controlling risk where you must. The approach requires strategic thinking about sequencing, honest assessment of capabilities, and discipline in execution.

This chapter breaks down all three timing models: parallel, serial, and semi-parallel. We will examine the trade-offs each model creates, the organizational capabilities each demands, and the decision framework for choosing your path. The methodology comes from the field, developed for the client whose call opened this chapter. It has been tested. It works. Now we document it.

The Parallel Model
All at Once

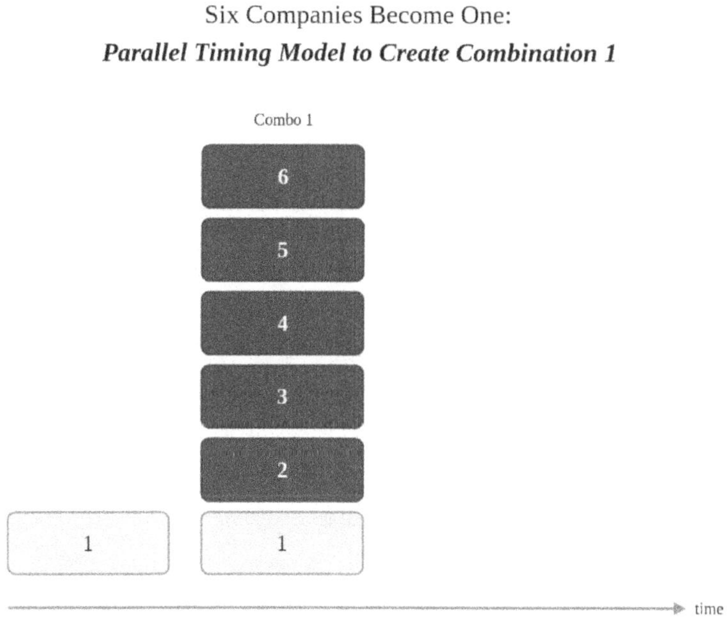

Figure 5.2. Parallel integrations.

The parallel model integrates everything simultaneously. Maximum speed. Maximum complexity.

You close five deals. You launch five integration workstreams. You build one combined entity from six separate companies, all at the same time. The logic is compelling: you reach your strategic end state fastest, you realize cost savings immediately, and you minimize the period of uncertainty. One massive push creates the new organization. Then you are done.

The execution challenge is enormous. You need integration resources for all five targets simultaneously. That means five integration leaders, five sets of functional workstreams, five streams of decision-making. Your best people are split across multiple deals. Your executives are making decisions about five integrations in parallel. Your systems team is connecting five different platforms. Your HR team is handling five retention programs. Your accounting team is tracking five sets of books.

The organizational load is crushing. Every function is maxed out. Sales is managing five sales force integrations. Product is combining five roadmaps. Engineering is merging five development organizations. Operations is consolidating five sets of facilities and supply chains. The day-to-day business struggles because everyone is focused on integration. Customers notice. Employees feel it. Competitors attack.

When Parallel Works

Parallel integration works in specific circumstances. Know the prerequisites.

First, all five targets must be similar. Same business model, same customer base, same operating model. If they are identical, you can use one integration playbook across all five. Your teams learn once and execute five times. The complexity is additive, not multiplicative. Five similar integrations are hard. Five different integrations are impossible.

Second, you need massive organizational capacity. Deep bench of integration talent. Experienced functional leaders who have integrated before. Strong program management capabilities. Robust change management resources. This is not normal organizational capacity. This is surge capacity. If you are at normal staffing levels, parallel integration will break you.

Third, your strategic imperative must demand speed. The market opportunity is time-sensitive. Competitors are moving. Customers are making decisions. Waiting six months for serial integration means losing the game. You need the combined entity operational immediately. Speed is not a preference. It is a requirement.

Fourth, you must accept high risk. Parallel integration maximizes execution risk. Problems compound across five integrations simultaneously. Customer attrition, talent loss, system failures, cultural clashes, all multiplied by five. Some things will break. Count on it. The question is whether you can contain the damage and keep moving.

The Trade-Offs

Parallel delivers speed but sacrifices everything else.

Time to a strategic thesis is the shortest. You reach your target end state in six to nine months. All targets are integrated. All integration gains are realized. The strategic vision is reality. This speed creates a competitive advantage. You have transformed while competitors are still planning their next strategic move.

Revenue continuity is lowest. Five simultaneous integrations create five times the customer disruption. Account coverage gaps multiply. Service quality issues compound. Sales force distraction accumulates. Some revenue loss is inevitable in any integration. In parallel, it is guaranteed and substantial. Budget for it upfront or be surprised by the damage.

Customer experience suffers the most. Your customers are dealing with system changes, account team transitions, and process modifications all at once. They cannot get consistent answers because your organization is in flux across the board. Customer support quality drops as everyone learns new tools and procedures. Customer success suffers. Some customers decide it is easier to switch vendors than to endure the chaos.

Talent retention is the hardest. Your people see constant change, unclear priorities, and overloaded teammates. The best employees have options. They use them. Retention becomes a numbers game. You will lose some percentage of your talent. The question is whether you lose the right people or the critical ones. Usually, it is the critical ones. They are the most marketable.

Controllability is lowest. You cannot closely manage five integrations simultaneously. Issues surface across all five at once. Decisions pile up faster than you can make them. Some problems slip through cracks. Others get inadequate attention because you are firefighting elsewhere. You are steering five ships in a storm. Some drift off course. Bet on it.

Visibility is worse. You cannot see everything happening across five integrations. Your dashboards show red flags, but you cannot always tell which are critical and which are noise. Teams are making decisions without full context. Coordination suffers. Duplication happens. The organization loses cohesion under the load.

A healthcare services roll-up learned these trade-offs the hard way. The platform closed six clinic groups in five months and integrated all six at once, on the sponsor's thesis that speed to scale would justify the chaos. The integration team split across six workstreams. Physician retention packages went out late in four of the six groups because no one owned the calendar. By month nine, the platform had lost 20% of its physicians and one regional payer contract, and the sponsor extended its hold period by two years to repair the damage. The scale arrived on schedule. The value did not.

The Serial Model

One at a Time

The serial model integrates sequentially. One target is fully integrated before starting the next.

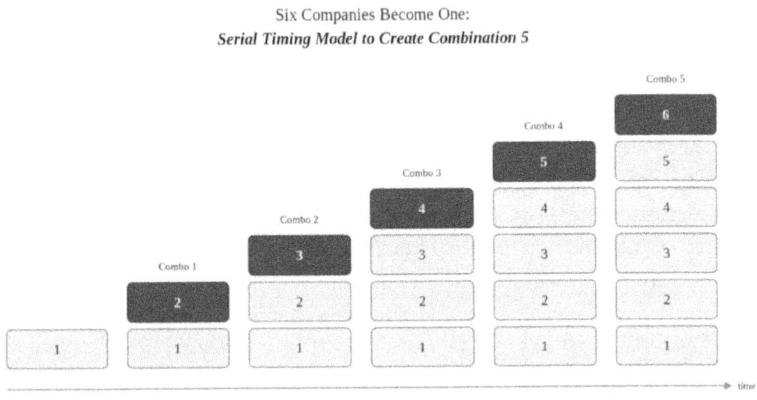

Figure 5.3. Serial integrations.

You close five deals. You integrate the first one completely: systems, processes, people, customers. Then you move to the second. Then the third. One combination builds on the previous. Each integration learns from the last. By the time you reach the fifth target, you are integrating into a progressively larger, more stable base.

The logic is control. You focus your integration resources on one target at a time. Problems get full attention. Decisions get proper consideration. Customers are managed carefully. Employees get clear direction. Each integration receives the organizational capacity it needs. Quality is high. Execution risk is minimized. But time stretches out significantly.

The timeline is long. Assume four months per integration. Five targets means twenty months total. That is approaching two years from first close to final integration. Market conditions change over that timeframe. Competitive dynamics shift. Some of your strategic assumptions might no longer hold by the time you finish.

When Serial Works

Serial integration works when control matters more than speed.

First, the targets must be distinct from one another. Different markets, different business models, different customer bases, different platforms. Each integration requires unique approaches. Doing them simultaneously would create coordination nightmares. Serial sequencing lets you tackle each integration with the specific approach it requires.

Second, you have limited integration capacity. You cannot surge resources. Your integration team is small. Your functional leaders are already loaded. Your change management capabilities are constrained. Serial integration matches your work to your capacity. You do each integration properly instead of five integrations poorly.

Third, integration complexity is high. These are not simple tuck-ins. They are complex, multi-geography, cross-platform integrations with significant customer and employee impacts. Each demands careful execution. Rushing would destroy value. Taking time to do it right preserves what you acquired.

Fourth, time pressure is moderate. Yes, you want to move quickly. But the market is not forcing immediate action. Your competitive position is not immediately at risk. Customers are not making immediate switching decisions. You have time to integrate properly. Use it.

The Trade-Offs

Serial maximizes control but sacrifices speed.

Time to the strategic thesis is the longest. Twenty months to reach your end state. By then, market conditions have changed, competitive dynamics have shifted, and your original strategy might need revision. The integrated entity you envisioned eighteen months ago might not be optimal for current market realities. You are building something for yesterday's world.

Revenue continuity is highest. You disrupt one business at a time. The other four targets continue operating normally while the first integrates. Customers barely notice. Sales teams stay focused. Revenue flows. By the time you integrate the second target, the first is stable and growing again. Cumulative revenue impact is minimized.

Customer experience is best. Each target's customers go through integration once, with full organizational attention. Support quality stays high. Communication is clear. Issues get resolved quickly. Customer satisfaction remains stable. Retention stays strong. You are managing change carefully, not forcing it rapidly.

Talent retention is highest. Employees see one integration at a time. They understand what is happening and why. They see colleagues from the previous integration who succeeded. They have time to adapt. Key talent stays. Cultural integration proceeds naturally. You are building one combined culture through staged integration, not forcing six cultures to merge simultaneously.

Controllability is highest. You can see everything happening. Problems surface with full visibility. Decisions get proper attention. Integration quality stays high. Nothing slips through cracks. You are managing one complex integration, not five. The complexity is high but manageable.

Time to competitive position is the longest. You will not have full market impact until all five integrations are complete. Competitors have time to respond. Market opportunities might pass. First-mover advantages erode. The careful execution that preserves value might allow competitors to capture opportunities you planned to own.

Serial discipline carries its own bill. A specialty chemicals firm acquired three regional competitors with the intent of integrating them one at a time, four to six months each. The execution was clean. Customer attrition remained near zero, and not a single plant manager left. But the third integration finished twenty-two months after the first close, and by then a larger rival had completed its own consolidation and locked up the two national accounts that had anchored the original thesis. The firm preserved everything it bought and lost the position it bought it for.

The Semi-Parallel Model

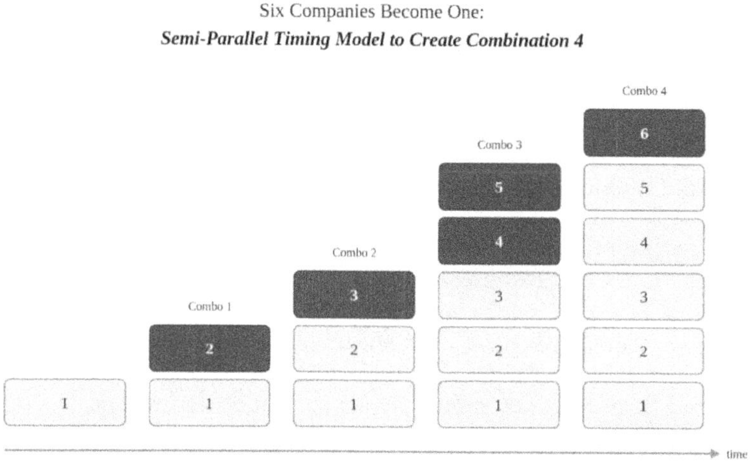

Figure 5.4. Semi-parallel integrations.

The Balanced Path

Semi-parallel integration sequences deliberately. Some targets integrate in parallel. Others integrate serially. Strategic choices about what to combine and when.

You might integrate two similar targets simultaneously, then add a third after those stabilize, then bring in the fourth and fifth as another pair. Or you integrate the simplest target first, then tackle two moderate-complexity deals in parallel, then sequence the most complex ones. The pattern depends on your specific targets, capabilities, and strategic priorities.

The logic is optimization. You are balancing speed against complexity, moving fast where you can while controlling risk where you must. Easy integrations happen quickly. Complex integrations get proper attention. Critical integrations receive focused resources. You are matching integration approach to deal characteristics systematically.

The execution requires planning. You need to assess each target's integration complexity, determine which targets can be paired, and sequence the combinations strategically. This planning happens before first close. You are deciding the sequencing strategy based on deal characteristics, not defaulting to parallel or serial based on organizational habit.

Sequencing Logic

Four factors drive sequencing decisions in semi-parallel integration.

First, target similarity determines pairing. Similar targets can integrate in parallel because they use the same playbook. Different targets need serial integration because they require unique approaches. Look at the business model, customer base, platform, and operating model. High similarity enables parallel integration. Low similarity forces serial.

Second, integration complexity determines timing. Simple integrations go first or pair together. Complex integrations get dedicated attention later or happen serially. Do not pair two complex integrations. You will overload your organization. Pair simple ones, or deliberately sequence complexity.

Third, strategic priority determines sequence. The most strategically important target might integrate first to realize value fastest. Or it might integrate last after you have learned from others. The decision depends on whether speed or quality matters more for that specific deal. Be explicit about the choice.

Fourth, organizational capacity determines batch size. How many integrations can you run simultaneously? Two? Three? Be honest about limits. Push beyond capacity, and quality suffers. Stay within capacity, and you maintain control. Match integration load to organizational capability.

The Trade-Offs

Semi-parallel balances all factors. You give up the extremes to capture the middle.

The time to strategic thesis is moderate. Twelve to fifteen months typically. Not as fast as parallel, not as slow as serial. Fast enough to capture market opportunities, slow enough to maintain quality. You are reaching your end state in a reasonable timeframe without destroying everything along the way.

Revenue continuity is moderate. You disrupt two or three businesses at a time, rather than one or five. Some revenue impact is inevitable. But it is manageable. You are not creating chaos across the entire organization. You are staging disruption in digestible chunks. Customers can handle it. Sales teams can manage it. Revenue stays relatively stable.

Customer experience is acceptable. Not perfect like serial. Not chaotic like parallel. Your customers go through integration in waves. Some experience change early. Others later. Each wave is manageable. Support quality stays reasonable. Communication stays clear. You are not creating perfect customer experience, but you are avoiding disaster.

Talent retention is moderate. Better than parallel, worse than serial. Employees see staged change. Some uncertainty exists, but it is time-limited. Key talent has time to evaluate and decide. You will lose some people, but not your entire bench. Retention programs can focus on critical employees in the current integration wave. Others can wait.

Controllability is moderate. Better than parallel, worse than serial. You are managing two or three integrations instead of five, so visibility is better. Problems get attention. Decisions get made. But you are still juggling multiple balls. Some things will slip. The question is whether they are important or trivial. Mostly, they are trivial if you sequence well.

Time to competitive position is moderate. You reach meaningful scale in nine months instead of six or twenty. Market impact happens in stages as each wave integrates. Competitors see you moving but have less time to respond than serial gives them. You are building competitive advantage progressively instead of all at once.

Making the Choice

The Assessment Framework

Seven factors determine which model fits your situation. Rate each factor for parallel, semi-parallel, and serial.

1. The framework scores three models, parallel, serial, and semi-parallel, against seven dimensions. Time to strategic thesis measures how quickly you reach your target end state: parallel is fastest, serial slowest, semi-parallel in between, so if market timing is critical, parallel scores higher, while if quality matters more, serial wins.

2. Time to investment thesis measures how quickly you realize your financial targets, with the fastest and slowest. A deal model that requires quick value realization favors parallel, while one that can absorb a slower ramp can tolerate serial. Revenue continuity measures how well you maintain existing revenue during integration. Here, serial protects revenue best, while parallel puts most at risk, so in competitive markets where customer retention is fragile, serial may be mandatory regardless of time pressure.

3. Customer experience follows the same logic: serial delivers the best experience and parallel the worst, so when customer success drives retention and retention drives value, you prioritize serial or semi-parallel rather than sacrificing customers for speed.

4. The remaining three dimensions complete the picture. Time to competitive position measures how quickly you achieve your strategic market position, where parallel is fastest. If competitors are moving and windows are closing, speed matters. If you have time to build position carefully, quality matters more. Talent retention measures how well you keep critical employees: serial retains best, and parallel loses most, so if the target's value lies in its people, protecting talent aggressively may make serial integration mandatory, whereas if talent is replaceable, you have more flexibility. And controllability measures how well you can manage execution, with serial offering the most control and parallel the least. If integration complexity and execution risk are high, controllability matters, while experienced teams running straightforward integrations can tolerate less risk.

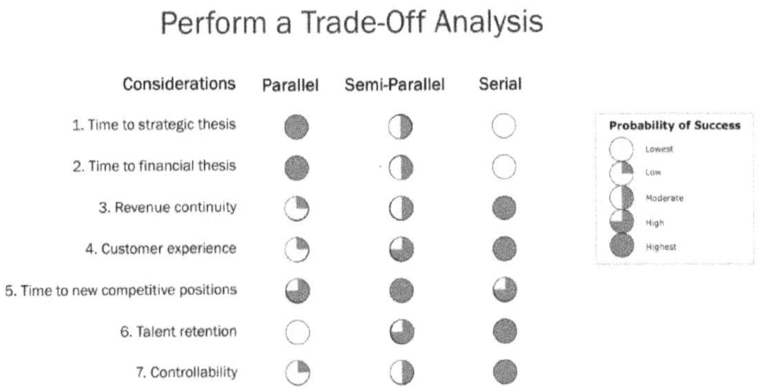

Figure 5.5. Decision support tool.

The Decision Process

Rate each factor for each model. Use a simple scale: lowest, low, moderate, high, highest.

Then aggregate. Which model scores best across the factors that matter most for your situation? That is your answer. But do this systematically. Do not just pick your preferred model and rationalize the scores to support it. Be honest about the trade-offs. Each model sacrifices something important.

Consider bringing in an objective third party for the assessment. Internal teams have biases. The corp dev team wants parallel because they want to move fast. Business units want serial because they want control. Functions want semi-parallel as a compromise. An external advisor can evaluate objectively based on deal characteristics and organizational capability.

Present the assessment to executives for a decision. Show all three models. Show the rating for each factor. Show the trade-offs explicitly. Let leadership choose based on strategic priorities. Some will prioritize speed. Others will prioritize control. Both are legitimate. The choice must be conscious and informed.

Document the decision and the logic. When problems emerge during integration, people will second-guess the choice. Having a documented rationale prevents revisionism. You chose parallel because speed was critical despite the risks. Or you chose serial because talent retention was mandatory despite the time. Own the choice and its consequences.

Addressing the Gaps

The assessment will reveal gaps. Factors where your probability of success is low.

Do not just accept the low scores. Shore them up. If controllability is low in your chosen model, build better program management. If talent retention is low, create stronger retention programs. If customer experience is low, invest in customer success resources. The model choice sets your baseline. Risk mitigation improves it.

Target your two or three lowest-scoring factors for intensive risk mitigation. You cannot fix everything. But you can improve the biggest risks. If parallel integration gives you the lowest scores on talent retention and controllability, build exceptional retention programs and world-class integration program management. Do not accept the weaknesses as inevitable.

Monitor these factors obsessively during execution. You identified them as high-risk. Track them religiously. Talent retention gets weekly reporting. Controllability gets daily dashboards. Customer experience gets constant measurement. Early warning lets you intervene before problems become crises. Late detection means damage is done.

Execution Implications

Different Models, Different Organizations

Each timing model demands different organizational approaches.

Parallel requires centralized integration management. You need a strong Integration Management Office coordinating across all five deals. Without central coordination, the integrations fragment. Decisions conflict. Resources duplicate. Opportunities get missed. The IMO provides synchronization, consistency, and control.

Serial allows decentralized integration and ownership. Business units can own integration because you are only doing one at a time. Corporate provides oversight and resources, but does not need to coordinate across multiple simultaneous integrations. This lighter governance structure works because complexity is sequential, not simultaneous.

Semi-parallel needs hybrid governance. Some aspects are centralized. Others decentralized. You coordinate across the integrations happening in parallel while allowing some autonomy for business unit execution. The governance structure adapts to the specific sequencing pattern you have chosen. Two targets integrating in parallel need more coordination than when those same targets integrate serially.

Communication Strategy

Communication requirements differ dramatically across models.

Parallel requires intense, comprehensive communication. You are changing everything simultaneously across five organizations. Employees need constant updates. Customers need repeated reassurance. Partners need ongoing guidance. The communication load is massive. You need dedicated communication resources and executive air cover. Everyone feels uncertain. Communication reduces anxiety.

Serial allows focused communication. You communicate intensely about the current integration. The other targets wait their turn. This concentrated approach is clearer and more manageable. Employees know what is happening and when. Customers receive targeted updates. The communication is deeper but narrower. Quality can be higher.

Semi-parallel needs staged communication. You communicate about current integrations intensely while preparing stakeholders for upcoming waves. Each stage has its own communication plan. Stakeholders know which wave they are in and what to expect. The staging creates predictability without overwhelming everyone with simultaneous changes.

Resource Allocation

Resource demands peak differently in each model.

Parallel front-loads everything. You need maximum resources immediately and sustain that level for six to nine months. The peak is high and sustained. You are staffing five integrations simultaneously. This requires surge capacity: hiring contractors, pulling people from other projects, or accepting degraded performance elsewhere. The resource spike is intense but time-limited.

Serial spreads resources across time. The peak demand is lower because you are only integrating one target at a time. But the duration is much longer. You need integration resources for twenty months instead of nine. The total resource consumption might be similar to parallel, just distributed differently. This can work better if you cannot surge but can sustain.

Semi-parallel creates multiple moderate peaks. Resources surge with each wave, then partially release before the next. The peaks are higher than serial but lower than parallel. The duration is longer than parallel but shorter than serial. This pattern often matches organizational reality better than the extremes.

Implications for the CEO

Multiple simultaneous acquisitions force a choice. Parallel, serial, or semi-parallel. There is no default answer.

Parallel maximizes speed and minimizes time to the strategic thesis. It also maximizes complexity, minimizes controllability, and puts revenue and talent at the highest risk. Choose parallel when market timing is critical, organizational capacity is massive, and you are willing to accept high execution risk for fast results.

Serial maximizes control and protects revenue and talent. It also maximizes time, delays competitive position, and extends strategic realization. Choose serial when integration complexity is high, organizational capacity is limited, and quality matters more than speed.

Semi-parallel balances factors. Moderate speed, moderate complexity, moderate control. No extremes in either direction. Choose semi-parallel when you need reasonable speed without destroying controllability, when organizational capacity is good but not unlimited, and when you can sequence strategically.

The framework provides structure for the decision. Assess seven factors across three models. Rate probability of success for each factor in each model. Identify which model scores best on the factors that matter most. Bring in an objective third-party assessment to prevent bias. Present options to executives for informed decision.

Then execute with discipline. The model choice sets your baseline approach. Risk mitigation addresses your weakest factors. Organizational structure matches your chosen model. Communication strategy adapts to your sequencing pattern. Resource allocation aligns with your timing peaks. Execution quality matters as much as model selection.

Most importantly, decide consciously. Do not default to parallel because it seems fast or serial because it seems safe. Look at your specific situation. Assess your actual capabilities. Identify your true priorities. Then choose the model that matches reality. Parallel works in specific circumstances. Serial works in others. Semi-parallel often splits the difference effectively.

Return to the client whose call opened this chapter. The firm needed a framework to think through sequencing. We built this. They used it. It worked. The assessment revealed that parallel execution was too risky given the complexity of their integration and organizational capacity. Serial was too slow, given their competitive timing. Semi-parallel sequenced strategically, pairing simple integrations while staging complex ones.

They reached their strategic end state in fourteen months instead of six or twenty-four. They maintained revenue continuity better than parallel would have. They achieved a competitive position faster than serial would have. They kept critical talent. They maintained reasonable control. The balanced approach worked because they chose it deliberately and executed it with discipline.

That is the lesson. When you are integrating multiple acquisitions, sequence matters as much as strategy. Think through the timing deliberately. Assess the trade-offs honestly. Choose the model that fits your situation. Then execute with focus. The framework gives you structure. Your judgment determines success.

Multiple deals create multiple choices. Choose wisely.

Chapter 6
Acquisition End-State Vision

Figure 6.1. Without a finish line, an integration can linger forever.

Many acquisitions fail because executive teams fail to develop and then adhere to an end-state vision. Think about your team beginning a journey with no destination. Any direction for the first step will do. But you are not a vagabond with nowhere to go.

You close the deal. Integration begins. Teams start working. But ask five executives what success looks like in two years, and you will get five different answers. The CFO sees consolidated financials. The COO sees integrated operations. The head of sales sees standalone units with loose coordination. The CEO sees something ambitious. Everyone is rowing hard, but in different directions.

This ambiguity is not an oversight. It is strategic cowardice. Leaders avoid defining the end-state because committing to one path means rejecting others. That creates conflict. It forces hard conversations. It exposes disagreements. So, they use vague language about expected gains and strategic fit and let integration teams figure it out. The teams cannot. They thrash. Value evaporates.

The end-state vision framework solves this. It defines four distinct integration models: Standalone, Synergy, Consumption, and Transformation. Each represents a fundamentally different destination. Each requires a different integration approach, timeline, and risk profile. Each creates value through different mechanisms. The choice is not right or wrong. It is explicit or implicit. Explicit choices create accountability. Implicit choices create chaos.

This chapter breaks down all four models. We will examine what each looks like, when it makes sense, and what it demands from your firm. We will explore the progression path from lighter to heavier integration. We will confront the trade-offs honestly. The goal is not to tell you which model to choose. It is to force you to choose and own the consequences.

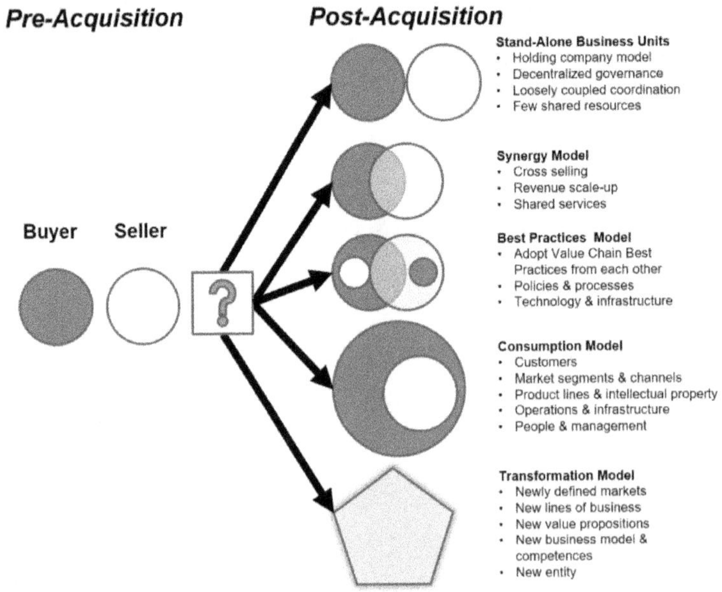

Figure 6.2. All stakeholders need a shared vision of the ultimate end-state.

The Standalone Model
Minimal Integration by Design

The Standalone Model keeps acquired firms separate. Deliberately.

This is not an integration failure. It is not an integration choice. You operate as a holding company with decentralized governance. The acquired business runs independently with its own leadership, systems, processes, and culture. Coordination is loose. Shared resources are minimal. The firms remain distinct entities under common ownership.

This model makes sense in specific situations. You acquire for portfolio diversification, not operational efficiency. The target operates in a different industry or geography where your expertise does not apply. The acquisition brings management talent you want to retain, and integration would drive them away. The target's culture and speed are assets you would destroy through integration. The regulatory environment requires operational separation. The business model depends on entrepreneurial autonomy that corporate processes would kill.

Private equity firms use this model extensively. They buy firms, improve them individually, and sell them separately. The holding company provides access to capital, strategic guidance, and governance oversight without operational integration. Each portfolio company optimizes independently. Success is measured company by company, not through combined performance.

Berkshire Hathaway built an empire on this approach. They acquire strong businesses with excellent management, then leave them alone. No value targets. No integration plans. No corporate mandates. Just capital, governance, and freedom to operate. The model works because they acquire quality, not potential. They are not buying turnarounds or betting on integration value.

Value Creation Mechanisms

Standalone value creation is financial, not operational.

The primary mechanism is capital efficiency. You provide cheaper capital than the standalone business could access independently. Your balance sheet, credit rating, and access to capital markets create financing advantages. The target reduces debt costs, optimizes capital structure, and funds growth initiatives that were previously unaffordable. This is real value, just not the combined value most people imagine.

Portfolio effects matter too. Investors value diversified portfolios differently from concentrated bets. Multiple revenue streams reduce volatility. Exposure across industries, geographies, or customer segments creates stability. This portfolio premium shows up in your valuation multiple. You are creating shareholder value through risk management, not cost reduction.

Strategic optionality has value. Owning businesses in adjacent spaces gives you options. You can enter new markets, shift resources, or pursue opportunities that were previously unavailable. These options have value even if you never exercise them. They are insurance against market shifts and competitive threats.

Management teams leverage scale. Your better practices (we say 'better' because no practice is ever truly best, and improvement is continuous) in governance, capital allocation, and strategic planning can spread across portfolio companies without operational integration. You are exporting knowledge, not systems. The target adopts what works for it and ignores what does not. This creates value without the friction of forced integration.

Execution Requirements

Standalone integration is simple but not easy.

The governance model is critical. You need clear boundaries between parent-company oversight and operating-company autonomy. What decisions require board approval? What is delegated to management? What metrics drive accountability? These lines must be explicit. Ambiguity creates friction, second-guessing, and micromanagement that destroy the autonomy you are trying to preserve.

Leadership retention matters more than in other models. The target's management team is running the show. If they leave, value evaporates. This requires thoughtful retention packages, equity incentives aligned with long-term performance, and cultural respect. You cannot treat acquired executives as employees. They are partners running businesses you own but do not operate.

Financial reporting needs standardization even when operations stay separate. You need consolidated financials for public reporting, capital allocation decisions, and performance monitoring. This means chart-of-accounts alignment, reporting calendar synchronization, and audit coordination. The back-office work is real, even if front-office operations remain independent.

The hardest challenge is restraint. Corporate functions want to help. They see inefficiencies and want to fix them. They propose shared services, system consolidation, and process standardization. Each idea makes sense individually. Collectively, they destroy the standalone model. You need discipline to resist integration creep. Set clear boundaries and defend them.

When Standalone Fails

The standalone model breaks down in predictable ways.

Investors question the strategy. If you are not integrating, why acquire? Why not just invest in the firm as a financial stakeholder? The holding company discount becomes real. Your stock trades below the sum-of-parts value because the market does not see strategic logic. This pressure pushes toward integration even when Standalone is the right choice.

Operational independence breeds strategic divergence. The acquired business optimizes for its objectives, not yours. They make decisions that conflict with your strategy. They compete with your other businesses. They develop capabilities that duplicate yours. Without integration, alignment is voluntary. Voluntary alignment is fragile.

Cost pressures mount. Maintaining separate systems, processes, and firms is expensive. Every shared service you do not consolidate is overhead duplication. Every system you do not integrate is tech debt. Every process that is not standardized is inefficient. These costs are real. The question is whether eliminating them destroys more value than it creates.

Talent mobility stagnates. People cannot move between businesses without friction when systems and processes are different. Career paths are siloed. Knowledge does not transfer between buyer and seller. Your ability to develop talent and build organizational capability suffers. This matters more over time as the initial management team ages out.

The standalone model works when you are buying quality assets that do not need fixing and where integration would destroy value. It fails when an integration value exists, but you lack the courage to pursue it. Know which situation you are in.

The Synergy Model

Selective Integration for Value

The Synergy Model is the default acquisition playbook. Integrate selectively. Capture obvious value. Preserve what works.

This model operates businesses as strategic business units within a larger corporate structure. You pursue cross-selling opportunities. You consolidate shared services. You reduce redundant costs. You combine balance sheets to optimize capital. But you maintain distinct brands, separate go-to-market motions, and independent product organizations. Integration is purposeful, not comprehensive.

The logic is straightforward. Some functions benefit from integration. Finance, HR, IT infrastructure, and procurement scale efficiently. Consolidating these creates measurable cost savings without disrupting customer-facing operations. Other functions benefit from coordination without integration. Sales teams can cross-sell products while maintaining separate quotas and compensation. Product teams can share roadmaps while developing independently. You integrate where it helps, coordinate where it matters, and leave alone what works.

Most public company acquisitions target this model. They promise specific numbers, usually 20% to 30% of the target's cost base. They identify integration opportunities by function. They create workstreams for finance consolidation, IT rationalization, and procurement leverage. They build business cases showing payback within eighteen to twenty-four months. The model is well-understood, relatively low-risk, and produces quantifiable results.

The Synergy Toolkit

Synergy value comes from five sources. Master these, and you will capture most of what is available.

Cross-selling is the most valuable and hardest to achieve. Your sales team sells the target's products. The target's sales team sells yours. Revenue per customer increases. Sales efficiency improves. Customer relationships deepen. But execution is complex. Sales teams need training on new products. Compensation systems need alignment. Channel conflicts need resolution. Early attempts often fail. Success requires patience and realistic expectations.

Cost reduction is easier. Eliminate redundant overhead. Close duplicate facilities. Consolidate vendors. Standardize processes. These savings are tangible, achievable, and quick. They form the backbone of most value cases. The challenge is avoiding cuts that damage the business. Easy cost reductions happen in the first year. Deeper cuts risk muscle, not just fat.

Shared services create efficiency at scale. Combined finance organizations, HR functions, IT operations, and back-office processes serve both businesses from centralized teams. This eliminates duplication and enables automation investments that were not viable at a smaller scale. But implementation is complex. Systems need integration. Processes need standardization. Service levels need definition. The benefits are real but distant.

Balance sheet combination optimizes capital. You refinance the seller's debt at lower rates. You redeploy cash more efficiently. You access capital markets on better terms. You optimize working capital across businesses. These are financial engineering benefits, but they are legitimate value creation. The combined entity has lower capital costs and more financial flexibility than the separate firms.

Procurement leverage scales purchasing power. Combined volume increases negotiating power with suppliers. You can consolidate vendors, negotiate better terms, and standardize specifications. This creates immediate, measurable savings. It is low-risk, assuming the seller was buying similar goods and services. The challenge is coordinating procurement without disrupting supplier relationships that matter to the business.

Integration Sequencing

Sequence matters. Integrate in the wrong order, and you destroy the value you are trying to create.

Start with back-office consolidation. Finance, HR, IT, and legal can integrate without affecting customers or revenue operations. These functions are support, not core business. Disruption is internal. You can work through problems without customer impact. The gains are quantifiable, and the timelines are manageable. This creates early wins that build momentum.

Next comes process and system harmonization. Standardize where it creates value. Accept diversity where it does not. The goal is not uniformity. It is efficiency. Some processes should be identical across businesses. Others work better when tailored to specific contexts. The decision framework is simple: does standardization reduce costs or improve quality enough to justify the disruption? If yes, standardize. If no, leave it alone.

Revenue initiatives come last. Cross-selling, channel integration, and go-to-market coordination happen after operational stability is achieved. Revenue gains are fragile. They depend on customer trust and sales force effectiveness. Both are damaged by internal chaos. Get the back office working before you ask the front office to take on new tasks. The revenue gains will be there when you are ready.

This sequencing violates most executive instincts. Leaders want revenue growth immediately. They downplay back-office work as administrative. But the data is clear. Firms that stabilize operations first achieve higher value realization than those that chase revenue gains while their back offices remain broken. Patience with operational integration creates capacity for revenue growth.

A business services firm demonstrated the sequence under pressure. It acquired a competitor at roughly a quarter of its revenue, with a business case built on shared services and cross-selling. Sales leadership wanted cross-sell campaigns to run in the first ninety days. The integration leader refused, on the strength of a prior deal in which the firm had pushed revenue programs while the back office was still split, and had watched its own sales force burn credibility quoting prices from two systems. This time, finance, HR, and the service platforms consolidated first. Cross-selling launched in month eight, into an organization that could quote, contract, and deliver as one firm. Synergy realization reached 85% of the announced case by month twenty. The earlier deal had reached barely half. Same firm. Same playbook on paper. Different sequence in practice.

The Synergy Trap

The value model fails when you count every possible benefit and assume they are all additive.

Value estimates are usually optimistic. Cross-selling projections assume perfect execution. Cost reduction targets assume no revenue impact. Shared services benefits assume smooth implementation. Each assumption is individually reasonable. Collectively, they are fantasy. Real value realization runs 60% to 70% of initial estimates. Factor that in upfront, or the deal does not work at actual results.

Integration creates costs that people ignore in business cases. You need duplicate staffing during transition. You pay severance for eliminated positions. You invest in system integration and process redesign. You lose productivity during change. You incur one-time costs for facility closures and vendor transitions. These costs are real cash outlays that reduce net deal value. Budget for the costs explicitly.

Some gains conflict. Aggressive cost reduction damages customer service and sales effectiveness. Rapid integration drives talent attrition. Procurement consolidation disrupts supplier relationships. You cannot maximize every value category simultaneously. Trade-offs are inevitable. The question is whether you are making them consciously or discovering them accidentally.

The biggest risk is distraction. Integration consumes management attention. The team that should be running the business is in integration meetings. Customer relationships suffer. Product development slows. Market opportunities get missed. Competitors attack. You capture gains but lose momentum. The net result might be value destruction rather than creation. Protect the base business while pursuing gains.

The Consumption Model
Full Integration for Scale

The Consumption Model eliminates the target as a separate entity. You absorb it completely.

Product lines merge. Market segments combine. Distribution channels integrate. Technologies consolidate. Operations unify. Infrastructure becomes shared. Management structures collapse. One entity emerges from two. The target's brand might survive in the portfolio, but the firm ceases to exist as an independent entity.

This model makes sense when you are acquiring in your core business. Same industry. Similar customers. Overlapping products. Redundant infrastructure.

The target has capabilities or market presence you want, but maintaining them separately creates inefficiency. Integration unlocks value that separation wastes.

Scale economics drive the logic. Two sales forces covering the same territory are a waste. Two manufacturing facilities making similar products is excess capacity. Two R&D teams developing parallel technologies is duplication. Two back offices processing similar transactions are overhead bloat. Consumption eliminates all of it. You create a single, more efficient operation.

Market consolidation follows this model. You buy a competitor, integrate operations, and emerge as the market share leader. This is how industries mature. Dozens of regional players consolidate into a few national leaders. Those leaders join forces to create global giants. Each acquisition follows the consumption playbook: absorb, integrate, optimize, move on.

Integration Depth

Consumption requires integration at every level. Half measures do not work.

Product portfolios merge completely. You rationalize SKUs, consolidate platforms, and create unified roadmaps. Redundant products get eliminated. Overlapping features get combined. Development resources get pooled. The result is a streamlined portfolio with clearer positioning and better resource utilization. But the transition disrupts customers who liked the old products and developers who built them.

Go-to-market integration combines sales forces, marketing teams, and channel programs. You eliminate territory overlap, merge account teams, and unify messaging. Some customer relationships survive. Others do not. Some sales reps thrive. Others leave. Channel partners consolidate or exit. The combined organization is more efficient, but the transition is chaotic.

Technology stack consolidation is brutal. You pick one CRM, one ERP, one collaboration platform, and one data architecture. Everything else goes away. The migration is complex, expensive, and risky. Data needs to be moved. Integrations need rebuilding. Users need retraining. Business processes need redesigning. Count on twelve to eighteen months of disruption and productivity loss.

Operations integration optimizes facilities, supply chain, and service delivery. You close redundant locations. You consolidate manufacturing. You merge distribution networks. You unify service operations. This generates significant cost savings but requires workforce reduction, facility closures, and geographic rationalization. The human and community impact is real.

The management structure becomes a single hierarchy. No more separate leadership teams. No more dual reporting. No more matrix coordination. One organization chart. One set of executives. One decision-making process. This clarity is valuable, but the process of creating it is political and painful. People lose jobs, status, and autonomy.

Value Creation at Scale

Consumption creates value through ruthless efficiency.

Cost savings are massive. You eliminate all redundant overhead, duplicate facilities, and parallel operations. The savings run 30% to 50% of the target's cost base. These are not projections. They are proven math. Two firms become one. Half the executives, half the facilities, half the systems. The costs disappear. The challenge is capturing them without destroying revenue.

Market position strengthens decisively. You are now the largest player in your space. Your scale advantages are insurmountable for smaller competitors. Your market coverage is comprehensive. Your product portfolio is complete. Your financial resources are superior. This position is defensible and valuable. Competitors cannot catch you without their own consolidating acquisitions.

Operational excellence becomes achievable. With a single organization, you can implement better practices consistently. You can invest in automation and technology at scales that were not viable before. You can standardize processes and train teams consistently. You can build capabilities systematically. The integrated organization can be better than either of its predecessors.

Customer value improves if you execute well. The combined portfolio serves customers better. The unified service organization is more responsive. The consolidated R&D delivers better products faster. Geographic coverage is broader. The value proposition strengthens. But only if integration does not disrupt customer relationships in the process.

Execution Demands

Consumption is hard. The most complex integration model. The highest execution risk.

Speed matters more than in other models. You need to move fast before talent leaves, customers defect, and competitors attack. But you also need to move carefully, because mistakes at this level of integration are costly. The balance between speed and quality is delicate. Most firms err on the side of caution and lose momentum. Better to move fast, accept some mistakes, and correct course rapidly.

Decision rights need clarity immediately. Who decides which products survive? Which systems win? Which facilities close? Which people stay? These decisions cannot wait for consensus. They cannot be committee-driven. You need empowered leaders who can make tough calls quickly and stick with them. Indecision kills consumption integrations.

Change management is massive. You are asking people to abandon familiar systems, processes, and relationships. You are reorganizing reporting structures. You are changing compensation. You are redefining roles. You are closing offices. Every employee is affected at both the buyer and seller. Without exceptional change management, you lose the people you need most. They are the ones with options elsewhere.

Customer communication is critical. Your customers are watching. They are worried about service disruption, relationship changes, and product continuity. They are getting calls from competitors offering to help them through this difficult transition. You need proactive, honest, frequent communication. Silence breeds doubt. Doubt breeds defection. Talk to your customers constantly.

The consumption model delivers the highest potential value and the highest integration risk. Get it right, and you dominate your market. Get it wrong, and you destroy two businesses instead of one.

Consumption done well looks like this. A building products manufacturer acquired its closest regional rival, a firm roughly 60% of its size, with overlapping plants, distributors, and product lines. Leadership declared full consumption on the day of the announcement and named the future organization within thirty days, including which of the five plants would close and on what schedule. The clarity was brutal and merciful at once. People knew. Severance terms were published early and honored fully. Two plants closed over fourteen months, with relocation offers and extended notice for the affected workforce. Distributors received a single consolidated catalog by month six. The combined firm emerged as the cost leader in its category, with savings above 40% of the target's cost base. The CEO later credited one decision above the rest: declaring the destination on day one, so that every hard call afterward was execution rather than debate.

The Transformation Model

Creating Something New

The Transformation Model is not about integrating what exists. It is about building what does not.

You combine the two firms' capabilities in novel ways to create new business lines, new value propositions, or entry into new industries. The goal is not efficiency or cost reduction. It is innovation at the business model level. You are using the acquisition as raw material for re-invention.

This model is rare. It requires vision, courage, and execution capabilities, which most firms lack. You are not following a playbook. You are writing one. The path is not clear. The outcomes are not predictable. The risks are substantial. But when transformation works, it creates industry-changing value that other models cannot touch.

Think about Amazon buying Whole Foods. Amazon did not just run a grocery chain. They transformed it using Amazon's logistics, technology, and Prime membership. They created a new retail model that blends digital and physical in ways neither firm could achieve alone. That is transformation, not integration.

Or consider Disney acquiring Marvel and Pixar. Disney did not just add content libraries. They integrated those creative capabilities with Disney's distribution, merchandising, and theme park operations to create new entertainment experiences and revenue streams. The whole became genuinely greater than the sum of the parts through intentional transformation.

The Transformation Thesis

Transformation requires a specific strategic insight about combined capabilities.

You see something nobody else sees. A way to combine the target's strengths with yours to create a new offering, serve a new market, or build a new business model. This is not obvious. If it were, competitors would do it. The insight is genuinely novel. It is risky because novel things might not work. But the potential value justifies the risk.

Core competencies must be complementary in non-obvious ways. You are not just adding capabilities. You are multiplying them. Your technology enables their products. Their customer relationships unlock your services. Your operational scale makes their business model viable. Their innovation culture transforms your firm. The combination creates possibilities neither firm could pursue independently.

Market opportunities must be substantial. You are investing heavily in creating something new. The payoff needs to justify that investment. You are not optimizing existing businesses. You are building new ones. The addressable market for the transformed entity must be significantly larger than what either firm serves today. Otherwise, the math does not work.

Timing is critical. Market conditions need to support the new business model. Customer needs must exist even if they are not yet well-articulated. Technology enablers must be mature enough to execute. Competitive dynamics must create an opening. The regulatory environment must permit the new approach. Miss any of these, and the transformation fails regardless of execution quality.

Integration as Innovation

Transformation integration does not follow standard playbooks.

You are not implementing better practices. You are inventing new ones. Standard integration approaches optimize for efficiency and value capture. Transformation integration optimizes for capability combination and innovation. You need different teams, different metrics, different timelines, and different tolerances for risk and failure.

The integration team becomes a startup within the larger firm. They have clear objectives but significant autonomy on methods. They can challenge corporate standards when those standards would constrain innovation. They can move faster than normal governance allows. They can experiment with approaches that might fail. This requires air cover from senior leadership and protection from corporate antibodies that attack anything different.

Resource allocation shifts from cost optimization to capability building. You are investing in new platforms, new teams, and new market development. These are growth investments, not efficiency plays. The business case is not solely based on cost reduction. It is about creating new revenue streams that did not exist before. The ROI timelines are longer, and the uncertainty is higher.

Talent strategy becomes critical. You need the best people from both firms working on the transformation. Not the people you can spare. The people you cannot afford to lose. This creates tension with running the base business. But transformation without top talent fails. Make the hard choice. Staff transformation with A players.

The Transformation Gamble

Transformation is the highest-risk, highest-reward integration model.

Most attempts fail. The strategic insight proves wrong. The capabilities do not combine as expected. The market does not materialize. Execution stumbles. Competitors respond. The firm rejects the change. Any of these kills the transformation. The failure rate is high because you are attempting something genuinely difficult and novel.

Success creates category-defining firms. You establish new markets, set industry standards, and capture first-mover advantages that compound for years. Your competitive position becomes unassailable because you are competing in a space you created. The value creation is massive and durable. But success requires vision, execution excellence, and luck.

The decision to pursue transformation must be conscious and committed. You cannot start with transformation, get scared, and retreat to value capture. You cannot try transformation, fail, and pivot to consumption. Transformation requires sustained commitment through inevitable setbacks. Leadership must believe in the end-state vision enough to persist when others doubt. Without that conviction, choose a different model.

Firms capable of transformation are rare. It requires strategic insight, execution capability, change management excellence, and cultural tolerance for risk. Most firms have one or two of these attributes. Few have all four. Be honest about your capabilities before committing to transformation. Better to excel at value capture than fail at transformation.

Choosing Your Path

The Decision Framework

Four models. One choice. How do you decide?

Start with strategic intent. What are you trying to achieve? Portfolio diversification points toward standalone. Operational efficiency suggests the Synergy Model. Market dominance indicates consumption. Industries undergoing major change demand a transformation model. The answer flows from strategy, not convenience.

Assess organizational capability honestly. Integration complexity increases from standalone through transformation. Each step demands more capability. Standalone requires financial management and governance. Synergy needs project management and change leadership. Consumption demands full integration expertise. Transformation requires innovation and risk tolerance. Choose a model you can execute. Ambitious failure is still failure.

Consider the seller's characteristics. Strong standalone businesses with excellent management resist integration. Weak businesses with operational problems need heavier intervention. Targets in your core market invite consumption. Targets with complementary capabilities enable transformation. The target constrains your options even if your strategy does not.

Factor in timing and context. Market conditions matter. Regulatory environment constrains choices. Competitive dynamics create urgency or allow patience. Internal capacity determines bandwidth. These contextual factors are not excuses. They are inputs to realistic decision-making. Ignoring them leads to choosing models you cannot execute in current circumstances.

The Progressive Path

You can progress through models sequentially. Light integration first, heavier later.

This reduces risk. You start with standalone or synergy to stabilize the acquisition. You learn the business, retain key talent, and maintain customer relationships. Once stable, you evaluate whether heavier integration makes sense. You might progress from standalone to synergy as opportunities emerge. Or from synergy to consumption as confidence grows. Or from consumption to transformation as capabilities combine.

The progression is not automatic. Each step requires a conscious decision and capability-building. Moving from Synergy to consumption requires developing expertise in full integration. Moving to transformation means building innovation capabilities. These do not emerge naturally. They require investment and commitment.

Progressive integration takes longer but reduces execution risk. You are not betting everything on a single integration approach. You are learning, adapting, and making decisions with better information. The cost is time. The benefit is optionality. Choose this path when you are uncertain about the target's potential or your ability to integrate.

But do not confuse progressive integration with deferring decisions. You still need an end-state vision. You are just reaching it through stages instead of immediately. Each stage has objectives and timelines. You are not wandering. You are leading your firm on a planned path with checkpoints.

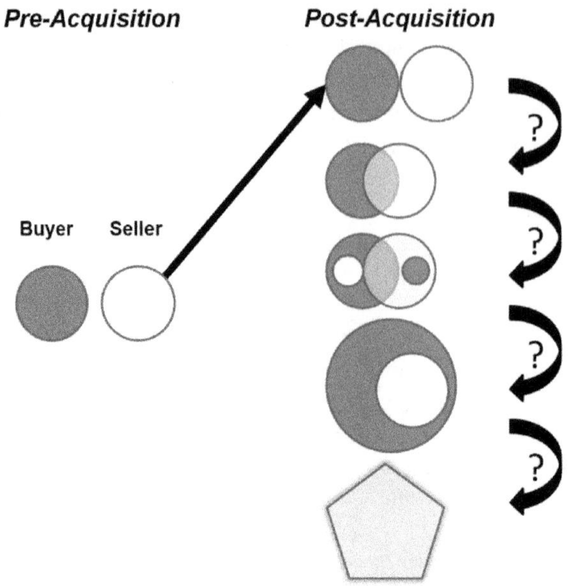

Figure 6.3. A firm's progression towards a transformed entity. How far? How fast?

The Commitment Problem

The biggest failure mode is failing to choose an end-state vision.

A diversified industrial manufacturer acquired a niche automation firm whose founder had built a fiercely independent engineering culture. The CEO told the board the deal would deliver cost and revenue growth targets within two years. The same week, he assured the founder that the business would run as a standalone entity, with its own systems, brand, and roadmap. Both statements were sincere. Both could not be true.

For two years, the firm executed neither model. Corporate finance consolidated reporting, which the founder read as the first betrayal. Corporate IT proposed a system migration, withdrew it after the founder escalated, then proposed it again under a new name. The value targets stayed in the board deck, unowned. The autonomy promise stayed in the founder's memory, unfulfilled. In month nineteen, the founder left, and her two best engineers followed within the quarter. The firm ended up holding the costs of both models and the benefits of neither. Integration expense without results. Autonomy erosion without integration.

The failure was not the choice of the wrong model. No model was ever chosen.

Leaders use vague language about flexibility and keeping options open. CEOs tell their boards they will pursue value gains while telling the seller they will maintain autonomy. They avoid committing to an end-state because commitment creates accountability. If you declare consumption and fail to integrate, that is a visible failure. If you never declare a model, you can claim you are making progress regardless of results.

This ambiguity kills value. Integration teams do not know what they are trying to achieve. They work on everything and nothing. Cost savings happen haphazardly. Revenue growth never materializes. The target stays partially independent but loses the benefits of autonomy. The acquirer invests in integration but does not capture full value. You get the costs of integration without the benefits. The worst outcome.

Choosing creates clarity. It aligns the firm. It enables measurement. It creates accountability. You might choose wrong. That is fixable. You can pivot to a different model when you learn more. But you cannot fix ambiguity. Ambiguity just persists, destroying value quarter after quarter.

Make the choice. Communicate it clearly. Hold yourself accountable for executing it. Change it if circumstances warrant. But choose. Your firm is waiting for direction.

Common Mismatches

Certain choices consistently fail. Recognize the patterns and avoid them.

Do not choose standalone when you need cost reduction to justify the price. If your deal model requires cost savings or revenue growth to meet return targets, a standalone end state will not work. You are creating a built-in failure. Either pay less or choose a different integration model. Do not expect integration gains for standalone execution.

Do not choose consumption for innovation acquisitions. The integration will destroy what you acquired. Startups thrive on autonomy, speed, and culture. Consumption eliminates all three. You lose the talent, kill the innovation, and end up with some code and a customer list. That is not why you bought the firm. Choose synergy or standalone for innovation deals.

Do not choose a transformation without supporting capabilities. Vision without execution is fantasy. If you lack an innovative culture, risk tolerance, and integration expertise, transformation will fail. Your firm will reject the changes. Your leadership will lose confidence during setbacks. You will retreat to consumption and salvage what you can. Better to acknowledge capability limits upfront.

Do not let the target choose the model. Their preference reflects their interests, not yours. The seller's management wants autonomy. They will argue for a standalone end-state. But you paid for value creation that might require deeper integration. Listen to their input. Respect their concerns. Then make the strategic choice based on value-creation logic, not on politics and emotion.

Implications for the CEO

Integration without vision is chaos. Vision without commitment is theater. Commitment without capability is delusion.

The end-state vision framework forces clarity. Four models. Different value creation logic. Different integration approaches. Different capabilities required. Different risk profiles. Choose one. Own the choice. Execute with discipline.

Standalone works when you are buying quality that does not need fixing. Keep it separate. Provide capital and governance. Let good management run good businesses. The value is financial, not operational. That is legitimate if you pay standalone prices and have standalone expectations.

Synergy delivers when selective integration creates measurable value. Cross-selling, cost reduction, shared services, and balance sheet optimization are real. The execution is well understood. The risks are manageable. The timelines are reasonable. This is the default model because it works for most deals. Master it before attempting more ambitious integration.

Consumption creates scale advantages through full integration. One organization. One set of systems. One operating model. The cost savings are massive. The market position is dominant. The execution is complex and risky. But done right, you emerge as the category leader. Competitors cannot match your economics. That position is valuable and defensible.

Transformation builds something new from combined capabilities. New business lines. New value propositions. New markets. The vision is ambitious. The execution is difficult. The failure rate is high. But success creates a category-defining combination and industry-changing value. Attempt this only if you have the vision, capability, and commitment to persist through setbacks.

The choice matters more than you think. Your end-state vision shapes integration priorities, resource allocation, and success metrics. It determines which talent you retain, which systems you keep, and which processes you preserve. It creates the filter through which you make thousands of integration decisions. Get the vision wrong and every downstream decision compounds the error.

70% of acquisitions fail due to execution issues, not strategic flaws. But execution failures often trace back to vision ambiguity. Teams cannot execute a plan if the end-state does not exist. They cannot make good decisions without clear objectives. They cannot measure progress without defined destinations. The end-state vision provides all of this. It is the foundation for everything else.

The framework is simple. The choice is hard. The execution is harder. But firms that master this create systematic acquisition capabilities. They know which models work for different deal types. They have built the capabilities to execute each model. They recognize mismatches and avoid them. They commit to chosen paths and deliver results.

Start with strategy. What value are you creating and how? Match the model to the value logic. Assess your capabilities honestly. Choose a model you can execute. Communicate it clearly. Hold yourself accountable. Adjust when learning demands it. But choose. The worst outcome is avoiding the choice and discovering three years later that you have drifted nowhere.

Know where you are going. That is the necessary first step to getting there.

Chapter 7

Adoption of Better Practices

Figure 7.1. It does not have to be a contest. Better practice can come from either side or from combining both.

The integration steering committee convenes for its monthly review. The agenda item: 'Operational Best Practices Integration.' The COO from the acquiring company presents first. His slides show the buyer's manufacturing processes. Lean methodology. Six Sigma. World-class safety record. Proven results across fifteen plants on three continents.

The plan is clear: roll out the buyer's practices to all acquired facilities. Timeline: six months. Budget: allocated. Training: scheduled. Questions?

The acquired company's VP of Operations raises his hand. 'Our defect rate is thirty percent lower than yours. Our safety record is better. Our throughput per employee is higher. Why are we adopting your practices?'

Silence.

This moment repeats in acquisitions everywhere. The assumption: the buyer has better practices. The buyer paid the premium. The buyer is larger. Therefore, the buyer's way is the right way.

This assumption destroys value.

This chapter presents a framework for deciding which practices to adopt, which to integrate, and which to keep separate. The framework prevents two failure modes: forcing inferior practices onto superior organizations and creating operational chaos by trying to integrate everything.

Another strategic initiative during which better practices are a key theme is the formation and implementation of shared services. Certain functions, such as information technology, human resources, and accounting, are consolidated across multiple operating business units. Whose processes to adopt, integrate, or transform. The choices are not easy.

The Arrogance Problem

Acquirers develop blind spots. The company succeeded. It grew. It generated the cash to buy others. Success breeds confidence. Confidence becomes assumption. The assumption: our way works, therefore it is the best way.

This logic fails. The buyer's practices enabled success in the buyer's context. That does not make them universally superior. The acquired company succeeded, too. It built something valuable enough to buy. Its practices enabled that success.

Consider what gets lost when buyers force their practices onto acquired companies without evaluation:

Innovation methods that produced the acquired company's differentiated products get replaced by the buyer's stage-gate process. The stage-gate process is rigorous and scalable. It is also slower and more bureaucratic. The innovation that made the acquisition valuable slows to a crawl.

Customer service approaches that generated industry-leading satisfaction scores get replaced by the buyer's centralized call center model. The call center is cost-efficient. It also cannot handle the complexity of the acquired company's custom solutions. Customer satisfaction drops. Customers defect.

Supply chain methods that enabled rapid responses to demand fluctuations get replaced by the buyer's planning-driven approach. The planning approach optimizes inventory costs. It also cannot respond to the acquired company's volatile market. Stockouts increase. Revenue suffers.

These failures share a pattern. The buyer had better practices for the buyer's business. But the acquired company operates in a different context. Different customers. Different products. Different market dynamics. Different success factors. Forcing one set of practices onto a different context destroys what made the acquisition valuable.

The Integration Complexity Problem

The opposite failure mode is equally destructive. Some integration teams recognize that both companies have valuable practices. They decide to integrate everything. Take the best elements from each side. Create hybrid processes that capture the strengths of both.

This sounds sophisticated. It creates chaos.

Integrating practices is expensive. It requires analysis, design, testing, training, and deployment. It creates transition risk. During integration, neither the old practice nor the new practice works fully. Performance degrades. Errors increase. People become confused about which process to follow.

Integration also creates dependencies. When you integrate sales processes, you must integrate sales systems. When you integrate sales systems, you must integrate customer data. When you integrate customer data, you must integrate data governance. One integration decision cascades into dozens of connected changes.

Organizations cannot absorb unlimited change simultaneously. Trying to integrate everything means integrating nothing well. Resources fragment. Attention diffuses. Simple implementations become multi-year programs. Value realization delays. Costs escalate.

The solution requires selectivity. Some practices should be adopted wholesale. Take one side's approach and roll it out to the other side. Some practices should be integrated. Analyze both approaches, design a better one, and deploy it everywhere. Some practices should remain separate. Let each side keep what works for them.

The framework that follows provides a method for making these choices systematically.

Three Strategic Intents

The better practices framework serves three purposes. Each purpose addresses a specific integration challenge.

Intent One: Identify What Should Be Adopted or Integrated

The first intent is inventory. Map all the practices that matter. Not just the obvious ones. Marketing and sales practices. Innovation and engineering practices. Operations and supply chain practices. Customer service practices. Support function practices.

For each practice area, ask four questions:

Does this practice create competitive advantage? If yes, it matters. If no, it is administrative hygiene.

Does this practice differ significantly between the companies? If the practices are already similar, integration is trivial. If they differ fundamentally, integration is complex.

Does this practice need to be consistent across the combined entity? Some practices require consistency. Financial controls must be consistent. Others benefit from variation. Sales approaches can vary by geography or customer segment.

Does integration create value or just cost? Some integration efforts unlock real value. Consolidating procurement practices reduces costs. Other integration efforts consume resources without clear benefit. Harmonizing innovation processes might not improve innovation.

These questions filter the universe of practices. They identify which practices warrant attention and which can be left alone.

Intent Two: Drive Thinking About Whose Practices to Adopt

The second intent is evaluation. Once you know which practices matter, assess them objectively. Whose practice is better? The buyer's? The seller's? Neither?

Objective assessment requires criteria. Not politics. Not organizational hierarchy. Not who paid the premium. Criteria tied to performance.

Different practice areas require different metrics:

For manufacturing: defect rates, throughput, safety records, cost per unit, flexibility, time to market.

For innovation: time from concept to launch, success rate of new products, R&D productivity, patent generation, and customer adoption rates.

For sales: win rates, sales cycle length, customer acquisition cost, average deal size, customer retention, and sales productivity.

For customer service: resolution time, first-call resolution rate, customer satisfaction scores, cost per interaction, escalation rates.

Compare the companies on these metrics. Be honest. Sometimes the buyer is better. Sometimes the seller is better. Sometimes neither is good enough, and both need improvement.

This evaluation forces uncomfortable conversations. The buyer's leadership must acknowledge when the acquired company has superior practices. The acquired company's leadership must acknowledge when the buyer's approach is more effective. Both must accept when integration is the right answer, even though it is the hardest path.

Intent Three: Ensure True Better Practices Are Embedded

The third intent is institutionalization. Decisions about better practices are meaningless without execution. The framework must lead to action.

When you decide to adopt a practice, adoption must happen. This requires change management. Training. Process documentation. System enablement. Leadership reinforcement. Measurement. The practice must become the new normal, not a parallel experiment that people ignore.

When you decide to integrate practices, integration must produce something better than either starting point. This requires design. Piloting. Refinement. Deployment. The integrated practice must capture the strengths of both approaches while eliminating weaknesses.

When you decide to keep practices separate, separation must be intentional and managed. This requires clear boundaries. Documentation of which practice applies where. Coordination mechanisms to prevent conflict. The separation must make sense operationally, not just politically.

The Capabilities Roadmap Framework

The framework is a roadmap. It maps capabilities across the value chain. For each capability, it specifies whether to adopt seller practices, adopt buyer practices, or integrate better practices from both.

The roadmap spans nine capability areas:

Customer Engagement and Experience. How the company interacts with customers. How it understands customer needs. How it delivers value.

Marketing and Brand. How the company positions itself. How it communicates value. How it builds brand equity.

Innovation and Engineering. How the company creates new products. How it solves technical problems. How it moves from concept to launch.

Sales, Channels, and Partners. How the company reaches customers. How it manages distribution. How it enables partners.

Supply Chain. How the company sources materials. How it manages suppliers. How it plans production. How it manages inventory.

Operations. How the company manufactures products. How it manages quality. How it ensures safety. How it maintains facilities.

Customer Service. How the company handles inquiries. How it resolves issues. How it maintains relationships post-sale.

Environmental, Safety, and Health. How the company manages environmental impact. How it ensures worker safety. How it maintains health standards.

General and Administrative Functions. HR, IT, Finance, Legal, Facilities. The support functions that enable the business.

For each capability area, the framework provides three options with clear definitions:

Option One: Adopt Seller Practice

Choose this option when the seller's practice is demonstrably superior to the buyer's. Superior means better performance on relevant metrics. Not different. Not interesting. Better.

When you adopt seller practices, the buyer changes. This requires humility. The buyer must acknowledge that the acquired company does something better. The buyer must learn from the acquired company. The buyer must adopt methods it did not invent.

This option works when the seller's practice is proven, documented, and transferable. It fails when the practice is tied to specific people who might leave or specific contexts that do not exist at the buyer.

Option Two: Adopt Buyer Practice

Choose this option when the buyer's practice is demonstrably superior to the seller's. This is the default assumption in most acquisitions. It should not be. But when the data supports it, execute decisively.

When you adopt buyer practices, the seller changes. This creates resistance. People at the acquired company resent being told their methods are inferior. They resist adoption. They slow-walk implementation. They maintain shadow processes.

Managing this resistance requires transparency. Show the data. Explain why the buyer's practice is better. Involve the acquired company's people in the rollout. Give them ownership of making it work. This transforms adoption from an imposed change into a collaborative improvement.

Option Three: Integrate Better Practices

Choose this option when both companies have valuable elements worth preserving. When neither practice is fully superior. When synthesis creates something better than either starting point.

Integration is the most complex option. It requires designing a new practice. Testing it. Refining it. Deploying it to both organizations simultaneously. It creates transition risk. Both organizations must abandon familiar methods and adopt something new.

Integration works when the value of the synthesized practice justifies the complexity. It fails when chosen as a political compromise rather than a performance optimization.

A warning: integration should be rare. Most practices should be adopted from one side or the other. Trying to change everything creates integration paralysis. Select integration only when the benefit clearly exceeds the cost.

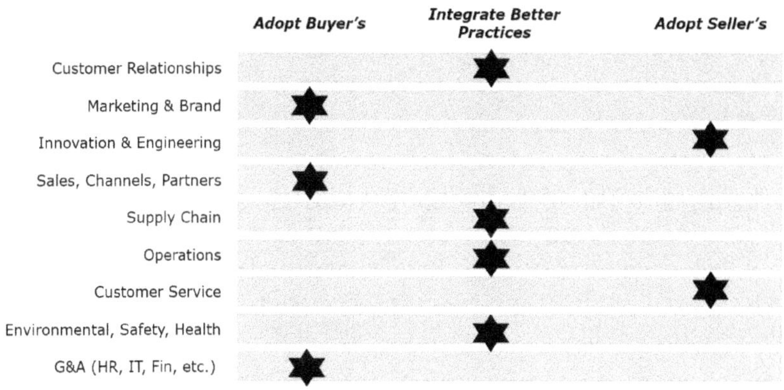

Figure 7.2. The capabilities roadmap: for each capability area, adopt the buyer practice, adopt the seller practice, or integrate to create a better practice.

Applying the Framework: A Detailed Example

Consider a technology company acquisition. A large enterprise software buyer acquires a fast-growing startup with innovative products but immature operations. The buyer brings scale, infrastructure, and established processes. The seller brings innovation, agility, and customer intimacy.

The integration team builds a capabilities roadmap. They assess each capability area against performance data. What they discover challenges initial assumptions.

Customer Engagement and Experience: Adopt Seller Practice

The data is unambiguous. The seller's Net Promoter Score is 72. The buyer's is 31. The seller's customer churn rate is 4 percent annually. The buyer's is 18 percent. The seller's expansion revenue is 135 percent of base. The buyer's is 103 percent.

Why? The seller organized around customer success. Every customer had a dedicated success manager who understood their business, tracked their outcomes, and proactively solved problems. The buyer organized around support tickets. Customers called when things broke. Problems got fixed. But no one owned the relationship. No one drove value realization.

The decision: adopt the seller's customer success model across the combined entity. This meant hiring success managers for the buyer's existing customers. This meant training hundreds of people on a new methodology. This meant changing compensation models. This meant building new systems.

Expensive. Disruptive. Necessary. The seller's approach drove retention and expansion. Those metrics drove lifetime value. Lifetime value drove valuation. The buyer's reactive support model was destroying value. Adoption was not optional.

Marketing and Brand: Integrate Better Practices

Marketing showed a split. The buyer excelled at enterprise marketing. Trade shows. Industry analyst relations. Reference customers. Sales enablement. The metrics proved it: higher-quality leads, better conversion rates on enterprise deals, and stronger brand recognition in Global 2000 accounts.

The seller excelled at digital marketing. Content creation. Community building. Social engagement. Product-led growth. The metrics proved it: lower customer acquisition cost, faster growth in the small and midsize business segment, stronger developer mindshare, viral product adoption.

Neither approach was fully superior. The buyer needed the seller's digital capabilities to reach small and mid-size customers efficiently. The seller needed the buyer's enterprise capabilities to move upmarket. The combined entity needed both.

The decision: integrate marketing practices. Create a unified marketing organization that combines enterprise rigor with digital agility. Preserve the seller's content engine and community programs. Adopt the buyer's analyst relations and enterprise event capabilities. Build hybrid campaigns that worked across segments. This took twelve months to design and deploy. It worked. Marketing efficiency improved across all segments.

Innovation and Engineering: Adopt Seller Practice

Innovation was stark. The seller shipped major releases every six weeks. The buyer ships annually. The seller had 95 percent of customers on the current release. The buyer had 60 percent of customers two releases behind. The seller's feature velocity was three times the buyer's. Customer satisfaction with the product roadmap was 25 points higher for the seller.

The buyer's process was rigorous. Stage gates. Business cases. Committee approvals. Risk assessments. This rigor prevented failures. It also prevented speed. By the time a feature went through the process, market needs had evolved.

The seller's process was lightweight. Small teams. Fast decisions. Continuous deployment. Customer feedback loops. This speed enabled innovation. It also created technical debt and occasional instability.

The decision: adopt the seller's innovation approach with selective controls. Move to continuous deployment. Empower small teams. Shorten feedback cycles. But add the buyer's security reviews and compliance checks. The speed mattered more than the rigor. The buyer's innovation velocity was destroying competitive position. The seller's approach was imperfect but better.

Sales, Channels, and Partners: Adopt Buyer Practice

Sales showed clear advantage to the buyer. The buyer had a mature sales organization. Defined methodologies. Territory management. Sales operations. Forecasting accuracy. Pipeline discipline. Deal review processes. The seller's sales organization was effective but informal. No CRM discipline. No forecasting rigor. High performer dependency.

The metrics supported the buyer. The buyer's win rate on competitive deals was 42 percent. The seller's was 38 percent. The buyer's sales cycle for similar deals was 20 percent shorter. The buyer's forecast accuracy was 91 percent. The seller's was 73 percent.

The decision: adopt buyer sales practices across the combined entity. Train the seller's sales team on the buyer's methodology. Implement the buyer's CRM system. Adopt the buyer's pipeline management and forecasting processes. The seller's team resisted initially. They viewed the buyer's approach as bureaucratic. But the data convinced them. Forecast accuracy improved within ninety days. Win rates increased within six months.

Supply Chain: Adopt Buyer Practice

Supply chain was not close. The buyer operated a sophisticated global supply chain. Supplier relationships. Volume discounts. Risk management. Quality assurance. Logistics optimization. The seller bought components at retail prices with minimal negotiation.

The decision: immediate adoption of buyer supply chain practices. Transfer all seller procurement to the buyer's team. Leverage the buyer's supplier relationships. Achieve immediate cost savings. This was the fastest adoption in the integration. The seller's team welcomed it. They knew their supply chain was weak. The buyer's capabilities created immediate value.

Operations: Integrate Better Practices

Operations showed mixed results. The buyer's operations were efficient at scale. Low cost per unit. High automation. Predictable output. The seller's operations were flexible and responsive. Fast changeovers. Rapid response to special requirements. Customer-specific customization.

The buyer's approach optimized for volume. The seller's approach optimized for variety. The combined entity needed both. Standard products at scale. Custom solutions where needed.

The decision: integrate operations practices. Segment the product portfolio. Standard products use the buyer's high-volume processes. Custom products use the seller's flexible processes. Create clear handoff protocols. This required redesigning production planning. It required new scheduling systems. It took nine months. The result: cost efficiency on standard products, responsiveness on custom products. Both metrics improved.

Customer Service: Adopt Buyer Practice

Customer service metrics favored the buyer. First-call resolution: buyer 76%, seller 62%. Average resolution time: buyer 4.2 hours, seller 8.7 hours. Customer satisfaction: buyer 4.3/5, seller 3.9/5. Cost per case: buyer 40% lower.

The decision: adopt buyer customer service practices. Migrate the seller's customers to the buyer's service platform. Train the seller's service team on the buyer's knowledge management and case routing systems. The transition took six months. Service quality improved. Costs decreased.

Environmental, Safety, and Health: Adopt Buyer Practice

ESH was non-negotiable. The buyer operated under strict regulatory requirements. Comprehensive safety programs. Environmental compliance. Regular audits. The seller had basic safety procedures but lacked formal programs.

The decision: immediate adoption of buyer ESH practices. This was regulatory compliance, not performance optimization. The seller's facilities were brought to the buyer's standards within ninety days. No debate. No integration. Adoption.

General and Administrative: Adopt Buyer Practice

G&A functions showed clear scale advantages to the buyer. Finance had sophisticated systems, controls, and reporting. HR had comprehensive programs, technology, and compliance infrastructure. IT had enterprise architecture, security, and operations capability. Legal had specialized expertise across domains.

The seller's G&A was lean but basic. Adequate for a startup. Insufficient for a scaled enterprise.

The decision: adopt buyer G&A practices across all functions. Migrate the seller to the buyer's systems. Adopt the buyer's policies and controls. Transfer the seller's administrative work to the buyer's shared services. This was standard integration work. The seller's team understood. Many welcomed access to better infrastructure.

Interpreting the Example

The example reveals several patterns about how better practice decisions should be made:

Pattern One: The Buyer Does Not Always Win

In nine capability areas, the buyer's practices were adopted in five. The seller's practices were adopted in two. Integration occurred in two. The buyer won more often, but not always.

The two areas where the seller won were strategic: customer engagement and innovation. These capabilities drove the acquisition thesis. The seller's customer success model produced superior retention and expansion. The seller's innovation velocity produced superior products. Forcing the buyer's practices onto these areas would have destroyed the value of the acquisition.

This pattern is common. Acquirers buy companies because they do something valuable. That something usually involves practices worth preserving. The framework forces explicit recognition of this reality.

Pattern Two: Integration Is Rare

Only two areas required full integration: marketing and operations. Everything else was adoption. This ratio is typical. Integration is complex and expensive. It should be selective.

The two integration decisions were justified. Marketing needed both enterprise and digital capabilities. Neither company had both. Synthesis created something neither could achieve alone. Operations needed both efficiency and flexibility. The buyer optimized for one. The seller optimized for the other. Integration enabled both.

When integration is chosen for political reasons rather than performance reasons, it fails. Every integration decision in this example had clear performance justification. Neither adoption option alone would achieve the required outcomes.

Pattern Three: Data Drives Decisions

Every decision referenced specific metrics. Customer satisfaction scores. Win rates. Cycle times. Defect rates. Cost per unit. Forecast accuracy. These metrics made decisions defensible.

Without data, better practice decisions become political. Whoever has more organizational power wins. With data, the better practice wins. This shifts the conversation from 'whose practice' to 'which practice performs better.'

Not all practices have clean metrics. Culture and leadership are harder to quantify. But most operational practices do have measurable outcomes. Use them. Let data settle debates.

Pattern Four: Context Matters

The decisions were contextual. Customer engagement adopted the seller's practice because the seller's model produced better outcomes. But sales adopted the buyer's practice because the buyer's discipline produced better outcomes.

Both decisions were correct because they fit the context. The seller's customer success model worked because it aligned with a subscription business model where retention drives value. The buyer's sales methodology worked because it aligned with the complex enterprise sales that require discipline and coordination.

There are no universal best practices. There are practices that work well in specific contexts. The framework forces explicit consideration of context. What works? Where? Why? When?

Pattern Five: Sequence Matters

The example shows varying implementation timelines. Supply chain adoption happened immediately. Innovation adoption took six months. Operations integration took nine months. Marketing integration took twelve months.

This sequencing was deliberate. Simple adoptions happened fast. Complex integrations took time. Risk-critical areas like ESH moved immediately regardless of complexity.

Sequencing prevents overload. Organizations cannot change everything simultaneously. The framework enables prioritization. Which practices must change immediately? Which can wait? Which require extended implementation?

Recommendations for Implementation

The framework works when implemented systematically. Seven recommendations based on repeated application:

Recommendation One: Start During Due Diligence

Do not wait until after close to assess practices. Start during due diligence. Identify the major capability areas. Gather preliminary data on both companies. Develop initial hypotheses about which practices are superior.

This early work serves two purposes. First, it influences deal valuation. If the target has demonstrably superior practices in strategic areas, those practices create value. Second, it accelerates Day 1 readiness. Teams know which practices to adopt and which to integrate. They can plan accordingly.

Recommendation Two: Use a Cross-Functional Team

The roadmap cannot be built by a single function. It requires perspectives from both companies across all major functions. Include operations leaders. Include functional experts. Include people who understand the metrics. Include people who understand the integration constraints.

This diversity prevents blind spots. A single function might not see where the target excels. A single company's perspective might miss opportunities for integration. Cross-functional dialogue surfaces the right answers.

Recommendation Three: Demand Data

Every adoption or integration decision must reference specific performance data. Not opinions. Not preferences. Not organizational hierarchy. Data.

When someone argues that the buyer's practice is better, ask for evidence. When someone argues that the seller's practice is better, ask for evidence. When someone argues for integration, ask for evidence that integration will outperform adoption.

This discipline prevents two problems. First, it prevents political decisions masquerading as performance decisions. Second, it forces teams to actually understand the practices they are evaluating. If they cannot produce data, they do not understand the practices well enough to make a decision.

Recommendation Four: Limit Integration Decisions

Integration should be rare. Most capabilities should adopt practices from one company or the other. Resist the temptation to integrate everything.

Use a forcing mechanism. Allow no more than 20 percent of capabilities to be designated for integration. If the team wants to integrate more, force them to choose. Which integrations matter most? Which can be converted to adoption decisions?

This constraint drives prioritization. It prevents integration from becoming the default answer when teams cannot agree. It forces hard choices about where synthesis truly creates value.

Recommendation Five: Validate with Operators

The roadmap should not be built in a conference room by executives. It must be validated by the people who execute the practices. Operators see details executives miss. They understand dependencies. They know what works and what breaks.

Share the draft roadmap with operational teams. Ask for feedback. Where do they disagree with the assessment? What risks do they see? What opportunities do they see? Incorporate their input. The roadmap becomes better, and adoption becomes easier.

Recommendation Six: Sequence Deliberately

Not everything can happen simultaneously. Some practices must change immediately for regulatory or risk reasons. Others can wait. Build a sequenced implementation plan.

Sequence based on three factors: urgency, complexity, and dependency. High urgency and low complexity happen first. High complexity and low urgency happen last. Dependencies determine ordering when practices must change together.

Make the sequence visible. Create a timeline. Show what happens when. This prevents the organization from being overwhelmed. It creates predictability. It enables resource planning.

Recommendation Seven: Track and Adjust

The roadmap is a hypothesis. Some decisions will prove correct. Some will prove wrong. Track actual outcomes against expected outcomes. When adoption fails to deliver expected improvements, investigate why. When integration proves more complex than expected, adjust the approach.

Build a review cadence. Quarterly is typical. Review what has been implemented. Review whether it worked. Review what comes next. Adjust the roadmap based on learning. This prevents the organization from rigidly following a plan that reality has invalidated.

Implications for the CEO

Better practice decisions determine whether acquisitions create or destroy value. When buyers force inferior practices onto superior organizations, value evaporates. When integration teams try to integrate everything, execution fragments. The better practices framework prevents both failure modes.

Eight principles guide effective application. The first is to challenge the assumption that the buyer always has the better practice, because sometimes the buyer is better, sometimes the seller is, and sometimes neither is good enough; let the data decide. The second is to map capabilities systematically across the value chain, from customer engagement through operations to support functions, assessing each area independently, since different areas demand different decisions.

The third is to default to adoption over integration, because most practices should be adopted from one side or the other, and integration is complex and risky enough to choose only when synthesis clearly creates a superior outcome. The fourth is to use performance data, whether customer, financial, operational, or quality metrics, to settle debates about which practice is better.

The fifth is to consider context when evaluating practices because a practice that works well in one setting may fail in another. Understand why a practice succeeds and transfer the principle, not merely the procedure. The sixth is to sequence implementation deliberately, starting with high-urgency, low-complexity changes and delaying high-complexity, low-urgency ones while respecting dependencies.

The seventh is to involve operators in assessment and validation, because they execute the strategy and see the details executives miss. The eighth is to track outcomes and adjust, treating the roadmap as a hypothesis to be tested and reviewed quarterly. Validate or refute it based on what the evidence shows.

The capabilities roadmap creates clarity. It forces explicit decisions about which practices to adopt, which to integrate, and which to keep separate. It prevents the default assumption that the buyer is always right. It prevents the political compromise of integrating everything.

Most importantly, it ensures that better practices are embedded in the combined entity. Not just the buyer's practices. Not just the seller's practices. But the practices that actually perform better regardless of origin.

That is how acquisitions create value. By getting better, not just bigger.

Chapter 8
The Organization Heat Map
Making the Invisible Visible in Acquisition Integration

Figure 8.1. When the organization is under strain, the real problems are hard to see.

The integration team sits in the conference room staring at the org chart. Boxes and lines. Names and titles. The CFO points to Manufacturing. 'Any issues there?' The VP of Operations shrugs. 'Nothing unusual.' The CHRO flips through her notes. 'Turnover is normal. Maybe a little high in Engineering, but nothing alarming.'

Six months later, Manufacturing is hemorrhaging. Two plant managers quit. The quality system collapsed. Customer complaints tripled. Engineering lost half its senior designers to competitors. Supply chain coordination broke down because no one understood the legacy planning tools.

The issues were there from the beginning. Hidden. Dispersed across functions. No single metric captured them. No executive owned all of them. The org chart showed structure. It did not show risk.

This chapter introduces a tool that makes organizational risk visible: the integration heat map. It identifies issues before they become crises. It focuses attention on what matters. It tracks progress as integration unfolds.

The Problem with Organizational Invisibility

Acquisitions concentrate attention on the obvious. Revenue targets. Cost synergies. System migrations. Product roadmaps. These elements are measurable, plannable, and trackable. They show up in integration plans with owners, milestones, and deliverables.

But organizations are not just plans and deliverables. They are people, processes, knowledge, relationships, and culture. These elements do not fit neatly into project plans. They resist simple measurement. They cross functional boundaries. They matter enormously but remain invisible until something breaks.

Consider what integration stress reveals:

The Sales organization looks healthy on paper. Revenue is steady. The pipeline is full. But half the sales force is updating resumes because they do not trust the new comp plan. The other half is confused about which products they are supposed to sell. The VP of Sales knows this. No one else does. The issue stays local until the quarter ends and revenue collapses.

Engineering appears stable. The product roadmap is on track. Projects are on schedule. But the legacy team uses tools that the acquiring firm does not support. IT wants to migrate everyone to the new platform. Engineering resists because the new tools do not support their workflow. The conflict simmers. Productivity drops. Deadlines slip. By the time leadership notices, the roadmap is six months behind.

Operations seems fine. Plants are running. Output is normal. But the acquired firm's quality system uses different standards. Operators trained on one system now work under another. Confusion grows. Defects increase. No one connects the dots until a major customer threatens to switch suppliers.

These failures share a pattern. The issues exist early. They span multiple dimensions: leadership, culture, processes, systems, and talent. They affect specific organizations disproportionately. But they remain invisible because no tool captures them in their entirety.

The organization heat map solves this problem. It makes the invisible visible.

Three Purposes of the Heat Map

The heat map serves three distinct purposes. Each addresses a specific failure mode in integration.

Purpose One: Identify Issues and Risks by Organization

The first purpose is diagnostic. The heat map systematically examines each organization across multiple dimensions. It asks, "Where are the problems?" How severe are they? Which organizations face the greatest risk?

This matters because integration risk is not distributed evenly. Some organizations face minimal disruption. Others face existential challenges. The heat map identifies which is which.

Consider two organizations in the same acquisition. Finance faces systems integration, process harmonization, and reporting consolidation. Complex work, but the issues are well understood. Standard integration playbooks exist. The path forward is clear.

Now consider Sales. Sales faces systems integration plus cultural conflict plus leadership turnover plus comp plan changes plus product portfolio confusion plus customer retention risk. The issues compound. They interact. They create cascading failures.

Without a heat map, leadership treats both organizations the same. With a heat map, leadership sees that Sales needs disproportionate attention. Resources flow where they matter most.

Purpose Two: Support Targeted Interventions

The second purpose is strategic. Once issues are visible, decisions become clearer. Where should integration focus? Which interventions deliver the greatest impact? What can wait?

Integration resources are always constrained. Time is limited. Money is limited. Executive attention is limited. The heat map prevents diffusion. It concentrates effort on the organizations and issues that matter most.

This is not about perfection. It is about triage. Some organizations are healthy and need minimal intervention. Some face moderate challenges that can be addressed with standard solutions. Some face severe, compounding challenges that require immediate, customized action.

The heat map makes triage explicit. It prevents the trap of treating all organizations equally. It enables a differentiated strategy.

Purpose Three: Track Progress Over Time

The third purpose is measurement. The heat map is not a one-time snapshot. It is a periodic diagnostic. Create it at the start of integration. Update it monthly or quarterly. Track how groups move from black circles to gray circles to white circles.

This tracking serves two functions. First, it measures intervention effectiveness. If a group stays at black circles despite focused attention, the interventions are not working. Try something different. Second, it maintains visibility. Integration teams change. Leaders rotate. New people join. The heat map preserves institutional memory. It prevents the organization from forgetting what it learned.

Most integrations track financial metrics obsessively. Revenue. Costs. Synergies. Those metrics are necessary but insufficient. They are lagging indicators. By the time financial performance deteriorates, organizational health has already declined. The heat map is a leading indicator. It shows problems before they hit the numbers.

How the Heat Map Works

The heat map is a matrix. Groups run down the left side. Workstreams run across the top. Each cell sits at the intersection of a group and a workstream, and a severity circle indicates whether issues exist there: a white circle for no issues, a gray circle for issues, and a black circle for significant issues.

The groups capture the entities and segments that the integration must bring together. The enterprise as a whole and the acquired target each get a row, so leadership can see issues at the combined level and at the target level side by side. Major business units (BUs) each have their own rows, labeled BU 1, BU 2, and BU 3. Geographic regions also get rows, since a workstream that looks healthy at the enterprise level can hide serious regional problems: Americas, EMEA, APAC, China, and LATAM each receive a row. The aim is a group list that mirrors how the firm actually runs and where accountability actually sits.

The workstreams span nine areas:

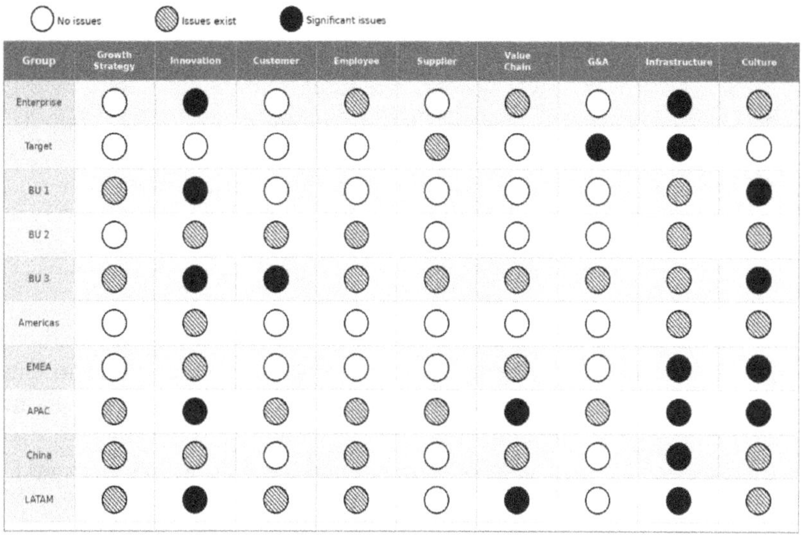

Figure 8.2. The organization heat map reveals issues across groups and workstreams.

Growth Strategy

Do the two firms share a coherent view of where growth will come from? Are the deal thesis and the operating plan aligned, or does each side expect different value drivers? Growth Strategy is the workstream that asks whether the combined entity knows how it intends to win. When a group shows issues here, every downstream workstream inherits the ambiguity, because teams cannot execute toward a destination that no one has defined.

Innovation

Where do new products, services, and ideas come from, and will the acquisition help or hurt that capability? Innovation covers research, design, and the pipeline of what comes next. It is often the reason a firm is acquired and just as often the first thing an integration breaks, because creative teams are sensitive to disruption, tooling changes, and loss of autonomy. Significant issues here threaten the future revenue the deal was meant to secure.

Customer

Are customers retained, served, and grown through the transition? The Customer workstream covers acquisition, retention, service, and the commercial relationships on which revenue depends. Integration noise reaches customers quickly through confused account ownership, changed terms, or slipping service levels. Issues in this workstream tend to convert into lost revenue faster than issues anywhere else.

Employee

Are the people who matter informed, retained, and able to do their work? The Employee workstream covers talent, retention, communication, and change readiness across the group. Organizations cannot execute what they do not understand, and they cannot execute at all if the people who hold critical knowledge leave. Issues here are leading indicators of trouble in every other workstream.

Supplier

Can the combined firm source what it needs on stable terms? The Supplier workstream covers procurement, inbound relationships, and the continuity of supply. Acquisitions disrupt supplier arrangements through renegotiated contracts, vendor consolidation, and shifting volumes. Issues here surface as cost increases, delivery delays, or single points of failure that were invisible before the deal.

Value Chain

Do the activities that create and deliver the product fit together across the two firms? The Value Chain workstream covers the core flow of work, from inputs through operations to delivery, and the coordination required to keep it moving. Issues here mean the combined operation does not yet function as one system, and the seams show up as duplicated effort, broken handoffs, and degraded throughput.

G&A

Can the support functions sustain the combined firm without friction? G&A (general and administrative functions such as finance, legal, human resources, and reporting) is the connective tissue of the enterprise. The work is rarely the source of competitive advantage, but issues here, in consolidated reporting, in compliance, in payroll, create drag that distracts leadership and erodes confidence during integration.

Infrastructure

Are the systems, tools, and physical and digital platforms compatible, and can they be integrated on a sensible timeline? Infrastructure covers the technology backbone and the facilities on which the organization runs. Systems integration consumes enormous resources, and dependence on legacy platforms varies widely across groups. Significant issues here often require an enterprise-level solution rather than a fix confined to one group.

Culture

How different are the cultures, and does the difference create friction or strength? Culture encompasses how teams work, what they value, and whether they regard one another with respect or suspicion. Culture clashes are real but hard to measure, so the heat map forces the question. It makes leaders state plainly where culture is aligned, where it diverges, and where divergence will undermine the rest of the integration.

Building the Heat Map

Building the heat map requires judgment, not just data. It is not a mechanical exercise. It requires people who know the organizations, understand the issues, and can assess risk realistically.

Five steps:

Step One: Assemble the Right Team

The heat map team includes functional leaders from both firms, the integration lead, and HR. Do not delegate this to staff. Leaders must do the assessment. They have the context. They see the patterns. They know the history.

Include skeptics. Include people who will challenge rosy assessments. The heat map only works if it is honest. Optimistic heat maps are worse than no heat map. They create false confidence.

Step Two: Define Organizations

List every major organization that will be impacted by an acquisition. Use the organization chart as a starting point, but do not be bound by it. Some chart boxes can be grouped. Some need to be split.

The goal is granularity without overwhelming detail. Ten to twenty organizations are typical. Fewer than ten and important differences get hidden. More than twenty and the heat map becomes unwieldy.

Step Three: Assess Each Cell

For each group, assess each workstream. Use a simple three-level scheme shown with severity circles:

A white circle means no issues. The group is strong on this workstream. Issues are minor or nonexistent. Minimal intervention needed.

A gray circle means issues exist. They are manageable with standard interventions. Attention required but not urgent.

A black circle means significant issues. There is potential for serious risk and disruption. Urgent, customized intervention required.

Debate each cell. Require evidence. When someone marks a cell as a white circle, ask why. When someone marks it as a black circle, ask what specifically makes it significant. Force specificity. Document the reasoning.

Avoid the temptation to make every cell a gray circle. The gray circle is safe. It says some risk, but nothing terrible. Too many gray circles produce a heat map that tells you nothing. Be willing to mark a black circle when issues are significant. Be willing to mark a white circle when a group is genuinely sound.

Step Four: Identify Patterns

Once the heat map is complete, step back. Look for patterns.

Which groups show mostly black circles? These need immediate, comprehensive intervention. Which groups show mostly white circles? These can be deprioritized. Which groups show mixed patterns? These need selective intervention on specific workstreams.

Which workstreams show black circles across most groups? These are systemic issues. They require enterprise-level solutions, not group-specific fixes. Which workstreams vary widely? These suggest the issue is local, not systemic.

The patterns tell you where to focus. They reveal whether integration challenges are concentrated or dispersed. They show whether issues are isolated or interconnected.

Step Five: Develop Intervention Plans

For each black-circle cell, develop a specific intervention plan. Not a vague intention. A plan. Who owns it? What will they do? By when? How will success be measured?

For gray-circle cells, decide which merit attention now and which can wait. Not everything can be addressed simultaneously. Sequence the work based on risk and dependency.

For white-circle cells, validate the assessment. Is it truly clear, or are you missing something? If it is genuinely sound, document why. What makes this group resilient? Can those factors be replicated elsewhere?

Case Example: A Global Industrial Acquisition

Consider an acquisition in which a global industrial firm bought a sizable competitor with strong products and a broad international footprint. The deal thesis combined product reach with geographic expansion. The integration team built the heat map sixty days before close, assessing each group against all nine workstreams. What the map showed reshaped the integration plan.

What the Heat Map Revealed

The black circles did not scatter at random. They clustered in two workstreams and in a handful of groups, and that clustering told the integration team where to look.

Innovation carried the heaviest concentration of significant issues. The enterprise as a whole, BU 1, BU 3, APAC, and LATAM all showed black circles on Innovation, signaling that the pipeline of new products was at risk in the very places the deal counted on for growth. This was not a local problem to be managed by a single unit. It cut across the combined entity.

Infrastructure showed the second concentration. The enterprise, the target, BU 3, EMEA, APAC, China, and LATAM all carried black or gray circles, with the regions hit hardest. The acquired firm ran on platforms that did not match the acquirer's, and the mismatch was most acute in the regions farthest from headquarters.

Culture showed significant issues at BU 1, BU 3, EMEA, and APAC. The acquired business units and the international regions did not yet share working norms with the acquirer, and where Culture and Innovation both showed black circles, the risk compounded.

Other intersections were calmer. The Customer and Supplier workstreams were largely sound across the enterprise, the target, and the Americas, which meant the commercial base and the supply relationships could bear the weight of the integration while attention went elsewhere.

The Pattern Analysis

Three patterns emerged from the map.

First, the risk concentrated by workstream. Innovation and Infrastructure accounted for most of the black circles. That concentration argued for enterprise-level responses in those two workstreams rather than a separate fix negotiated group-by-group.

Second, the risk also concentrated by group. BU 3 and APAC showed issues across most of their workstreams, while the Americas and the Customer-facing workstreams stayed sound. Resources could flow to the groups that needed them without disturbing the parts of the business that were working.

Third, the most dangerous cells were the ones where a troubled workstream met a troubled group. BU 3 and APAC each combined Innovation and Culture issues, so a fix aimed at one without the other would not hold. These intersections needed coordinated, not piecemeal, intervention.

Recommendations Implemented

The heat map drove five integration decisions. Each targeted a specific concentration of black circles.

Recommendation One: An Enterprise Innovation Plan

Innovation showed significant issues across the enterprise, BU 1, BU 3, APAC, and LATAM. Treating each separately would fragment the response. The intervention created a single enterprise innovation plan with a single owner, protecting the acquired firm's design teams from disruptive tooling changes for 12 months while a shared pipeline and a common roadmap were built. Pushing the change down to each unit independently would have lost the talent the deal was meant to secure.

Recommendation Two: An Enterprise Infrastructure Workstream

Infrastructure showed black or gray circles in seven groups, concentrated in the regions. The intervention stood up a dedicated infrastructure workstream with a comprehensive road map: it mapped every platform, every integration point, and every dependency, then sequenced the migration so the hardest-hit regions, EMEA, APAC, China, and LATAM, received support first. A single source of truth tracked migration status and prevented the work from splintering into disconnected regional projects.

Recommendation Three: Culture Work in the Business Units
Culture showed significant issues at BU 1, BU 3, EMEA, and APAC. The intervention paired leaders from the acquirer and the target in each affected group to surface working-norm differences early, rather than waiting for them to harden into conflict. Where Culture and Innovation both showed black circles, in BU 1, BU 3, and APAC, the culture and innovation work were run together so that neither undermined the other.

Recommendation Four: A Regional Triage for APAC and LATAM
APAC and LATAM carried issues across most workstreams. The intervention gave each region a single integration lead with the authority to sequence the local work and access to enterprise resources to execute it. This prevented distant regions from being managed by remote control, which is how regional problems usually grow unseen until they impact financial results.

Recommendation Five: Protect the Sound Workstreams
Customer and Supplier were largely sound across the enterprise, the target, and the Americas. The intervention here was restraint: leave these workstreams stable, avoid unnecessary change, and use their steadiness as the platform from which the harder work in Innovation, Infrastructure, and Culture could proceed. Not every cell needs an intervention. Some need protection.

Results

The heat map was updated quarterly. By month six, the pattern had shifted.

Innovation shifted from black circles to gray circles at the enterprise level and in BU 1 as the shared pipeline took hold and the design teams remained. BU 3 and APAC improved more slowly because cultural and innovation issues had to be addressed together.

Infrastructure improved in the regions as the sequenced migration reached EMEA and APAC on schedule. China and LATAM remained gray circles while their migrations were still underway, but their trajectories were clear. The work stayed visible.

Culture moved from black circles toward gray circles in BU 1 and EMEA as the paired-leader work built trust. BU 3 and APAC stayed harder, and the heat map kept them in view so resources did not drift away prematurely.

By month twelve, most cells showed white or gray circles. A few black circles remained, concentrated where Innovation and Culture had compounded in BU 3 and APAC, and both were improving. The acquisition met its growth targets and investment thesis. Leadership credited the heat map for forcing early identification of the right problems and enabling targeted, sequenced action.

Common Pitfalls and How to Avoid Them

The heat map works when used correctly. It fails when misused. Four common pitfalls:

Pitfall One: Making Every Cell a Gray-Circled One

Teams default to the gray circle because it is safe. It says there is some risk, but we are handling it. A heat map that is 80% gray circles tells you nothing.

Solution: drive critical thinking and force choices. Limit the number of gray-circle cells. Require teams to mark a black circle when issues are significant and a white circle when a group is sound. If someone argues that everything is a gray circle, ask them to rank-order those cells. The top third becomes black circles. The bottom third becomes white circles. This creates a useful distinction.

Pitfall Two: Building It Once and Ignoring It

The heat map is not a one-time exercise. It is a tracking tool. Teams build it, present it, file it, and forget it. The heat map becomes a static artifact instead of a living diagnostic.

Solution: schedule updates. Monthly for the first six months. Quarterly after that. Make the update process lightweight. Do not rebuild from scratch. Review each black-circle and gray-circle cell. Has it improved? Has it worsened? Update the circles. Track the changes. Keep it visible.

Pitfall Three: Confusing Data with Judgment

Teams want to make the heat map objective. They create scoring rubrics. They define metrics. They automate the ball assignment based on data. This sounds rigorous. It produces garbage.

The heat map requires judgment. Leadership instability is not measurable by a simple metric. Culture clash is not quantifiable. Integration complexity is not reducible to a formula. The heat map works because experienced people assess these factors holistically.

Solution: embrace subjectivity. Use data where it exists, but do not let the absence of data prevent assessment. Bring the right people into the room. Debate the ratings. Document the reasoning. Trust judgment.

Pitfall Four: Focusing on the Heat Map Instead of the Interventions

The heat map is a diagnostic tool. It is not the solution. Teams spend enormous amounts of energy trying to make the heat map perfect. They debate ratings. They refine definitions. They produce a beautiful matrix. Then they do nothing with it.

Solution: move quickly from diagnosis to action. The heat map does not need to be perfect. It needs to be good enough to drive decisions. Once you have identified the black-circle cells, develop intervention plans. Assign owners. Set deadlines. Execute. The value is in the interventions, not the heat map itself.

Implications for the CEO

The organization heat map is a tool for making organizational risk visible. It serves three purposes: identifying issues and risks by organization, supporting decisions about where to focus integration efforts, and tracking progress over time.

Eight principles guide effective use. The first is to start early by building the heat map before close rather than after, and to use it to shape the integration strategy while there is still time to adjust. The second is to be honest: a black circle means significant issues, and groups that face serious challenges need serious interventions, because false optimism destroys value. The third is to focus on patterns, looking for concentrations of risk and systemic issues, since patterns reveal where to focus resources and whether a problem calls for a local or an enterprise-level solution.

The fourth is to differentiate the interventions, because different organizations face different risks, and engineering talent risk requires a different remedy than manufacturing process risk. The fifth is to update the map regularly, monthly or quarterly, treating it as a living tracking tool rather than a snapshot, so that improvement is visible and new risks surface early. The sixth is to trust judgment over metrics, because organizational health is not fully quantifiable; bring experienced people together, let them assess, document their reasoning, and resist forcing false precision.

The seventh is to move from diagnosis to action quickly, identifying the black-circle cells, developing interventions, assigning owners, and executing, so the heat map never becomes an end in itself. The eighth is to use it as a communication tool, because the map creates a shared understanding of where risk lives, aligns leadership, and focuses executive attention when it is shared widely and referenced in every integration meeting.

The heat map does not prevent all integration failures. But it prevents a specific, common failure mode: the slow-motion collapse of organizations whose problems were visible early but remained invisible because no tool captured them systematically.

Organizations are complex. Integration makes them more complex. The heat map cuts through complexity. It makes risk visible. It enables focused action. It tracks progress. It works.

Use it.

Chapter 9
Tailor-Made Tools

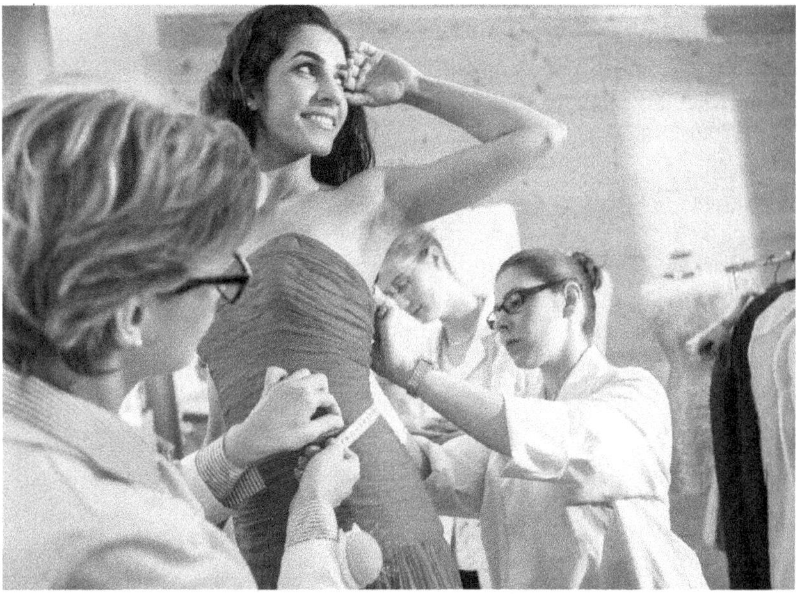

Figure 9.1. Tailor-made or off-the-rack? Your choice.

The integration consultant opens her laptop. The slide deck appears. Same frameworks everyone uses. Deal Thesis Decomposition. Integration heat maps. Better practices matrices. Value driver trees. The tools are solid. Proven. Used in hundreds of acquisitions.

The CEO stops her on slide three. 'I've seen this before. Our last acquisition. The consulting firm before you showed me the same thing. This doesn't capture what makes our situation different.'

He is right. He is also only half right.

Notice what made his objection possible. He recognized the deal thesis decomposition on slide three because he had learned to read one. He knew the integration heat map was generic because he had seen a specific one done well. The standard frameworks did not fail him in that moment. They trained him. A CEO who had never worked through the discipline of the preceding chapters would have nodded along, reassured by the polish, and missed entirely what the slides did not capture. Fluency in the standard tools is what lets him feel the gap.

This is the relationship between the frameworks already developed in this book and the tools this chapter introduces. The standard frameworks are not training wheels to be discarded once an executive grows sophisticated. They are the foundation. They solve the problems they were designed to solve. They solve them reliably across thousands of integrations. We do not abandon them. We build on them.

What follows is not an argument that standard frameworks are weak. It is an argument that every tool has a design envelope (the range of situations it was built to handle), and that the most demanding acquisitions occasionally push past that envelope. When they do, the executive who has mastered the standard frameworks is precisely the one equipped to recognize the boundary and to commission something custom. The tailor-made tool is the next move for the practitioner who has already made the standard tools second nature, not a replacement for the practitioner who never learned them.

Standard frameworks solve standard problems. They work with the common patterns. The predictable challenges. The issues that repeat across deals. But some acquisitions face unique situations. Unique industries. Unique strategies. Unique complexities that standard tools do not capture.

This chapter explores when standard tools fail and custom tools succeed. It presents a method for creating tailor-made integration tools that address specific situations. Tools that become competitive advantages because competitors do not have them.

The Limits of Standard Frameworks

Standard frameworks are valuable. They codify lessons from thousands of integrations. They prevent reinventing solutions to solved problems. They provide structure when chaos threatens.

But every framework has a design envelope, and standard frameworks are no exception:

They are built for common problems, not unique situations. A standard heat map shows organizational risk across standard dimensions. It works when risks follow standard patterns. It fails when risks are specific to an industry, strategy, or organizational structure that differs from the norm.

They standardize thinking. Standard frameworks shape how people see problems. Teams using the same frameworks develop the same insights, make the same decisions, and achieve the same outcomes as their competitors. Nothing differentiates them.

They are diagnostic by design, not aspirational. Frameworks identify what is broken. They help fix it. But some acquisitions are not about fixing problems. They are about creating something new. Building capabilities that do not exist yet. Pursuing visions that standard frameworks cannot represent.

They lose force through familiarity. When everyone uses the same tools, the tools lose impact. Executives glaze over. They have seen it before. The framework might be correct, but it does not engage. It does not provoke new thinking. It does not inspire action.

These boundaries are easiest to see in practice. Later in this chapter, we examine three acquisitions where standard frameworks reached their limits and the custom tools we built to go beyond them.

What Makes a Tool Tailor-Made

Tailor-made tools differ from standard frameworks in five ways. Understanding these differences clarifies when to build custom tools and when to use standard ones.

Custom Designed for Your Deal

Standard frameworks are generic by design. They work across industries and situations. Tailor-made tools are specific. They incorporate the unique elements of your industry, your strategy, your organization, your challenges.

The connected car concept map was specific to automotive and internet convergence. It showed vehicle systems, internet protocols, supply chain logistics, and customer experiences in one integrated view. No standard framework could do this because none combined these domains.

This specificity creates clarity. Teams see their situation, not a generic abstraction. They recognize themselves in the tool. This recognition drives engagement and action.

Incorporate Aspirations in Addition to Problems

Most integration frameworks are diagnostic. They identify what is broken. Organizational risks. Process gaps. System incompatibilities. Cultural conflicts. They help you fix problems.

Tailor-made tools can be aspirational. They show not just what is broken but what could be built. Not just risks but opportunities. Not just today's state but tomorrow's vision.

The connected car tool showed a future that did not exist in 1998. Vehicles communicating with infrastructure. Operating systems enabling services. Data flowing between car and cloud. This was an aspiration, not a diagnosis. The tool helped people see what they were building, not just what they were fixing.

Rapid Visualization and Application

Tailor-made tools emphasize visual communication. Not dense text. Not complex matrices. Not bullet-heavy slides. Visual representations that convey complex information quickly.

This matters because integration requires shared understanding across diverse stakeholders. Engineers and marketers. Operators and strategists. Both companies. Multiple levels. Visual tools create shared mental models faster than reports and text-based frameworks.

The shipping disruption tool was a single large-format visual. Disruption vectors. Strategic options. Capability requirements. Market dynamics. Everything visible on one page. Teams could point, discuss, and debate. The visual itself became the medium for strategic conversation.

Reusable for Future Acquisitions

Tailor-made does not mean one-time use. Well-designed custom tools become reusable assets. They get added to the organization's integration playbook. They get applied to future acquisitions in the same industry or facing similar challenges.

This reusability creates leverage. The investment in developing a custom tool pays dividends across multiple deals. The organization builds institutional knowledge encoded in tools that capture its specific integration challenges and solutions.

Competitive Advantage Through Uniqueness

When competitors use the same standard frameworks, they develop similar insights and make similar decisions. Differentiation comes from execution, not strategy. Everyone sees the same things. Everyone does roughly the same things. Whoever executes with speed, predictability, and control wins.

Custom tools create differentiation. Competitors do not have them. Competitors cannot copy them because they are specific to your situation. The tools enable insights and strategies competitors cannot see. This creates competitive advantage.

The connected car concept map gave the automotive manufacturer a framework for thinking about internet-vehicle convergence that competitors lacked. While competitors struggled to articulate the vision, this company had a visual language. This language enabled faster decision-making and clearer communication.

Strategic Concept Maps: An Advanced Form

The most sophisticated tailor-made tools are strategic concept maps. These are not simple diagrams. They are advanced, highly evolved frameworks that render complex information artistically.

Strategic concept maps have six defining characteristics:

Render Broad, Complex Information from Multiple Sources

Concept maps integrate information that normally lives in separate documents. Market data. Competitive intelligence. Technical architectures. Organizational structures. Strategic options. Financial projections. Customer insights. All synthesized into one coherent visual.

This synthesis matters because integration decisions require seeing connections across domains. Marketing decisions affect product decisions. Product decisions affect operations decisions. Operations decisions affect financial outcomes. The concept map shows these connections explicitly.

Engage Viewers in Rich Discussion

Good concept maps provoke conversation. They raise questions. They surface disagreements. They force people to articulate assumptions. The map becomes a medium for dialogue, not just a presentation tool.

In the connected car example, executives would point to different parts of the map. How does the operating system connect to the supply chain? Where does customer data flow? What partnerships enable this? The map structured these conversations. It prevented them from fragmenting into parallel discussions that never connected.

Enable Multiple Cognitive Styles

Integration teams include both analytical thinkers and visual thinkers. Left-brain people who process information sequentially and logically. Right-brain people who process information holistically and intuitively.

Standard frameworks favor analytical thinkers. Lists. Matrices. Sequential logic. Visual thinkers struggle with them. Concept maps work for both. Analytical thinkers can follow the logical connections. Visual thinkers can see the patterns and relationships. Both groups engage with the same content in their preferred way.

This cognitive inclusivity expands the range of perspectives. When more people can engage with the material, more insights emerge. Better decisions follow.

Foster Alternative Perspectives

Linear frameworks guide thinking in one direction. Start here. Move to here. Conclude there. This structure helps prevent confusion, but it also constrains exploration. Teams follow the framework's logic. They miss alternatives.

Concept maps are non-linear. Multiple entry points. Multiple pathways through the information. Different people see different patterns. Multiplicity surfaces alternatives that linear frameworks hide. Teams discover options they would not have considered.

Scale to Large Format

Concept maps work best when printed large. Wall-sized. Teams gather around them. They point. They discuss. They sketch additions. The physical scale changes the dynamic from presentation to collaboration.

Laptop screens constrain. One person controls. Others watch. Large-format prints, for example, ANSI E size, democratize. Everyone sees everything. Everyone can point. Everyone can mark up the printout. Everyone participates. The map becomes shared property, not one person's presentation.

Compatible with Modern Approaches

Concept maps align with contemporary methods. Big data visualization. Design thinking. Systems thinking. Agile planning. These approaches emphasize visual representation, iterative refinement, and collaborative sensemaking. Concept maps provide a medium for applying these methods to acquisitions.

This compatibility matters as integration practices evolve. Teams trained in design thinking or agile methods recognize concept maps as familiar territory. They know how to work with visual frameworks. They know how to iterate and refine. The tool fits their working style.

Three Cases in Practice

Theory is abstract. Cases make it concrete. Three real acquisitions show how tailor-made tools addressed specific integration challenges. Each begins with a situation that standard frameworks could not resolve completely and ends with the custom tool that did.

Case One: The Connected Car Vision

An automotive manufacturer acquired a software company in 1998. The acquisition thesis: build connected car capabilities before competitors move first. Enable vehicles to communicate with infrastructure, with other vehicles, and with the internet.

The challenge: no one understood what a connected car meant. The automotive executives thought in terms of manufacturing, supply chains, and dealer networks. The software executives thought in terms of operating systems, protocols, and data flows. No common language existed. No shared vision.

Solution: a strategic concept map illustrating the connected-car ecosystem. The map had four layers. The physical layer showed vehicle components and manufacturing. The network layer showed connectivity protocols and infrastructure. The service layer showed applications and customer experiences. The business layer showed revenue models and partnerships.

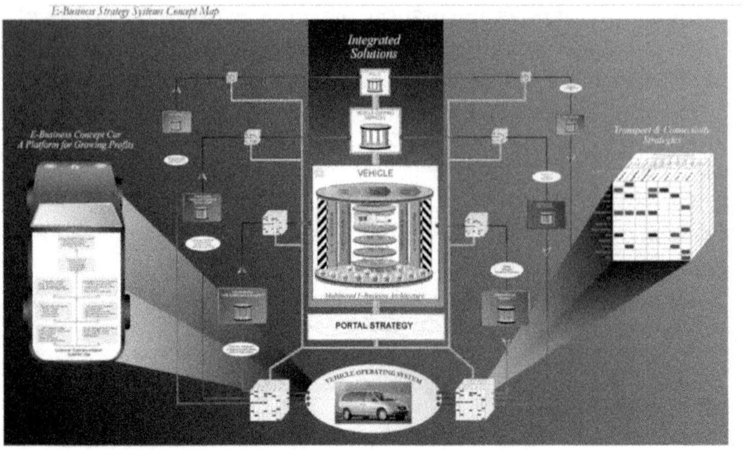

Figure 9.2. Concept map of the connected car, 1998.

The map made visible how internet capabilities would integrate with automotive systems. Engineers could see where software would touch hardware. Software developers could see where their code would run. Business leaders could see how services would generate revenue. Everyone saw the same future from their own perspective.

Impact: the map became the primary framework for acquisition and integration planning. Teams referenced it in every major decision. Where should the operating system team sit within the organization? Look at the map. Which partnerships mattered most? Look at the map. What capabilities to build versus buy? Look at the map. The tool created a shared language that did not exist before.

Case Two: The Disrupted Shipping Industry

A private equity firm acquired a traditional shipping company. The industry was being disrupted. Digital platforms were changing how shipping capacity was bought and sold. Customer expectations were shifting. Legacy business models were breaking.

The challenge: develop a strategy for surviving disruption. The acquisition created scale and efficiency. But scale and efficiency were not enough. The company needed to understand the vectors of disruption. Where was the industry going? What business models would work? What capabilities to build? What partnerships to form?

Solution: a disruption game plan visualized as a strategic map. The map showed five disruption vectors radiating from the center. Digital platforms. Customer expectations. Competitor moves. Regulatory changes. Technology evolution. For each vector, the map showed response strategies, required capabilities, and timeline considerations.

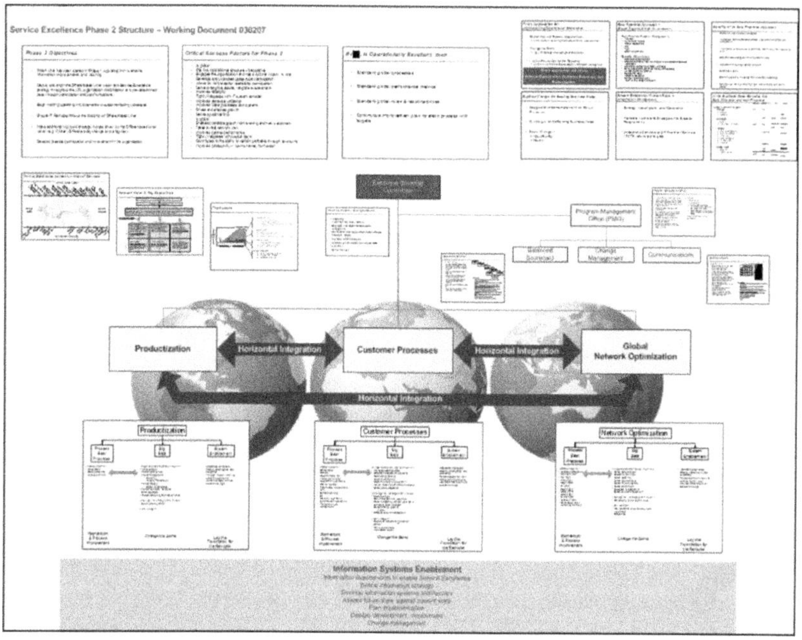

Figure 9.3. Concept map to visualize an industry disruption strategy and execution.

The map also showed interdependencies. Responding to digital platforms required building new technology capabilities. Meeting customer expectations required operational changes. Competitor responses required strategic positioning decisions. Everything connected. The map showed how.

Impact: the map forced strategic choices. The company could not address all five vectors simultaneously. The map made trade-offs explicit. Which vectors posed the greatest threat? Which response strategies delivered the most value? Where should the company invest first? The visual format enabled rapid scenario planning. Teams could sketch alternative strategies directly on the map.

Case Three: The New Practice Launch

A consulting firm emerged from an acquisition with a new capability in energy and environmental consulting. The integration was complete. Systems were merged. Organizations were aligned. But the market did not know this new practice existed.

The challenge: go-to-market strategy. Which clients to target? Which services to lead with? Which partnerships to form? How to position against competitors? How to build credibility fast?

Solution: a go-to-market concept map organized around three dimensions. The client dimension showed target industries and decision-makers. The service dimension showed offerings arranged by complexity and value. The partnership dimension showed alliances and channel relationships.

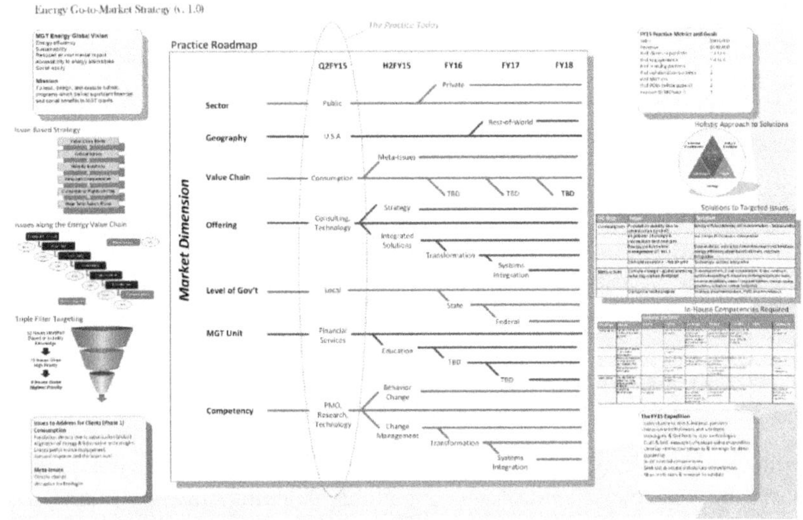

Figure 9.4. Concept map for a new energy consulting service.

The map connected these dimensions. Certain clients needed services delivered through partnerships. The connections were explicit, enabling the team to design integrated go-to-market campaigns rather than separate initiatives across sales, marketing, and partnerships.

Impact: the map became the strategic plan. Every go-to-market decision referred to it. Which trade shows to attend? Look at the map to see which clients and partners would be there. Which thought leadership to develop? Look at the map to see which services need market education. Which partnerships to prioritize? Look at the map to see which partnerships enabled access to priority clients. The practice achieved profitability eighteen months after launch, faster than typical for new consulting practices.

The Development Process

Tailor-made tools do not emerge fully formed. They require a deliberate development process. The process has four phases, each building on the previous one.

Phase One: Research

Research gathers raw data. Research asks: what information matters for this integration? What problems need solving? What aspirations need articulating? What perspectives require inclusion?

Research methods vary. Current and future customer requirements. Interviews with executives from both companies. Document review of strategies and plans. Analysis of competitive landscape. Assessment of industry trends. Customer research. Technical deep dives. The goal is a comprehensive understanding of the integration context.

Research should over collect data, facts, information, and perceptions. Gather more information than will ultimately be included in the map. Breadth enables synthesis in later phases. Narrow focus too early, and critical connections get missed.

Phase Two: Analyze

Analysis finds structure in the research. What are the key dimensions? What are the major categories? What are the critical relationships? How does information cluster?

This phase requires analytical discipline. Look for patterns. Test different organizational schemas. Some ways of structuring the information will be more illuminating than others. The right structure makes complexity comprehensible. The wrong structure obscures it.

In the connected car example, analysis identified four layers as the organizing structure: physical, network, service, and business. Other structures were considered. Product-centric. Customer-centric. Technology-centric. But the four-layer model best captured how the internet and automotive capabilities would integrate.

Phase Three: Interpret

Interpretation adds meaning to the structure. What does the fact pattern mean? What insights emerge? What decisions does this enable? What questions does this raise?

This is the creative phase. Facts have been gathered. Structure has been found. Now comes the work of making sense. What story does the data tell? What future does it point toward? What actions does it suggest?

Good interpretation requires domain expertise and strategic judgment. Someone who understands the industry. Someone who has seen similar situations. Someone who can connect dots that others miss. This is not mechanical work. It is knowledge work at its most sophisticated.

Phase Four: Render

Rendering creates a visual artifact. How do we represent information visually? What metaphors work? What visual language clarifies rather than confuses?

Visual design matters enormously. Poor design obscures good analysis. Good design illuminates it. The visual choices are not cosmetic. They are substantive. Color conveys meaning. Placement conveys relationship. Size conveys importance. Typography conveys hierarchy.

Rendering requires both analytical and artistic capability. Understanding what needs to be shown. Knowing how to show it clearly. Balancing completeness with simplicity. Including enough detail to be useful without overwhelming the viewer.

The rendering phase also involves iteration. Draft the visual. Test it with stakeholders. Gather feedback. Refine. Test again. The first version is never the final version. Each iteration clarifies and improves. A concept map is dynamic.

Recognize Patterns Throughout

Pattern recognition is not a separate phase. It occurs throughout the process. During research, patterns emerge about what matters most. During analysis, patterns appear in how information clusters. During interpretation, patterns reveal insights. During rendering, patterns guide design choices.

Effective tailor-made tools surface patterns that were always present but never visible. The connected car tool surfaced the pattern of layered integration. The shipping disruption tool surfaced the pattern of interdependent responses. The go-to-market tool surfaced the pattern of integrated campaigns. These patterns were not invented. They were discovered and made visible.

When to Build Tailor-Made Tools

Tailor-made tools are not always necessary. Sometimes traditional frameworks work perfectly. Building custom tools requires time and expertise. Invest in custom tools when the situation demands it.

Five indicators suggest custom tools are warranted:

Indicator One: Unique Strategic Context

When your acquisition operates in a unique strategic context, standard tools fail. The context might be a converging industry. An emerging technology. A new business model. A regulatory shift. Something that creates complexity, traditional frameworks do not address.

The connected car case exemplified this. In 1998, the convergence of the internet and the automotive industry was unique. No standard frameworks existed. A custom tool was necessary to make the strategic context comprehensible.

Indicator Two: Complex Interdependencies

When the integration involves complex interdependencies across multiple domains, visualization helps. Technical interdependencies. Organizational interdependencies. Market interdependencies. Everything connects to everything else.

Standard frameworks break complex problems into components. This decomposition works when components are independent. It fails when components are tightly coupled. Tailor-made tools can show coupling explicitly.

Indicator Three: Need for Shared Language

When the two organizations speak different languages, standard frameworks do not help. They use one vocabulary or the other, favoring one organization and alienating the other.

Tailor-made tools can create new shared vocabulary. Not the buyer's language. Not the seller's language. A third language that includes both perspectives. This linguistic bridge enables communication that was previously impossible.

Indicator Four: Aspirational Vision Required

When the integration aims to create something new rather than fix something broken, aspiration matters. People need to see the future. They need to understand what they are building. Text-based diagnostic frameworks typically identify value drivers in cost, revenue, and cash flow that are tied to the valuation of a combined firm.

Tailor-made tools can be aspirational. They can show futures that do not exist yet. They can make visions tangible. This matters for acquisitions driven by transformation rather than consolidation.

Indicator Five: Competitive Differentiation Opportunity

When the integration creates unique capabilities that competitors cannot match, differentiation becomes strategic. Standard tools are available to everyone. Custom tools are available only to you.

If your acquisition creates truly unique capabilities, develop unique tools to capture them. These tools become part of your integration intellectual property. They enable insights and strategies competitors cannot replicate.

Implications for the CEO

Standard frameworks solve standard problems. Tailor-made tools solve unique problems. Knowing when to use which determines integration success.

Eight principles guide the development and use of tailor-made tools. The first is to recognize when standard frameworks are insufficient: when the situation is unique, when complexity demands custom visualization, when aspirations matter as much as problems, and when competitive differentiation requires proprietary tools. The second is to design for your specific context, incorporating your industry dynamics, your strategic situation, your organizational characteristics, and your integration challenges, because specificity creates relevance and engagement.

The third is to emphasize visual communication, since complex integrations require shared understanding across diverse stakeholders, and visual tools create shared mental models faster than text-based frameworks. The fourth is to enable multiple cognitive styles so that analytical and visual thinkers both engage, because a good concept map shows logical connections and visual patterns at once. The fifth is to follow the development process systematically: research gathers the raw material, analysis finds the structure, interpretation adds meaning, and rendering creates the visual artifact, with pattern recognition running throughout.

The sixth is to invest in both analysis and design, because analytical rigor without visual clarity produces confusion, while visual appeal without analytical depth produces mere decoration. The seventh is to build reusable assets, since tailor-made for one deal does not mean disposable; well-designed custom tools join the integration playbook and serve future acquisitions facing similar challenges.

The eighth is to understand the value proposition: custom tools require more investment than standard frameworks, but they create competitive advantage, enable insights competitors cannot see, and support decisions standard tools cannot, so the investment pays dividends when the situation demands it.

The choice between traditional and tailor-made tools is not either-or. From my work, successful acquisitions use a blend of both. Traditional frameworks for common challenges. Custom tools for unique situations. The art is knowing which is which.

Think of it this way: would you choose Chanel or Nordstrom Rack? Haute couture or off-the-rack? Both have their places. Off-the-rack works for many situations. Haute couture is for occasions that demand exceptional decision-making and execution.

Integration is the same. Standard frameworks work for most situations. Tailor-made tools are for integrations that demand something exceptional. The strategic ones. The complex ones. The ones that create sustainable competitive advantage. Know the difference. Build accordingly.

Chapter 10
Building Institutional Capability

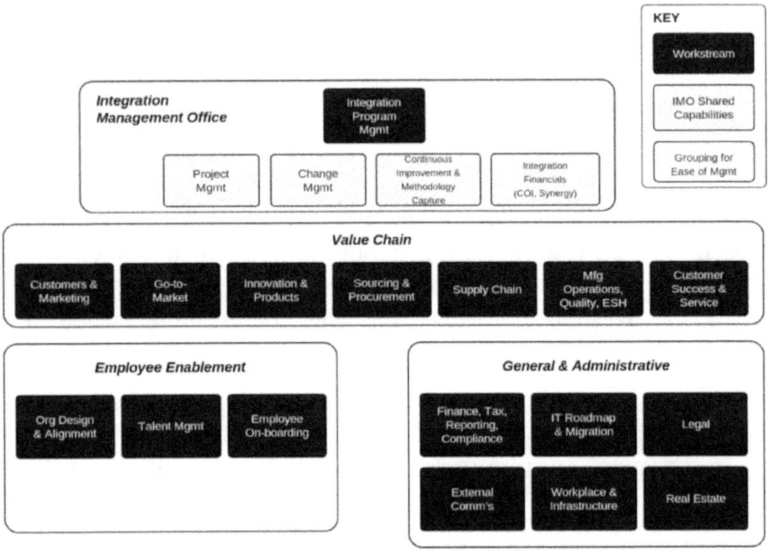

Figure 10.1. Acquisition integration workstream structure inspired by Cisco Systems.

An industrial technology firm closed its first significant acquisition in 2016. The integration succeeded, and most of the credit belonged to one person: a vice president of operations with a gift for program management who improvised a playbook as she went. She sequenced the ERP cutover after the customer migrations, locked in retention packages before the announcement, and maintained a weekly cadence that caught problems early. The deal delivered. The board congratulated the team. Then she accepted an offer from a private equity firm, and the playbook left in her head.

Three years later, the firm acquired again. A new integration leader, chosen for availability rather than experience, ran the ERP cutover first because the IT roadmap said so. Customer shipments stalled for three weeks. Retention offers were sent out after the announcement, when the target's best engineers were already taking recruiter calls. None of these mistakes was new. Every one of them had been made and corrected in 2016. The firm had paid for the lessons once and owned none of them.

This pattern describes most acquirers. Each deal is an adventure. Each integration is improvised. Experience accumulates in people, and people leave. The organization never gets systematically better at M&A.

Serial acquirers cannot afford this approach. When you buy multiple companies per year, when M&A is a core growth strategy rather than an occasional event, you need institutional capability. Repeatable processes. Reusable frameworks. Trained teams. Documented knowledge. Continuous improvement. This chapter shows how to build it.

From Deal-by-Deal to Institutional Discipline

The shift from occasional acquirer to serial acquirer requires fundamental change. Not just doing more deals. Doing deals differently. Building capability that persists between acquisitions.

The Occasional Acquirer Pattern

Occasional acquirers follow predictable patterns. Deal emerges opportunistically. Executive team forms *ad hoc* integration committee. Someone gets assigned the integration leader role, usually whoever has bandwidth. The team hires consultants to guide them. Deal closes. Integration happens. Team disperses. Knowledge walks away.

Three years later, another acquisition appears. Different executives. Different integration leader. Different consultants. They start fresh. Previous lessons are lost. Previous mistakes repeat. The organization learns nothing systematically.

This approach works, barely, when acquisitions happen rarely. It fails completely for serial acquirers. When you buy three companies per year, when PE firms manage portfolios of fifty companies, when technology platforms acquire monthly, ad hoc approaches cause chaos.

The Serial Acquirer Requirement

Serial acquirers need three things that occasional acquirers do not:

First, dedicated capability. Not borrowed resources. Not ad hoc teams. Permanent roles. Standing organizations. People whose job is M&A integration. They develop expertise. They accumulate experience. They get better over time.

Second, documented processes. Not tribal knowledge. Not "the way we did it last time." Written playbooks. Standard frameworks. Reusable templates. Codified lessons. Knowledge that persists when people leave.

Third, continuous improvement. Not repeating past approaches. Learning from each deal. Refining methods. Updating playbooks. Getting systematically better. Treating M&A as a discipline rather than a series of unique events.

Building these three elements transforms occasional capability into institutional capability. Deals execute faster. Integration quality improves. Value capture accelerates. M&A becomes a competitive advantage.

Integration Playbook Development

The integration playbook is the foundation of institutional capability. Not a binder that sits on a shelf. A living document that guides every acquisition.

What a Playbook Contains

A comprehensive integration playbook has five sections:

Section One: Integration Strategy Framework. This section documents your approach to categorizing acquisitions. The classes of integration. Decision criteria for choosing an approach. Resource requirements for each class. Timeline expectations. Risk factors. This framework enables rapid classification of new deals.

Section Two: Executive Alignment Tools. This section contains the frameworks and tools from this book: Deal Thesis Decomposition, End-State Vision, Integration Classes, Timing and Probabilities, Assumptions and Decisions, Heat Maps, Better Practices, and Tailor-Made Tools. Include instructions for applying each framework. Templates for documenting outcomes. Examples from previous deals.

Section Three: Workstream Playbooks. This section provides detailed guidance for each integration workstream: Finance, IT, HR, Legal, Operations, Sales, Marketing, Product, and R&D. For each workstream, the playbook provides key activities, decision points, deliverables, timelines, risks, and success metrics. These playbooks enable workstream leads to execute without starting from scratch.

Section Four: Communication Framework. This section guides all integration communication: employee communications, customer communications, partner communications, and investor communications. Message templates. Timing guidelines. Channel selection. Approval processes. Consistent communication prevents confusion.

Section Five: Lessons Learned Repository. This section captures knowledge from previous acquisitions. What worked. What failed. What to repeat. What to avoid. Organized by deal type and integration class. This repository prevents repeated mistakes and enables sharing successes.

How to Build the Playbook

Building a playbook takes a minimum of six months. Longer for complex organizations. Follow this sequence:

Month One: Assess current state. Interview executives who led previous integrations. Review integration documentation. Identify what exists. Document what worked and what failed. Understand current capabilities and gaps.

Month Two: Define target state. Decide which frameworks to adopt. Determine the level of detail required. Identify what can be standardized versus what must remain flexible. Design playbook structure.

Months Three and Four: Develop content. Write framework instructions. Create templates. Document processes. Build workstream playbooks. Draft communication guidelines. This is intensive work that requires subject-matter expertise.

Month Five: Validate and refine. Share the draft playbook with executives. Conduct workshops to review key sections. Gather feedback. Identify gaps. Revise content. Ensure the playbook is practical, not just comprehensive.

Month Six: Deploy and train. Publish the final playbook. Train integration teams. Conduct workshops with executives. Make playbook accessible: digital, searchable, well-organized. A playbook nobody can find is worthless.

Keep It Living

Playbooks become obsolete the moment they are published. Markets change. Regulations evolve. Technologies advance. Organizations learn. The playbook must evolve, too.

Assign playbook ownership to your integration capability leader, the person responsible for institutional M&A capability. They maintain the playbook. Update it after each acquisition. Add new lessons learned. Refine frameworks based on experience. Remove outdated content.

Schedule formal playbook reviews annually. Gather integration leaders from recent deals. Review what worked and what needs updating. Make deliberate improvements. Version the playbook so people know which version they are using. A living playbook gets better. A static playbook dies.

Training Integration Teams

The playbook exists. Now you need people who can use it. Training converts the playbook into capability.

Who Needs Training

Three groups require training, each with different needs:

Executives who sponsor integrations need a strategic understanding. They do not need to know every detail. They need to understand frameworks, make informed decisions, and hold teams accountable. Train them on the eight alignment tools. Show them how the playbook works. Explain their role in integration governance.

Integration leaders who coordinate across workstreams need comprehensive knowledge. They must understand the entire playbook. Know when to apply which frameworks. Facilitate executive workshops. Coordinate workstream activities. Track progress. Escalate issues. Train them on everything.

Workstream leads who execute specific functions need deep functional knowledge. Finance leads need to know the finance playbook. IT leads need to know the IT playbook. They do not need a comprehensive understanding of other workstreams. Train them on their domain, plus enough context to coordinate with others.

Training Approach

Training should be practical, not academic. Executives learn by applying, not listening.

For executive training: Run half-day workshops. Walk through one complete alignment framework using a real or realistic scenario. Have them use the tool. Document decisions. Experience what good alignment feels like. Learning by doing works better than learning by reading.

For integration leader training: Run a two-day intensive program. Day one covers strategic frameworks and executive alignment tools. Day two covers workstream coordination, progress tracking, and issue escalation. Include case studies from previous deals. Role-play difficult scenarios. Prepare them for reality.

For workstream lead training: Run function-specific half-day sessions. Focus on their playbook. Walk through activities, deliverables, and timelines. Show examples from previous integrations. Address common problems. Make it immediately applicable.

Certification and Standards

Consider formal certification for integration leaders. Not bureaucracy for its own sake. Standards that ensure consistent capability.

Define what certification requires. Complete training program. Participate in at least one integration as workstream lead. Lead one integration successfully. Demonstrate proficiency with playbook and frameworks. Submit lessons learned. Get endorsed by an executive sponsor.

Certification creates a pool of qualified integration leaders. When the next acquisition happens, you have trained people ready to lead. No scrambling to find someone with bandwidth. No starting from scratch with inexperienced leaders. Capability is ready.

Ongoing Development

Training is not a one-time event. Capability requires ongoing development.

After each major acquisition, conduct a retrospective workshop. Gather integration leaders and key workstream leads. Review what worked and what did not. Extract lessons. Update playbook. Share learnings across the organization. This converts experience into institutional knowledge.

Quarterly, run integration community sessions. Bring together everyone involved in M&A: past integration leaders, current workstream leads, and executives who sponsor deals. Share experiences. Discuss challenges. Solve problems collectively. Community enables peer learning and builds an integration culture.

Capturing Lessons Learned

Every acquisition teaches lessons. The question is whether you capture them.

When to Capture Lessons

Capture lessons at three points, not just at the end:

At Day 100: Conduct mid-integration review. What is working? What is failing? What adjustments are needed? Capture these insights while integration is active.

Waiting until the end loses detail. Day 100 lessons enable course correction on the current deal and inform planning for the next deal.

At Day 365, conduct the final integration review. Assess full results. Compare outcomes to objectives. Identify root causes of successes and failures. Document comprehensively. Day 365 lessons capture the complete picture after integration effects fully manifest.

Continuously: Capture significant lessons as they emerge. Do not wait for formal reviews. When something important happens, whether a major success, a major failure, or an unexpected insight, document it immediately. Create a mechanism for anyone to submit lessons anytime. Continuous capture prevents the loss of insights between reviews.

What to Capture

Good lessons learned have five elements:

Context: What was the situation? Deal type. Integration class. Key characteristics. Specific challenges. Without context, lessons cannot be applied appropriately to future deals.

Action: What did we do? Specific approaches. Decisions made. Resources deployed. Timelines followed. Actions must be concrete enough to replicate or avoid.

Outcome: What happened? Results achieved or missed. Intended consequences and unintended effects. Quantify when possible. Vague outcomes produce vague lessons.

Insight: Why did this happen? Root cause analysis. What factors drove the outcome? What would we do differently? Insight separates valuable lessons from mere history.

Application: When should this lesson apply? What future situations warrant using this lesson? What situations do not? Application guidance prevents misapplying lessons.

How to Organize Lessons

Lessons need structure, or they become an unsearchable pile of disconnected observations.

Organize by integration class, capturing lessons for Standalone Preservation, Synergy Capture, Full Consumption, and Strategic Transformation deals separately.

Organize by workstream, with finance, IT, HR, and the other functional integrations each holding their own lessons.

Organize by common challenge.

Multiple organization schemes help. The same lesson might appear in multiple categories. The Finance workstream lesson on cost savings might also appear in the value capture class lessons. Redundancy is acceptable if it improves findability.

Making Lessons Accessible

Lessons captured but not used waste effort. Make them accessible.

Create a lessons learned database. Digital. Searchable. Well-organized. Include all five elements for each lesson. Tag by integration class, workstream, challenge type. Enable keyword search. Make it part of the playbook so everything lives in one place.

Require integration teams to review relevant lessons during planning. Before starting finance integration, review finance lessons from previous deals. Before conducting an executive alignment workshop, review lessons on workshop facilitation. Make lesson review a mandatory part of integration preparation.

Share lessons broadly. Publish a quarterly summary of recent lessons. Present interesting cases at integration community sessions. Make lessons visible. Organizations that share knowledge openly build capability faster than organizations that hoard it.

Scaling Frameworks Across Multiple Deals

Serial acquirers run multiple integrations simultaneously. Managing one integration is challenging. Managing five requires a systematic approach.

The Portfolio View

Occasional acquirers focus on individual deals. Serial acquirers need a portfolio view. How many integrations are active? What resources are committed? Where are bottlenecks? What capabilities are stretched?

Create an integration portfolio dashboard. List all active integrations. Show status, timeline, resource commitment, and risks for each. Update monthly. Review with the executive team quarterly. Portfolio view enables intelligent resource allocation and prevents overcommitting organization.

Use the integration class framework to prioritize. Strategic Transformation deals need more executive attention than Standalone Preservation. Full Consumption deals require more resources than Synergy Capture. The portfolio view, combined with integration classes, enables smart prioritization when you cannot give equal attention to everything.

Resource Allocation

Resources are finite. Executive attention. Integration leader capacity. Functional expert availability. Capital for integration investments. Serial acquirers must allocate deliberately.

Establish resource allocation principles. High strategic importance gets more resources. Higher integration complexity results in a longer timeline. Larger deals get more dedicated support. Smaller deals leverage shared services. Principles prevent ad hoc allocation that leaves some deals under-resourced while others are over-served.

Build shared integration services. Create a pool of integration specialists who support multiple deals: communications experts, change management professionals, and system integration architects. Shared services enable expertise scaling without hiring dedicated resources for each deal. Small deals gain access to capabilities they could not justify on their own.

Sequencing Multiple Integrations

When acquiring multiple companies, integration sequencing matters. Integrate too many simultaneously, and quality suffers. Sequence too conservatively and value realization delays.

Assess organizational capacity honestly. How many major integrations can you run well simultaneously? Consider executive bandwidth, integration leader availability, functional capacity, and employee change tolerance. Most organizations can handle two to three major integrations concurrently. Beyond that, quality deteriorates.

Stagger integration starts when possible. Close deals at different times. Avoid five integrations launching on Day 1 simultaneously. Staggered starts enable lessons from early integrations to inform later ones. They prevent overwhelming the organization.

Use integration classes to inform sequencing. Start simple integrations first: Standalone Preservation and Synergy Capture. Build confidence and capability. Then tackle complex ones: Full Consumption and Strategic Transformation.

Sequential complexity build-up prevents overloading the organization with too much change too fast.

Maintaining Executive Alignment Across Portfolio

Executive alignment is hard for one deal. It is harder for five deals. Executives cannot maintain a detailed understanding of every integration. But they must maintain strategic alignment across the portfolio.

Conduct portfolio alignment sessions quarterly. Review all active integrations. Confirm strategic priorities. Reallocate resources if needed. Identify cross-deal issues. Make portfolio-level decisions. These sessions prevent individual deals from drifting in different directions.

Use consistent frameworks across all deals. When every integration uses Deal Thesis Decomposition, Assumptions and Decisions, and Heat Maps, executives can understand any deal quickly. Consistent frameworks enable efficient portfolio management. Unique approaches for each deal create confusion and prevent learning transfer.

Building the Integration Management Office (IMO)

Serial acquirers need permanent integration capability. The Integration Management Office (IMO) provides it.

IMO Purpose and Scope

The IMO owns institutional M&A integration capability. Not corporate development. They source and close deals. Not business units. They operate acquired companies. The IMO specializes in integration.

IMO responsibilities:

- The office maintains the integration playbook and frameworks, trains integration teams and workstream leads, provides integration leaders for major deals, and facilitates executive alignment workshops. It tracks integration portfolio status and risks, captures and shares lessons learned, provides shared integration services such as communications, change management, and program management, and reports portfolio metrics to the executive team.

The IMO acts as a center of excellence. It does not own integration execution, which belongs to the business units. But it owns integration methodology, capability, and knowledge.

Cisco Systems is the reference case, and the workstream structure in Figure 10.1 reflects its influence. Cisco has acquired more than two hundred firms since 1993, at times closing a deal nearly every month, and it could not have done so by improvising. The firm built a standing integration function with dedicated leaders, a documented playbook refined deal after deal, and a discipline of beginning integration planning during diligence rather than after close.

Acquired employees received their offer terms, reporting lines, and workspace assignments at a speed that became part of the firm's reputation because Cisco had learned early that talent retention determined whether technology acquisitions paid off. The capability compounded. Each acquisition taught the function something, the playbook absorbed it, and the next deal ran better. That is institutional capability. The knowledge belongs to the firm, not to whoever happens to be leading the current deal.

IMO Structure and Staffing

IMO size depends on M&A volume. Small acquirer: one or two people. Active acquirer: five to ten people. PE firm with a large portfolio: twenty or more people.

Core roles:

IMO Director: Owns integration capability. Reports to the CEO or CFO. Maintains playbook. Oversees training. Manages portfolio. Advises the executive team. Senior role requiring strategic judgment and operational expertise.

Integration Leaders: Lead major integrations. Coordinate workstreams. Facilitate executive workshops. Track progress. Escalate issues. Need broad business understanding and strong program management skills. Typically, three to five integration leaders for an active acquirer.

Integration Specialists: Provide functional expertise in communications, change management, and system integration. Support multiple deals. Enable capability scaling. Typically, two to four specialists.

Knowledge Manager: Maintains the playbook and lessons-learned database. Coordinates training. Manages documentation. Often combined with another role in smaller IMOs. Critical for preserving institutional knowledge.

IMO Evolution Over Time

Do not build full IMO immediately. Evolve capability as M&A activity grows.

Stage One (First few deals): Single integration leader who coordinates the first integration. Document what works. Build initial playbook. Capture first lessons. Establish foundation.

Stage Two (Multiple deals per year): Add a second integration leader. Formalize playbook. Establish a training program. Create shared services. Build portfolio management capability.

Stage Three (High-volume acquirer): Full IMO with the director, multiple integration leaders, specialists, and knowledge management. Sophisticated portfolio management. Continuous improvement process. World-class capability.

Staged build prevents over-investing before capability is needed. But do not wait too long to invest. IMO capability enables faster, better integrations. The ROI is substantial.

Continuous Improvement

Institutional capability requires continuous improvement. Static capability becomes obsolete. Markets evolve. Competition intensifies. What worked last year may not work next year.

Measure Performance

You cannot improve what you do not measure. Track integration performance systematically.

Key metrics:

- Value realization rate: Percentage of projected gains achieved
- Time to investment thesis accomplishment: How long to realize benefits
- Customer retention rate: Percentage of acquired customers retained
- Employee retention rate: Percentage of key talent retained
- Integration cost efficiency: Actual versus planned integration costs
- Timeline adherence: Percentage of milestones hit on schedule

Track these metrics for every integration. Compare across deals. Identify trends. Celebrate improvements. Investigate degradation. Metrics create accountability and enable learning.

Benchmark Against Other Practices

Internal metrics show progress over time. External benchmarks show how you compare to others.

Participate in M&A benchmarking studies. The M&A Leadership Council, consultancies, and research firms conduct periodic benchmarking. Compare your value realization rates, integration timelines, and cost efficiency against peer groups. Identify where you excel and where you lag. Benchmarking reveals blind spots.

Invest in Capability Development

Continuous improvement requires continuous investment. Budget for it.

Send integration leaders to external training programs. The M&A Leadership Council and others offer certifications. Universities offer executive programs. Consulting firms run workshops. External training brings fresh perspectives and prevents insular thinking.

Attend M&A conferences and forums. M&A Science and industry-specific M&A events. Networking with peers enables learning from others' experiences. Conference sessions share emerging practices.

Hire specialists when capability gaps exist. If change management is weak, hire a change management expert. If communications consistently fail, hire a communications professional. Build capability gaps rather than tolerating them.

Experiment and Innovate

Better practices capture the past. Innovation creates the future.

Encourage controlled experimentation. Try new approaches on smaller, lower-risk integrations. Test alternative workshop formats. Pilot new communication channels. Experiment with different integration sequencing. Learn what works. Scale successes. Drop failures.

Pay attention to technology. New tools emerge constantly: collaboration platforms, project management software, data analytics, and AI-enabled insights. Evaluate whether technology can improve acquisition team effectiveness. But do not chase technology for its own sake. Adopt technology that solves real problems.

Implications for the CEO

Institutional capability separates serial acquirers from occasional acquirers. Occasional acquirers treat each deal as a unique adventure. Serial acquirers build systematic capability that improves with each deal.

Integration playbooks codify knowledge. Comprehensive playbooks contain strategy framework, alignment tools, workstream guidance, communication templates, and lessons learned. Living playbooks evolve continuously. Static playbooks become obsolete.

Training converts playbooks into capability. Executives need strategic understanding. Integration leaders need comprehensive knowledge. Workstream leads need functional depth. Practical training through application works better than academic training through lectures.

Lessons learned enable continuous improvement. Capture lessons at Day 100, Day 365, and continuously. Document context, action, outcome, insight, and application. Organize by integration class, workstream, and common challenge. Make lessons accessible and require their use.

Portfolio management scales capability across multiple deals. Portfolio view enables intelligent resource allocation. Integration classes inform prioritization. Shared services enable expertise scaling. Consistent frameworks enable efficient portfolio management.

Integration Management Offices provide permanent capability. IMOs maintain playbooks, train teams, provide integration leaders, facilitate workshops, track portfolios, and capture lessons. IMO structure scales with M&A volume. Evolve capability as M&A activity grows.

Continuous improvement requires measurement, benchmarking, investment, and experimentation. Track performance metrics. Compare against peers. Invest in capability development. Innovate systematically. Organizations that improve continuously separate from those that repeat past approaches.

The serial acquirer's advantage is not whether the next deal closes. It is whether the firm is better at the next integration than it was at the last. When this year's acquisition arrives, the disciplined firm opens a playbook rather than improvising from memory. It applies the lessons of the last deal rather than rediscovering them at the same cost. And when the people who led its best integration walk out the door, their knowledge has already become the firm's. Build the capability. Make the learning belong to the institution, not the individual.

Chapter 11
Designing the Human-Machine Deal Team

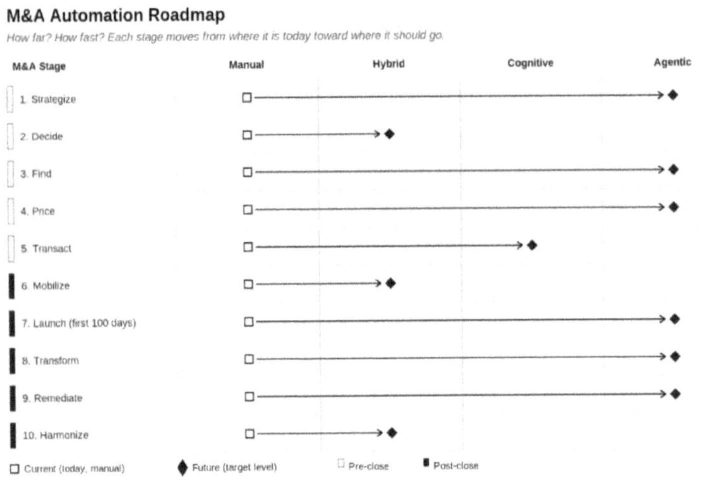

Figure 11.1. The M&A automation roadmap. Each stage moves from where it stands today toward the automation level that fits it.

A managing director stares at a data room. Four hundred files arrived overnight. Contracts, financial statements, supplier agreements, employment records, insurance binders, regulatory filings. The deal team has nine days to assess whether the target is worth what the seller wants. In a prior decade, the team would have divided the files among junior analysts, lost a weekend, and surfaced perhaps the obvious risks. Today, the managing director uploads the room to an analysis engine. Within twenty minutes, the system has tagged every document by category, extracted the financial metrics, flagged a customer concentration that the seller did not emphasize, and found a change-of-control clause buried in a footnote on page 211. The analyst who would have spent the weekend reading now spends the time thinking.

This is not the future. It is the present, unevenly distributed. Roughly half of dealmakers already report using artificial intelligence tools nearly every day, and adoption across private equity and venture firms climbed from under half to over 80% in a single year. The question facing the executive is no longer whether AI belongs in the deal process. The question is where it belongs, how far it should reach into each stage, and what must remain in human hands no matter how capable the machine becomes.

This chapter answers that question with a framework. We map artificial intelligence across the ten stages of the acquisition lifecycle, and for each stage, we ask how far automation should go. The answer is not the same for every stage. Some stages can be handed almost entirely to the machine. Others must stay close to human judgment, no matter how good the tools become. The art is in knowing the difference, and in designing the partnership so that silicon and carbon each do what they do best.

The Machine Is Neither Author Nor Tool

Most conversations about AI in dealmaking begin in the wrong place. They begin with technology and ask what it can do. The better starting point is the relationship and asking how it should be designed. We borrow a frame from control system design (the engineering discipline that models how a system holds a desired output through continuous feedback). A thermostat is a familiar example. The target temperature is the setpoint. The gap between the room and the setpoint is the error signal. The furnace is the controller. The thermometer that reports back closes the loop.

A deal team is a control system of exactly this kind. The investment thesis is the setpoint. The gap between what the team knows and what it needs to know is the error signal, experienced as the discomfort of an open question. The analysts and executives are the controller, generating the corrective response. And the feedback loop closes every time new information updates the thesis, which adjusts the next round of work. The discomfort of an unanswered question is not a failure. It is the system working correctly.

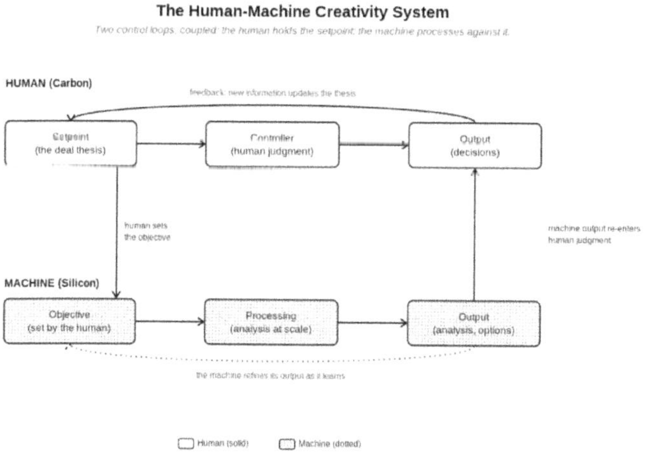

Figure 11.2. The human-machine creativity system. Two control loops, coupled: the human holds the setpoint and controller; the machine processes against it.

Artificial intelligence enters this loop at a specific point, and getting that point right is the whole game. The machine is not the author of the deal. It has no setpoint of its own. Remove the human thesis, and the machine has no target to optimize against; it generates output with no error signal to correct it. Nor is the machine a passive tool, a faster calculator that waits to be told what to compute. A tool does not close a feedback loop.

The machine sits between those two errors. It is an active participant in the loop, generating candidate outputs that re-enter the human system as fresh information, which the human evaluates, which drives the next iteration. The executive defines the objective. The machine processes against it. The result feeds back into human judgment. That cycle, not the raw capability of any model, determines whether the partnership produces something neither side could produce alone.

This framing rules out the two failure modes we see most often. The first is treating AI as an autonomous dealmaker, turning it loose to source, screen, and recommend, with the human reduced to a rubber stamp. A system with no human setpoint optimizes toward whatever proxy it was given, and proxies drift. The second is treating AI as a novelty tool, bolted onto one task such as document search, while the rest of the process runs as it always has. The first error abdicates judgment. The second wastes the capability. The design we propose keeps the human as the controller and the machine as an active participant whose output is always evaluated before it moves the deal forward.

Where in your current deal process is the feedback loop visible, and where has it gone silent? When the machine produces an answer, who evaluates it before the deal moves forward?

Four Levels of Automation

Before mapping AI across the lifecycle, we need a vocabulary for how far automation reaches into a given task. We use four levels, each a meaningful step beyond the last.

Manual process is the baseline. People do the work with conventional tools: spreadsheets, documents, meetings, phone calls. The human performs every step and holds every judgment. The acquisition lifecycle runs this way in most firms today.

Hybrid automation adds machine assistance to human work without changing who is in charge. The analyst still drives, but the machine accelerates discrete tasks: drafting a first memo, summarizing a document set, populating a model from extracted figures. The human reviews everything. This is where most serious adopters operate now.

Cognitive automation hands the machine a defined analytical task end-to-end, with the human setting the parameters and judging the result. The system does not merely assist; it produces a finished analysis, a valuation range, a risk profile, a benchmarked comparison, that the human then evaluates and approves. The human owns the decision. The machine owns the analysis that informs it.

Agentic automation goes further still. The system pursues a goal across multiple steps, makes intermediate decisions, calls on other tools and data sources, and returns a complete result with minimal human intervention along the way. The human sets the objective and reviews the output, but the machine orchestrates the path between them. Agentic systems are the newest level and the one that demands the most careful design, because the further the machine runs without a human in the loop, the more the design of the objective and the review of the result must carry the weight that continuous human oversight used to carry.

These levels are not a ladder that every task must climb to the top. The right level for a task depends on what the task requires. Pure analysis of well-structured data can run safely at the agentic level. Judgment that turns on relationships, trust, and tacit context should stay closer to the human, at the hybrid or cognitive level, no matter how capable the models become. The map that follows assigns each stage the level that fits it, not the highest level available.

The Ten Stages and How Far AI Should Reach

Framework Foundry organizes the acquisition into ten stages across two phases. The pre-close phase covers the first five: strategize, decide, find, price, and transact. The post-close phase covers the remaining five: mobilize, launch, transform, remediate, and harmonize. The transaction itself is the hinge between them. We walk each stage in turn, naming the automation level that fits and the reason it fits there.

Underneath these ten stages sit more than two hundred questions a disciplined acquirer should answer along the way. Do you have a clean room? Is your executive team aligned on the global, industry, customer, and product assumptions? What is your hurdle rate? Do you have an agreement on the selection criteria for a target? The value of AI is not that it replaces these questions. It is that it helps answer many of them faster and more completely, question by question, so the human attention left over can concentrate on the questions that only judgment can settle.

Stage One: Strategize (toward agentic)

Growth strategy formulation looks like the most human stage of all, and the strategic choice surely is. Yet the analytical work that feeds the choice is largely pattern recognition over large bodies of data, exactly what machines do well. An agentic system can scan an industry for consolidation patterns, map a firm's organic growth options against its competitors, model a five-year pro forma under several scenarios, and assemble the evidence base for a strategy discussion. The executive still decides the direction. The machine builds the analytical foundation under it. This stage can move from manual to agentic because the output is analysis, and the human retains the decision informed by that analysis.

Stage Two: Decide (toward hybrid)

Strategy decision-making is where the analysis becomes a commitment. Here, the automation level should stay low, at hybrid, and the reason is instructive. The decision turns on judgment, accountability, and the alignment of an executive team and a board, none of which the machine can hold. What the machine can do is sharpen the inputs: pressure-test the assumptions, surface the early-warning signs that one scenario is playing out rather than another, and keep the decision criteria honest. The machine informs the decision. It does not make it. A firm that lets an agentic system decide its growth strategy has confused the analysis with accountability, and only one of those can be delegated.

Stage Three: Find (toward agentic)

Target identification is among the strongest cases for full automation. The traditional approach to sourcing is notoriously narrow; by one benchmark, firms see only a small fraction of the relevant opportunities in their own target markets, because human networks and manual screens cannot cover the field. An agentic system can. It can scan websites, job postings, regulatory filings, and news across thousands of candidate firms, match them against the thesis, and surface targets a human team would never have found. In one documented pattern, a sourcing team scanning for companies expanding their field sales force, a proxy for new-market entry, had the system flag twenty-seven firms not previously on the radar, three of which advanced to signed agreements. This stage can run agentic, with the human defining the criteria and judging the shortlist.

Stage Four: Price (toward agentic)

Pricing the target combines two activities with different automation profiles. The analytical core, building the model, benchmarking the target against comparable firms, stress-testing the return-on-investment assumptions, and running probability-weighted scenarios, is well-suited to the machine. AI can compare a target's customer churn or overhead against hundreds of similar firms in moments and flag what looks out of line. That work can run at the agentic level.

The judgment that sits on top of it, what the firm is actually willing to pay and why, remains human. We treat this stage as agentic in its analytical work, with the explicit understanding that the number the analysis produces is an input to a human pricing decision, not the decision itself.

Recall the lesson of an earlier chapter: the most expensive failures in the history of dealmaking have come not from miscalculation but from a price decided in haste and an agreement never truly nailed down. The machine sharpens the math. It does not absolve the judgment.

Stage Five: Transact (toward cognitive)

The transaction is the hinge of the lifecycle, and it sits at an intermediate level for a clear reason. Diligence document review, contract analysis, and the mechanical assembly of the closing are tasks the machine performs with cognitive automation: it produces finished work product, the diligence summary, the flagged clauses, the verified figures that the human reviews and acts on. But the negotiation itself, the give-and-take that sets final terms, is a human contest of relationships and leverage that should not be handed to a machine. We place this stage at cognitive automation: the analytical and document-intensive work is largely automated, while the negotiating table stays human.

Stage Six: Mobilize (toward hybrid)

Mobilizing the buyer and seller for integration is fundamentally about people: aligning two leadership teams, establishing trust, and setting a shared direction before the work begins. This is relationship work, and it belongs close to the human, at the hybrid. The machine can help with the scaffolding, drafting the integration charter, assembling the workstream templates, and building the initial plan, but the alignment itself happens between people in a room. A firm that automates its way through mobilization will find it has built a plan that no one owns.

Stage Seven: Launch, the First Hundred Days (toward agentic)

The first hundred days are an execution sprint across many parallel workstreams, and execution at scale is where agentic automation earns its keep. The system can track hundreds of integration tasks against their timelines, flag the ones slipping before they slip visibly, route work, and surface the dependencies that human coordinators miss under pressure. The human leaders set the priorities and own the escalations. The machine runs the underlying operational machinery at a speed and level of completeness no manual coordination can match. This stage can run agentic, with the human leadership focused on the decisions that the tracking surfaces rather than on the tracking itself.

Stage Eight: Transform (toward agentic)

Transforming the combined firms, redesigning processes, consolidating systems, capturing the value that justified the deal is heavy analytical and operational work. Agentic systems can analyze the procurement and payment processes of both firms, identify the redundancies and the opportunities, and design a streamlined process that takes the better practice from each side. After the design, the same systems can automate routine execution, route tasks, flag anomalies, and predict problems before they surface. The human owns the design choices and the trade-offs. The machine does the analysis that reveals them and the execution that follows. This stage can run agentic.

Stage Nine: Remediate (toward agentic)

Remediation is the stage where things that went wrong get found and fixed, and it depends entirely on detecting problems early enough to act. This is a monitoring and anomaly-detection task that the machine performs continuously and tirelessly in ways humans cannot. Agentic systems track key performance indicators, detect deviations from the integration plan, and surface operational drift in real time, often before the responsible humans would have noticed. The system can even propose remediation paths based on what worked in prior deals. The human decides which fix to apply. The machine finds what needs fixing. This stage can run agentic.

Stage Ten: Harmonize (toward hybrid)

Harmonizing the combination is the long work of making two firms into one culture, one identity, one way of operating. It is the most human stage of the post-close phase, and it remains in a hybrid stage. The machine can measure and track employee sentiment across channels, monitor whether the combined firm is operating as intended, and flag where friction persists. But harmonization itself, the leadership, the symbolism, the patient work of building a shared identity, is human work that no system can perform. The machine tells the leaders where the friction is. The leaders do the harmonizing.

The Pattern in the Map

Step back from the ten stages, and a pattern appears. The stages that move all the way to agentic automation, strategize, find, price, launch, transform, and remediate share a common character: they are dominated by analysis, pattern recognition, monitoring, and execution at scale. These are the tasks where the machine's tireless speed and breadth genuinely exceed human capacity. The stages that remain at hybrid, decide, mobilize, and harmonize share a distinct character: they hinge on judgment, accountability, relationships, and trust. The single stage at cognitive automation, transact, is a deliberate blend, automating the document-heavy analysis while keeping the negotiating table human.

The pattern is not arbitrary, nor is it about the difficulty of the work. Deciding the growth strategy is harder than finding a target, yet finding goes agentic while deciding stays hybrid. The dividing line is not difficulty. It is whether the task is fundamentally analytical or fundamentally human. Analysis delegates well. Judgment, accountability, and relationship do not. A firm that understands this dividing line will automate aggressively where automation pays and hold the line where it must, rather than either fearing AI everywhere or trusting it everywhere.

This is also why the roadmap is properly a subject of debate rather than a fixed prescription. Reasonable executives will disagree about where a given stage should sit, and the disagreement is the point. A draft roadmap, marked with where each stage stands today and where it should move, is a tool for forcing that conversation in a specific firm with specific capabilities and a specific tolerance for risk. The map we have drawn is our considered draft. Your firm's map should be argued, not inherited.

AI and the Alignment Tools

Artificial intelligence does not replace the frameworks developed in this book. It accelerates them. Each of the eight alignment tools becomes faster and more complete when a well-designed machine partner does the underlying analytical work, leaving the human judgment the tool was built to support.

Deal Thesis Decomposition asks what value drivers justify the deal. An agentic system can assemble the evidence for each driver and test it against market data, so the executives debate a decomposition that is already grounded rather than one built from memory. End-State Vision and Integration Classes both depend on seeing the target clearly; AI sharpens that picture, but the choice of vision and the classification of the deal remain human.

Timing and Probabilitics is, at its core, scenario modeling, which the machine does well, leaving the executives to weigh the scenarios rather than build them. Assumptions and Decisions becomes more honest when a system surfaces the early warning signs that an assumption is failing. Heat Maps gain precision when AI populates them from real operational data rather than impressions.

Better Practices, the disciplined choice of whether to adopt the buyer's practice, the seller's, or a new combination, is exactly the kind of comparison agentic systems perform well, though the choice itself stays with the leaders who must live with it. And Tailor-Made Tools, the custom instruments built for deals that exceed the standard frameworks, are now faster to build than ever, because a capable machine partner can prototype a bespoke analysis in hours rather than weeks.

The thread running through all eight is the same control-system logic we began with. In every case, the machine does the analysis and the human holds the judgment. The tool defines the question. The machine helps answer it. The human decides what the answer means.

Designing the Partnership Well

If the machine is an active participant in a control loop, the quality of the partnership depends on the design of three connection points, and a firm can engineer each one or neglect it. The first is the definition of the objective. The machine optimizes against whatever target the human sets, so a vague or proxy objective produces confident output aimed at the wrong thing. The second is the machine's processing itself, which the firm must understand well enough to trust, including where the analysis is strong and where it is fragile. The third is the evaluation of the output, the moment the machine's result re-enters human judgment. A partnership that carefully defines the objective, honestly understands the process, and rigorously evaluates the output will outperform one that automates the same tasks without that discipline.

Two practical cautions follow. The first concerns oversight as automation deepens. At the hybrid level, the human reviews everything, so errors surface quickly. At the agentic level, the machine runs many steps before a human sees the result, which means the design of the objective and the rigor of the final review must carry the oversight that continuous human checking used to provide. The deeper the automation, the more the design has to compensate for the absent human in the middle. The second concerns the data. An agentic system reaching across thousands of documents and external sources can surface a firm's confidential information in places it should not go, and it can ingest sources whose reliability no one has checked. The discipline that governs what the machine may touch and what it may send outward matters more as the machine's reach grows.

None of this is a reason to hold back. The firms that win at dealmaking with AI are not the ones that adopt the most tools. They are the ones who deliberately design the human-machine partnership, stage by stage, with a clear view of where the machine should run far and where the human must stay close. Cisco, for instance, runs AI-powered dashboards to monitor post-acquisition progress across teams, systems, and workflows, a use squarely in the agentic execution-and-monitoring stages where the machine excels, while its leaders hold the judgment that the dashboards inform. Studies of post-merger integration report meaningfully faster integration timelines and higher value capture for firms that adopt AI and analytics well. The advantage is real. It accrues to design, not to enthusiasm.

Implications for the CEO

Artificial intelligence belongs in the deal process, and the executive's task is to decide where it belongs, stage by stage, rather than to embrace it everywhere or resist it everywhere. The machine is neither the author of the deal nor a passive tool. It is an active participant in a control loop, generating analysis that humans evaluate and act on. Design that loops well, and the partnership produces what neither side could alone. Design it poorly, by abdicating judgment to an autonomous system or by bolting AI onto a single task, and it produces either drift or waste.

The four levels of automation, manual, hybrid, cognitive, and agentic, give the executive a vocabulary for how far to reach into each task. The ten-stage map assigns each stage the level that fits it. The analytical, monitoring, and execution-heavy stages- strategize, find, price, launch, transform, and remediate- can run agentic. The judgment-and-relationship stages, decide, mobilize, and harmonize, stay at hybrid. The transaction sits between, at cognitive. The dividing line is not the difficulty of the work but whether the work is fundamentally analytical or fundamentally human.

The tools of this book are not displaced by AI. They are accelerated by it, with the machine analyzing each tool and the human holding the judgment that each tool was built to support. And the advantage goes to the firms that design the partnership with discipline: a clear objective, an honest understanding of the machine's processing, and a rigorous evaluation of its output.

When the next deal arrives, the disciplined firm has a deliberate map of where the machine runs far and where the human stays close. It does not automate by accident. It knows which of the ten stages belongs to the machine and which demands human judgment, and it does not confuse the two. And when the machine hands the team an answer, someone is accountable for deciding what it means. Design the partnership on purpose. Keep the human at the setpoint and let the machine do the rest.

Chapter 12
The Process: Agree Early, Agree Often

Figure 12.1. "Oh, dear! Oh, dear! I shall be too late!"

Two firms signed a letter of intent on a handshake and a shared sense that the logic was obvious. The strategic fit was clear. The price was within range. Both chief executives wanted the deal, and neither wanted to spoil the goodwill by raising the questions that might slow it down. So the hard questions waited. Who would run the combined commercial organization? Whose technology platform would survive? What the deal was actually supposed to produce, and how the two sides would know whether it had, remained to be seen. Everyone agreed to agree later.

Later, all arrived at once, three weeks after close, in a conference room where the goodwill had evaporated. The questions that would have been difficult to discuss during the courtship had become a contest for control during the marriage. The integration stalled. The gains slipped. The value that justified the deal leaked away while two leadership teams fought over what they had never actually decided.

This is the most common way acquisitions fail, and it is entirely preventable. The failure is not in the strategy or the price. It is in the timing of the agreement. The teams agreed late, when alignment was expensive, rather than early, when it was cheap. And they agreed once, treating alignment as an event to be completed rather than a discipline to be sustained. This book has given you eight tools for producing alignment. This chapter gives you the process that puts them to work: agree early and agree often.

What Early Agreement Protects

The reason to agree early is not only to save money, though it does. The deeper reasons are to protect the deal against the risk of missing its thesis and to preserve the growth that the deal was meant to produce.

An acquisition is a bet that the combined firm will grow in ways neither firm could alone, and that bet is expressed in the deal thesis. Every agreement deferred is a chance for the combined firm to drift away from that thesis, to execute something other than the strategy that justified the price. Agreeing early is how an acquirer keeps the deal pointed at the growth it bought while holding down both the risk of failure and the cost of getting there.

Three stakes ride on the timing of agreement, and they stand together rather than in rank. The first is risk: the probability that the deal misses its thesis. The second is value: the probability that the combined firm actually grows as promised. The third is cost: what the acquirer spends to resolve disagreements.

These are not a hierarchy in which one matters more than the others. They are three faces of the same coin, and deferral worsens all three at once. A deferred agreement raises the risk of missing the thesis, lowers the odds that the promised growth will be realized, and runs up the cost of the eventual resolution in a single motion. Early agreement improves all three together. We take them in turn only to show the mechanism of each, not to rank them.

Take risk first. Every deferred agreement raises the risk that the deal misses its thesis. The thesis names the value drivers, the specific sources of growth that justify the deal. When the parties defer agreement on how those drivers will be realized, on which products lead, on whose capabilities prevail, and on how the two organizations combine, they leave the thesis exposed to drift. The combined firm begins executing toward whatever the unresolved questions default to, which is rarely the thesis and never by design.

The most expensive failures in dealmaking are not miscalculations of price. They are theses missed because the agreements that would have realized them were deferred past the point of repair. A deal that comes in over budget but hits its thesis is a success. A deal that lands on budget but misses its thesis is a failure, and deferral is how the second outcome happens.

Take value next. Early agreement increases the probability that the combined firm will actually grow. When the parties settle the thesis, the end-state, and the integration approach while goodwill is high and the path is still adjustable, the integration that follows executes the growth strategy cleanly: resources flow to the right places, the two organizations move toward one destination, and the value the thesis promised has the best chance of being realized.

The valuation of the combined firm is ultimately a function of whether the growth strategy is successfully executed. Agreeing early is among the greatest levers an acquirer has over execution, and therefore over the value created. Deferral leaves growth on the table.

And take cost, because its mechanism is the clearest of the three. The cost of resolving a disagreement is not fixed. It rises steeply as the deal progresses. A disagreement revealed during the thesis stage costs a conversation. The same disagreement surfaced after close costs a renegotiation, a delay, a loss of trust, and sometimes the deal itself.

Early in a deal, the parties have maximum goodwill and minimum commitment; nothing is signed, nothing is announced, and a hard question is simply part of diligence. Late in a deal, the situation inverts: commitment is maximum, goodwill is spent, and a hard question is no longer diligence but a threat, resolvable only by expensive means because walking away has become catastrophic.

The discipline follows directly. For every consequential question a deal raises, ask when it must be answered, and then answer it earlier than that. Pull the hard conversations forward into the window where goodwill is high and commitment is reversible. The executive who masters this does not eliminate disagreement, which is impossible, but relocates it to the moment when it is cheapest to resolve, least likely to derail the thesis, and most likely to preserve the growth. Agreeing early is not about agreeing quickly. It is about agreeing while agreement is still cheap, still safe, and still able to protect the deal's value.

A single example makes all three stakes concrete. Suppose two firms disagree about which of their two overlapping product lines will survive the combination. Raised during the thesis stage, the disagreement is a planning question: the teams model both options, see which one the deal economics favor, and decide. The cost is a few analyst days. The risk to the thesis is nil because the decision is made in service of the thesis. And the value is protected because the combined firm will focus its growth on the winning line from day one.

Raised during diligence, after the price is set, the same disagreement is a valuation question, because the answer changes what the combined firm is worth. Resolving it costs weeks and some goodwill, and it puts the thesis at moderate risk because the price may no longer fit the revised plan.

Raised after close, the disagreement is a political contest: two product teams, two sets of customers, two general managers whose careers are attached to their respective lines, fighting in public while the market watches. The cost is months and lost people. The risk to the thesis is now severe because the combined firm is actively executing in two directions at once. And the value is bleeding away in real time as customers defect amid uncertainty, and the growth the deal promised slips out of reach.

Same disagreement. Resolved early, it costs little, threatens nothing, and protects the growth. Resolved late, it comes at a heavy cost, endangers the thesis, and destroys value. The discipline of agreeing early is nothing more than the refusal to let a cheap, safe, value-protecting decision become an expensive, dangerous, value-destroying one.

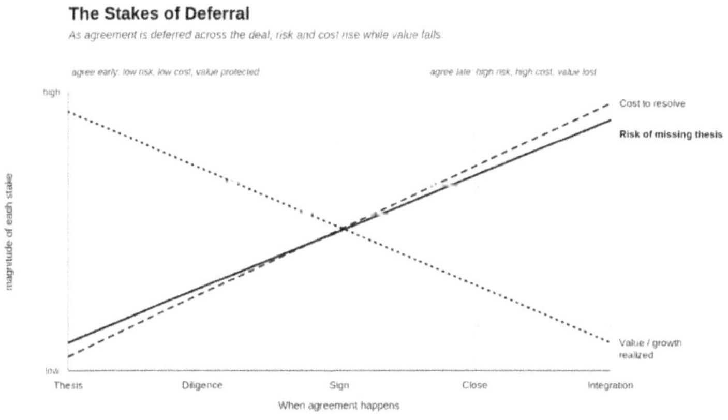

Figure 12.2. The stakes of deferral. As agreement is deferred across the deal, the risk of missing the thesis and the cost to resolve disagreement both rise, while the value and growth realized fall.

Why Often, Not Once

If early were the whole story, alignment would be a single event: gather the executives, work through the questions, document the decisions, and proceed. Many firms treat it exactly this way, and then they are surprised when the alignment they achieved in the spring has dissolved by the autumn. Alignment is not durable. It decays.

It decays for reasons no one can prevent. New information arrives that no one had at the outset, and it changes the calculus. Assumptions that everyone accepted prove wrong. Circumstances shift, a competitor moves, a market turns, a key executive departs. And memory itself erodes; people who agreed in the room remember different things three months later, each recalling the version that suits their interest. A one-time agreement, however carefully reached, begins degrading the moment the room empties.

This is why the discipline has a second half. Agreeing early gets the alignment. Agreeing often keeps it. Agreement is properly understood as a rhythm rather than an event, a cadence of returning to the consequential questions and confirming that the answers still hold. The firms that sustain alignment are not the ones that align hardest at the start. They are the ones that re-align steadily throughout, catching drift while it is small and correcting it before it compounds into the kind of misalignment that wrecks an integration.

Early and often are therefore two halves of one discipline. Early addresses when the first agreement happens. Often addresses how the agreement is sustained against the forces that erode it. A firm that agrees early but not often achieves a clean start and a messy finish. A firm that agrees often but not early spends the whole deal trying to settle questions it should have settled before commitment hardened. The process requires both.

A Lesson from the Factory Floor

This discipline has a distinguished precedent, and naming it lends the argument the authority of a proven system. The Toyota Production System, the manufacturing philosophy that reshaped global industry, rests on principles that map almost exactly onto agreeing early and agreeing often. Toyota did not discover these ideas in dealmaking, but the logic is the same, because the underlying problem is the same: a defect introduced early and left to flow downstream becomes vastly more expensive, dangerous, and value-destroying than the same defect caught at its source.

The first Toyota pillar is *jidoka*, often translated as automation with a human touch, and its operating rule is to stop the line. When a defect appears at any station, the worker halts production immediately rather than letting the flawed part flow to the next station, because a defect caught at its source costs almost nothing to fix, while the same defect discovered after it has been built into the finished vehicle costs a fortune. The principle traces to Sakichi Toyoda's self-stopping loom of 1924, which halted itself the instant a thread broke.

This is agreeing early, stated in the language of the factory. A deferred agreement is a defect allowed to flow downstream. The discipline of agreeing early is the discipline of stopping the line: surface the disagreement at the station where it appears, the thesis stage, the diligence stage, and resolve it there, before it is built into the combined firm, where the cost of correction multiplies.

Quality management captures the same truth in its widely cited rule of thumb that a defect costs one unit to prevent, ten to correct in production, and a hundred to fix after it reaches the customer. The acquisition cost curve obeys the same arithmetic.

The second principle is *kaizen*, continuous improvement through a steady cadence of small corrections rather than occasional large ones. Toyota does not improve its lines in annual upheavals; it improves them daily, in increments, through a disciplined rhythm of noticing and adjusting. This is agreeing often. Alignment, like quality, is not achieved once and banked. It is sustained through a cadence of small re-confirmations that catch drift while it is still small, exactly as the factory catches process drift before it becomes a defect.

And underneath both sits the elimination of *muda*, the Japanese term for waste, the wasted motion, wasted material, and wasted time that a well-designed system drives out. Agreeing early and often is, at bottom, a campaign against muda in the deal: against the wasted months of relitigating settled questions, the wasted value of gains that slipped away, the wasted effort of two teams executing in different directions. Do it right the first time, at the source, on a steady rhythm, and the waste disappears. The factory learned this lesson decades ago. The dealmaker is wise to learn it too.

The Rhythm of Agreement

The nine tools of this book are not a menu from which an executive selects. They are a sequence, a chain of agreements arranged so that each one comes early enough to be cheap and each one builds on the agreement before it. Walking the sequence shows what agreeing early actually looks like in practice, question by question, tool by tool.

The chain begins with Assumptions and Decisions, because the first thing two parties must agree on is what the deal is taking on faith and what it has actually resolved. Every acquisition rests on assumptions; the discipline is to name them, agree on which ones are load-bearing, and decide in advance what will signal that an assumption is failing. This agreement comes first because every later agreement depends on it; a team that has not examined its assumptions cannot meaningfully evaluate anything downstream. Settle the assumptions early, and the rest of the chain has a foundation. Defer them, and every later disagreement is really a disguised argument about something the team never surfaced.

Deal Thesis Decomposition comes next, because once the parties have named their assumptions, they must agree on what the deal is supposed to produce. The thesis names the value drivers and quantifies the contribution of each. This agreement comes early because every integration decision is, at bottom, a decision about whether it serves the thesis; a team that has not agreed on why it is doing the deal cannot meaningfully agree on anything downstream. Settle the thesis, and the rest of the chain has a destination. Defer it, and every later disagreement is really a disguised argument about the thesis.

Strategic Distortions follows, naming the nine cognitive shortcuts that quietly bend executive judgment during high-stakes deals. Either-or thinking. Amplifying. Discounting. Each distortion served humans well across millennia, and each now distorts strategy under pressure. This agreement comes early because distortions are cheapest to correct before they have shaped the decisions that follow. A team that names its distortions before it commits is a team that can reason clearly. A team that discovers them after the close is a team explaining to its board why the thesis missed.

Classes of Integration translates the thesis into a decision about how much the two firms will actually combine. Standalone Preservation, Synergy Capture, Full Consumption, or Strategic Transformation: the class sets the intensity of integration and, with it, the resources, the timeline, and the risk. This agreement comes early because it governs the scale of everything that follows, and a team that has not agreed on the class will discover, painfully, that some members were planning a light touch while others were planning a full absorption.

Timing of Multiple Acquisitions comes next, because once the parties know how much they will combine, they must agree on the sequence and the odds. Which integrations run in parallel, which run in series, and what is the realistic probability that each lands on time. This agreement comes early because sequencing decisions made late are sequencing decisions made under duress, when the chance to stage the work sensibly has already passed.

Acquisition End-State Vision follows, because once the parties agree on what the deal should produce and how intensely the firms will combine, they must agree on what the combined firm should become. The vision describes the organizational structure, the market position, the capability model, and the cultural approach of the entity that will exist on the far side of integration. This agreement comes early because it is the target that every integration decision aims for; teams that integrate without a shared end state are building toward different destinations and will collide at every junction.

Adoption of Better Practices comes next, settling the recurring question of whose way of working survives. For each capability area, the parties agree whether to adopt the buyer's practice, the seller's, or combine the two into a better practice that neither could achieve alone. This agreement comes early because the alternative, letting each function quietly default to its own incumbent habits, produces a combined firm that never actually combined.

The Organization Heat Map provides the parties with a shared picture of where integration risk concentrates. The map shows which functions, systems, and combinations pose the greatest danger, so attention and resources flow to the right places. This agreement comes early because an early-seen risk can be planned for, while a late-seen risk is a crisis being managed.

Tailor-Made Tools closes the chain for deals whose distinctive features exceed what standard frameworks can accommodate. When a deal presents a problem that the preceding tools do not address, the parties agree to build a custom instrument for it rather than forcing the deal into a framework that does not fit. This agreement comes last in the sequence because it is the exception that the practitioner reaches for only after the standard chain has revealed where it falls short.

Walk the chain, and the pattern is unmistakable. Each tool is a moment of agreement. Each moment comes as early as the deal allows. And each agreement, once reached, becomes the foundation on which the next one is built. This is the rhythm of agreeing early: not one grand alignment, but a sequence of specific agreements, each pulled forward to the cheapest moment it can occupy.

The Rhythm in Practice

Two contrasting deals show the discipline at work and at fault. Both are composites, drawn from the recurring patterns we have seen across many engagements rather than from any single transaction, but the patterns are real.

In the first, a software firm acquired a smaller competitor. The acquiring chief executive insisted on settling the thesis and the end state before signing, against the advice of bankers who wanted to move quickly. The two teams spent an uncomfortable week agreeing on what the combined firm would become, which product line would lead, whose engineering culture would prevail, and what the deal would have to deliver to justify its price. The discomfort was real, and the deal nearly broke twice over questions that, had they surfaced after close, would have broken it permanently.

Because they surfaced early, the parties could resolve them while walking away was still an option, which gave each side the leverage to be honest. The integration that followed was not easy, but it never stalled, because the hard questions had already been answered and documented before anyone announced anything. The firm then held the agreements to a monthly review for the first half-year, and twice caught an assumption drifting before it became a problem.

In the second, a manufacturer acquired a regional rival on a compressed timeline, deferring the contentious questions to preserve momentum. Whose enterprise system would survive waited. Which plants would consolidate waited. Whether the acquired brand would be retired waited. Each deferral felt prudent at the time, a way to keep a good deal moving.

After close, the deferred questions returned together, now entangled with the anxieties of two workforces and the expectations of customers who had been promised continuity. The integration consumed eighteen months of executive attention that should have gone to the market, lost a third of the acquired firm's senior engineers to the uncertainty, and delivered roughly half the value the thesis had promised. Nothing in the strategy was wrong. The failure was entirely in the timing of agreements.

The contrast is the lesson. The two deals differed not in the quality of their logic but in when the parties chose to agree. The first paid for alignment early, in the cheap currency of an uncomfortable week. The second paid for it late, in the ruinous currency of lost people, lost value, and lost time. Same kind of deal. Different rhythm. Different outcome.

Where Agreement Happens

These agreements are reached in rooms, and running those rooms well is a craft in its own right. The mechanics of executive facilitation, who belongs in the room, how to structure the discussion, how to surface the disagreement hiding behind polite consensus, and how to close on a decision that holds are a discipline we do not attempt to teach here, because they have already been taught better elsewhere.

The definitive guide is the work of Bob Frisch and the Strategic Offsites Group, whose book *Who's in the Room?* and whose *Harvard Business Review* articles, beginning with the seminal "Off-Sites That Work," are the better resources for any executive who wants to run the sessions where these agreements are forged.

We recommend that work to the reader and concentrate here on what is ours to contribute: not how to run the room, but what must be agreed in it, and when.

Sustaining the Agreement

Agreeing early builds the chain. Agreeing often protects it. The protection takes the form of a cadence, a deliberate rhythm of returning to the agreements to confirm they still hold against the forces that erode them.

The cadence has a natural shape. In the early phase of integration, when circumstances change fastest and drift accumulates quickest, the agreements deserve frequent review, often monthly. As the integration matures and the combined firm settles, the review can be extended to quarterly intervals. The point is not the precise interval but the discipline of the return. A firm that revisits its agreements on a known rhythm catches drift as a small correction. A firm that revisits them only when something breaks catches drift as a crisis.

What gets reviewed is the chain itself. Does the thesis still hold, or has new information changed what the deal can produce? Is the end-state still the right target? Have the load-bearing assumptions survived contact with reality, or has one of them failed in the way the team agreed to watch for? Each agreement in the chain is a candidate for re-confirmation or revision, and the cadence is simply the schedule on which the team asks.

Most agreements will hold most of the time, and the review confirms them quickly. The value is in the few that have quietly stopped being true, because those are the ones that wreck integrations when they go unexamined.

This is the second half of the discipline made concrete. Agreeing often is not an endless meeting; it is a light, regular, deliberate return to a small set of consequential agreements. It costs little, and it prevents the most expensive failure in dealmaking: the slow, unnoticed divergence of two teams who once agreed and no longer do.

Implications for the CEO

The promise on the cover of this book is a process, and the process is the executive's to enforce. Agreeing early and agreeing often is not a technique that a facilitator can supply, nor a tool that a team can purchase. It is a discipline that the chief executive models, demands, and protects because the chief executive is the only person with the authority to bring hard conversations forward against everyone's natural inclination to defer them.

What the discipline protects is three things at once: the thesis, the growth, and the cost. Deferring agreement raises the risk that the combined firm drifts off its thesis. It lowers the odds that the growth the deal promised is realized, because the strategy executes cleanly only when the fundamental questions are settled. And it runs up the cost, because disagreement gets more expensive as the deal progresses. These move together. The executive who agrees early is not trading one against another. The executive is protecting all three in the same motion, and, above all, protecting the reason the deal was done.

The factory floor learned this first. Toyota stops the line to catch defects at their source, improves through a steady cadence of small corrections, and drives out waste at every step. The dealmaker who agrees early stops the line on a disagreement before it flows downstream. The dealmaker who agrees often improves alignment through a steady cadence rather than an occasional upheaval. And the dealmaker who does both drives out the waste, the wasted time, effort, and money that deferral always produces. Do it right the first time, at the source, on a rhythm.

The twelve frameworks are the structure of the early agreement, a chain in which the thesis is settled first, and each later agreement builds on the one before. The cadence of re-confirmation is the structure of sustained agreement: a light, regular return to the chain to catch drift while it is still small. And the mechanics of the room, where the agreements are actually forged, are a craft the executive can learn from the work of Bob Frisch and others who have mapped it well.

The question for the executive is not whether the team will agree. Every team agrees eventually, in the room or in the wreckage, and the deal tells you which. The only question is when. So agree early, while the disagreement is still a conversation rather than a casualty. Agree often, because alignment decays, and a single consensus will not hold. Stop the line at the source, catch the drift before it becomes a defect, and pay for alignment in the cheap currency of an early conversation rather than the ruinous currency of a late one. Do the hard work early. That is the whole of it.

Conclusion

Remove the Blindfolds

Return to the parable that opened this book. Several blindfolded executives each lay hands on a different part of an elephant. One feels the trunk and declares it a snake. One feels a leg and declares it a tree. One feels the ear, the tusk, the side, the tail, and each declares something different. Every one of them is partially right. Every one of them is completely wrong. And the combined firm they are about to build will be assembled from these incompatible pictures, by people who do not yet know they disagree.

The solution was always simple to name and hard to do. Remove the blindfolds. Get the executives to see the same animal before they commit to building from it. This book has been an extended answer to a single question: how does a leadership team actually remove the blindfolds, early enough and often enough to matter? The answer is not exhortation. It is a discipline, supported by tools, governed by a process. We can now state the whole of it plainly.

What the Book Has Argued

The thesis is in the title. Agree Early, Agree Often. Behind those four words sits a claim about timing that runs against the instinct of most dealmakers. The instinct is to preserve momentum, to defer the hard questions, to save the contentious conversations for after the ink dries. The argument of this book is the reverse. The firms that succeed are the ones that surface the hard disagreements while the relationship still has the goodwill to absorb them, and that return to those agreements on a steady cadence as the deal unfolds.

The reason is a matter of stakes that move together. When agreement is deferred, three things worsen at once. The risk that the deal misses its thesis rises because the combined firm begins executing toward whatever the unresolved questions default to. The value the deal promised erodes because growth is realized only when the strategy executes cleanly. And the cost of resolution climbs because a disagreement that would have been a conversation during diligence becomes a contest after close. Agreeing early protects all three. It is the single discipline with the widest leverage over whether an acquisition creates the value that justified it.

This is not so much a new idea as an old one carried into a new domain. The factory floor learned decades ago that a defect caught at its source costs almost nothing, while the same defect discovered downstream costs a fortune. Stop the line early. Improve on a steady rhythm. Drive out the waste. The disciplined acquirer does the same: surface the disagreement at the station where it appears, resolve it before it is built into the combined firm, and return to the agreements often enough to catch drift while it is still small.

The Tools That Remove the Blindfolds

The discipline is made practical by eight tools, each removing a specific blindfold, each producing a specific agreement. We recall them here not to teach them again but to show how they chain together into a single act of seeing.

Deal Thesis Decomposition removes the blindfold over why the deal is being done, replacing vague strategic rationale with named value drivers and quantified benefits. End-State Vision removes the blindfold on what the combined firm will become, giving every executive a single destination to build toward rather than several. Integration Classes removes the blindfold over how much the two firms will actually combine, forcing an explicit choice among standalone preservation, synergy capture, full consumption, and strategic transformation. Timing and Probabilities removes the blindfold over speed and sequence, making the schedule and its odds explicit and testable rather than assumed.

Assumptions and Decisions removes the blindfold on what the team is taking on faith, naming the load-bearing assumptions and deciding in advance what will signal failure. Heat Maps remove the blindfold on where integration risk concentrates, so attention and resources flow to the dangerous cells rather than spreading evenly across the safe ones. Better Practices removes the blindfold of assuming the buyer always knows best, forcing an honest choice for each capability among the buyer's way, the seller's way, or a combination better than either. And Tailor-Made Tools remove the blindfold that standard frameworks can impose, building custom instruments for deals whose distinctive features the standard eight cannot capture.

Eight tools, eight blindfolds, one act of seeing. Used as a chain, each pulled forward to the earliest moment it can occupy, they let a leadership team look at the same elephant and, for the first time, agree on what it is.

A word on the newest member of the deal team. In the modern acquisition, a well-designed machine partner can do much of the analytical labor beneath each of these tools, scanning for targets, benchmarking a price, populating a heat map from real operational data, monitoring an integration for the first signs of drift, faster and more completely than a human team working alone.

I devoted a full chapter to how this partnership should be designed, and the central lesson bears repeating here: the machine is neither the author of the deal nor a passive calculator, but an active participant whose analysis the human must always evaluate before it moves the deal forward. Artificial intelligence makes the tools faster and the alignment more durable. It does not make the judgment, the accountability, or the agreement. Those remain, irreducibly, human work.

Used with that discipline, the machine is one more way to remove the blindfolds sooner.

The Intelligence Advantage

The discipline described in this book operates through human judgment: the executive who surfaces a buried assumption, the facilitator who reads the room and names the disagreement no one else will, the integration leader who insists on revisiting the deal thesis when the evidence is moving against it. That judgment remains irreplaceable.

But the environment in which that judgment operates is changing. Artificial intelligence has crossed a threshold in M&A relevance. AI-assisted document review processes contracts at a scale that no diligence team can match. Machine learning models trained on customer transaction data identify revenue opportunities within days of close. Workforce analytics platforms map talent risk before the integration management office holds its first meeting. Real-time KPI dashboards catch integration drift in month two, not month eight.

Chapter 12 addresses how AI enhances the eight alignment tools directly. But the AI opportunity in M&A extends beyond alignment to the full arc of value creation: accelerating innovation, driving revenue growth, managing costs, and achieving deal thesis objectives. We have examined that broader terrain in a companion white paper.

Readers who want to explore the AI opportunity across the full M&A lifecycle, including a 90-day pilot architecture for building AI integration capability and the four value creation domains where AI is delivering measurable results today, will find that analysis in The Intelligence Advantage: How AI Is Redefining Value Creation in Mergers and Acquisitions, available at frameworkfoundry.ai under A.I. The white paper is a companion to this book, not a prerequisite. The tools in these pages work without it. But firms that deploy the tools and technology together will compound their integration advantage faster than firms that deploy either alone.

Why Most Still Fail

The tools exist. The process is known. And still, most acquisitions fail to deliver the value that justified them. Decades of research put the failure rate somewhere between half and two-thirds or higher, depending on how failure is measured. One widely cited analysis from Deloitte's M&A practice found that fully 65% of major strategic acquisitions were failures. Against the trillions in deal value this book's opening pages described, the waste is staggering. The reason is not that the discipline is unknown. The reason is that it is hard.

Agreeing early is harder than dealmaking, harder than planning, harder than execution, because it requires confronting disagreements that everyone would rather avoid, making decisions when ambiguity feels safer, and forcing clarity when vagueness is more comfortable. Most teams skip the work. They rush from announcement to execution, paper over the disagreements with vague consensus, and proceed on a false alignment that holds until the first hard choice exposes it. Then, three months in, they discover that operations assumed one thing and finance another, that sales expected the brand to be preserved, and marketing expected it to be retired, and that the agreement they thought they had was never actually reached. By then, the cheap moment has passed, and the bill comes due at the late price.

The firms that succeed are not smarter or better funded. They are more disciplined. They align early; they use the tools to structure conversations that are hard to have without structure; they surface the disagreements they would rather avoid; and they return to their agreements on a cadence rather than trusting a single consensus to hold. That discipline, not intelligence or resources, is what separates the firms that create value from those that destroy it.

The Choice

Every executive who picks up the next deal faces the same choice, not whether to acquire. That decision is made elsewhere, on other grounds. The choice this book speaks to is how to agree: early, while agreement is cheap and the thesis is still protectable, or late, in the wreckage, where every team agrees eventually because reality forces the matter.

The path of the majority is to defer. Preserve the momentum, avoid the friction, hope the disagreements resolve themselves, and join the firms whose deals consume more value than they create. The other path is to do the hard work. Surface the disagreements early. Settle the thesis before the offer, the end state and the integration class before the close, and the assumptions and the risk map before the first day. Return to all of it on a steady rhythm as the integration unfolds. Build the institutional capability so that the next deal is run better than the last, and so that the knowledge does not walk out the door when the people who earned it do.

None of this is heroic. It is the opposite of heroic. It is the patient, unglamorous discipline of doing the small right thing early rather than the large expensive thing late. The factory learned it. The disciplined acquirer learns it too. And the firm that learns it does not merely avoid the common failure. It compounds an advantage that its less disciplined competitors cannot easily copy, because the advantage lives in a practice, not in a single clever deal.

The Final Word

The elephant is real, and the executives are touching it right now. Some hold the trunk, some the leg, some the tusk, and most do not yet know that the others feel something different. The blindfolds can stay on, and the firm can proceed with incompatible pictures toward the failure that incompatible pictures produce. Or the blindfolds can come off early, while there is still time to agree on what the animal is and build accordingly.

This book has argued that the difference between those two outcomes is neither luck nor genius. It is the timing of agreement, sustained by discipline and supported by tools. Agree early while it is cheap and safe, and to protect the value of the deal. Agree often, because alignment decays, and a single consensus will not hold. Remove the blindfolds, and keep removing them, because they grow back.

So, the matter is no longer whether your executives will agree. They will, in the room or in the wreckage, and the deal will tell you which. The only choice that was ever yours is "when?" Make it now, while agreement is still cheap, still safe, and still able to protect the growth you bought. Do the hard work early, before the elephant is built wrong. Agree early. Agree often.

Appendix: The Texaco-Getty-Pennzoil Case

The Handshake That Reshaped American Business Law

Readers may recall the story from the Introduction. The work my team led from 1989 to 1991 on the New Texaco rebuilt a firm that the Texaco-Getty-Pennzoil battle had nearly destroyed. The case itself, told here in fuller detail, is the deal whose failure taught me everything this book argues. It is, in a real sense, the case that triggered the book.

The fight among Texaco, Getty Oil, and Pennzoil ranks among the hardest corporate takeover battles in American history. At its center sat Getty Oil, the firm that billionaire J. Paul Getty built into one of the largest independent oil producers in the United States. Getty died in 1976. Control fractured. Family interests and the J. Paul Getty Museum trust each held a piece, and no single hand held the whole. By 1983, the firm carried deep strategic value, owing to petroleum reserves that included a stake in the Neutral Zone between Saudi Arabia and Kuwait. Pennzoil, a Houston oil firm run by chairman J. Hugh Liedtke, saw a chance to vault into the top rank of global energy. The path ran straight through Getty Oil.

On December 28, 1983, Pennzoil opened talks to buy Getty Oil at roughly $100 per share. The negotiations moved to New York's Plaza Hotel and ran hot. On January 3, 1984, the two sides reached what Pennzoil took to be a binding agreement, a transaction valued at nearly $112.50 per share, set forth in a signed memorandum of terms. Some merger documents remained unfinished. Pennzoil believed the deal was done. Getty's advisors thought otherwise, and they kept shopping the firm. Within days, Texaco's Chairman and CEO, John McKinley, stepped in with a richer offer, climbing toward $128 per share. Getty took it. The Texaco transaction came to roughly $10.1 billion, one of the largest acquisitions the country had seen.

Pennzoil sued. The suit landed in Texas state court, and the charge was blunt: Texaco had knowingly wrecked an existing contract between Pennzoil and Getty Oil. Lawyers call this tortious interference (the act of inducing one party to break a binding agreement with another). The case, *Pennzoil Co. v. Texaco Inc.*, turned on a question every dealmaker should sit with. When does a handshake become a contract? Texaco argued that no real contract existed because the parties had never executed the final acquisition papers. Pennzoil pointed to the signed memorandum and the public announcements, and it held that both sides had shown clear intent to close. The trial opened in Houston in July 1985. It drew a crowd: executives, attorneys, investment bankers, and legal scholars, all of them watching.

On November 19, 1985, the jury sided with Pennzoil without hesitation. The jury ordered Texaco to pay about $7.53 billion in compensatory damages and another $3 billion in punitive damages. The total cleared $10.5 billion. With interest running, the exposure passed $11 billion. No civil jury in American history had returned a number that large.

Then came the squeeze. Texas law required Texaco to post a bond for the full judgment before it could appeal. Texaco could not raise the money. No bond, no appeal. On April 12, 1987, the firm filed for Chapter 11 bankruptcy protection. Wall Street reeled. Texaco had stood for decades as one of the largest and most established oil firms on earth, and now it sat in bankruptcy court.

The fight ended in December 1987. Texaco, then led by Jim Kinnear, a new CEO, negotiated to pay Pennzoil $3 billion in cash, a sum far below the jury's number yet still among the largest legal settlements any firm had ever paid. Getty Oil vanished as an independent firm, swallowed up by Texaco. Texaco never truly recovered, neither in its balance sheet nor in its name. In 2001, Chevron acquired it, and the merged firm briefly carried the ChevronTexaco banner before returning to Chevron alone. Pennzoil drifted toward automotive lubricants and service work, and in 2002, it folded into Shell's U.S. operations.

The case still anchors American corporate law, and the reason is plain. A handshake can bind. When the parties' conduct shows clear intent, an informal agreement can carry the weight of a signed contract, even if the paperwork is unfinished. The verdict changed how dealmakers behave. It put a premium on precise documentation, on fiduciary duty (the legal obligation to act in another party's best interest), and on the cold arithmetic of legal risk. Business schools and law schools still teach the case, not as a triumph but as a warning. The contest for control of one firm can become a catastrophe for everyone who touches it. How much would Texaco have saved by treating that handshake as the contract it turned out to be? A different set of actions would have ensued with different consequences.

Notes

The notes below provide sources for specific facts, figures, and named references cited in the text, organized by chapter. They are not a comprehensive bibliography.

Introduction

Figures for global acquisition deal volume are drawn from Dealogic (2025); see Figure Credits for the specific attribution. The estimate of value lost to failed integrations reflects the author's analysis of the failure-rate literature discussed in the note to the Conclusion.

Chapter 2: Deal Thesis Decomposition / Chapter 6: Acquisition End-State Vision

The figure that 60% to 70% of acquisitions fail to deliver anticipated value is one of the most cited in the M&A literature and draws on a consistent body of research spanning several decades. Among the most frequently referenced studies are McKinsey & Company, "Where Mergers Go Wrong," *McKinsey Quarterly*, 2004; KPMG, "Unlocking Shareholder Value: The Keys to Success," 1999; and Mercer Management Consulting, "How Acquirers Fare Post-Merger: Analysis of 1990s Deals," 2003.

The figure in Chapter 6 attributing 70% of acquisition failures to execution issues rather than strategic flaws reflects the same body of research, with particular weight given to the McKinsey analysis. Because these studies span a range of methodologies, time periods, and deal populations, readers should treat the figure as a durable order-of-magnitude finding rather than a single precise measurement. More recent analyses, including work by Bain & Company and the Boston Consulting Group, confirm the range while extending the dataset into the post-2010 period.

Chapter 3: Strategic Distortions

The framework of cognitive distortions that underlies this chapter originates with David D. Burns, M.D., *Feeling Good: The New Mood Therapy* (New York: William Morrow, 1980; revised edition, New York: Avon Books, 1999). Burns identified systematic errors in thinking, including all-or-nothing thinking, overgeneralization, and catastrophizing, as primary drivers of depression and anxiety. His framework, rooted in cognitive behavioral therapy and the earlier work of Aaron T. Beck, has shaped clinical psychology and psychiatry for four decades.

The nine strategic distortions presented here were developed by the author beginning in 2007 by mapping Burns's clinical taxonomy onto business strategy contexts; the distortions are not Burns's own and should not be attributed to him.

The executive case examples in the Business Mindfulness Practices section draw on published sources for three of the eight leaders cited. Andy Grove's account of Intel's exit from memory chips and pivot to microprocessors is drawn from Andy Grove, *Only the Paranoid Survive: How to Exploit the Crisis Points That Challenge Every Business* (New York: Currency Doubleday, 1996). The account of Bill Campbell's advisory role and the estimate of value creation attributed to his coaching are drawn from Eric Schmidt, Jonathan Rosenberg, and Alan Eagle, *Trillion Dollar Coach: The Leadership Playbook of Silicon Valley's Bill Campbell* (New York: Harper Business, 2019). Ray Dalio's codification of decision-making principles at Bridgewater Associates is drawn from Ray Dalio, *Principles: Life and Work* (New York: Simon & Schuster, 2017).

Chapter 7: Adoption of Better Practices

The discussion of Toyota's production philosophy draws on the same sources detailed in the note to Chapter 12.

Chapter 8: The Organization Heat Map

The Global Industrial Acquisition case example is a composite drawn from the author's consulting engagements over four decades. Specific details, including company identity, geography, and financial figures, have been altered to preserve client confidentiality.

Chapter 11: Designing the Human-Machine Deal Team

The framing of a deal team as a control system draws on the standard vocabulary of control system engineering (setpoint, error signal, controller, feedback loop). Figures cited for the pace of artificial-intelligence adoption among dealmakers reflect industry surveys current at the time of writing; given how quickly adoption is changing, readers should treat specific percentages as indicative rather than fixed and consult the most recent surveys from the major advisory firms for current figures.

Chapter 12: The Process: Agree Early, Agree Often

On running the rooms where alignment is forged: Bob Frisch, *Who's in the Room? How Great Leaders Structure and Manage the Teams Around Them* (Hoboken, NJ: John Wiley & Sons, 2012); and Bob Frisch and Logan Chandler, "Off-Sites That Work," *Harvard Business Review*, June 2006. Frisch is the managing partner of the Strategic Offsites Group.

On the factory-floor lineage of agreeing early: the principle of jidoka ("automation with a human touch"), one of the two pillars of the Toyota Production System, originated with Sakichi Toyoda's automatic loom, which stopped itself the instant a thread broke. The Type G Automatic Loom dates to 1924. The principle was later generalized into a manufacturing methodology by Taiichi Ohno; see Taiichi Ohno, Toyota Production System: Beyond Large-Scale Production (Cambridge, MA: Productivity Press, 1988). The related cost-of-quality heuristic, that a defect costs roughly one unit to prevent, ten to correct in production, and a hundred to fix after it reaches the customer, is a widely used rule of thumb in quality management and is offered here as an illustration rather than as a precise empirical measure.

Conclusion

On acquisition failure rates: estimates vary widely with the definition of failure and the period studied. The figure that roughly sixty-five percent of major strategic acquisitions have been failures is associated with the work of Mark Sirower of Deloitte's M&A practice; see Mark L. Sirower, *The Synergy Trap: How Companies Lose the Acquisition Game* (New York: Free Press, 1997), and Mark L. Sirower and Jeffrey M. Weirens, *The Synergy Solution: How Companies Win the Mergers and Acquisitions Game* (Boston: Harvard Business Review Press, 2022). More recent data in the latter work indicates that roughly fifty-six percent of deals from 2012 to 2018 failed to achieve positive returns, and the authors caution against the commonly repeated but unsupported claim that seventy to ninety percent of deals fail.

Appendix: The Texaco-Getty-Pennzoil Case

On the Texaco-Getty-Pennzoil case: Steve Coll, *The Taking of Getty Oil: The Full Story of the Most Spectacular and Catastrophic Takeover of All Time* (New York: Penguin Books, 2008); *Pennzoil Co. v. Texaco Inc.*, 729 S.W.2d 768 (Tex. App. 1987). The narrative also draws on contemporaneous coverage of the 1985 verdict and the 1987 settlement in the *Los Angeles Times* and the *Washington Post*, as well as the Encyclopedia *Britannica* entry for the Pennzoil Company.

A Note on Process and Authorship

I wrote this book using the human-machine architecture described in Chapter 11 and shown in Figure 11.2. The human side of the loop, me, supplied the higher-order cognitive creativity, the frameworks, the four decades of consulting experience, the judgments about which stories to tell, the narrative arcs, the structural decisions, the voice rules, the style guide, the prose, and the editorial direction. On the machine side, Anthropic's Claude assisted with research, copyediting, and formatting across multiple sessions. Every chapter cycled through human evaluation before the next iteration moved forward.

A note on the cases as well. Except where firms are named, the cases in this book are either anonymous clients or composites drawn from recurring patterns that emerged from more than two hundred engagements, with identifying details altered to protect confidentiality.

Acknowledgements

A book about alignment is, by its nature, the product of many alignments. This one is no exception.

The frameworks in these pages were built in the field, not the halls of academia. They exist because hundreds of executives trusted me with their most consequential decisions. I owe a debt to every client over more than forty years of practice who was willing to ask the hard questions about their firms' transformations and acquisitions. Their willingness to do the difficult work of alignment, even when it was uncomfortable and slowed things down, is the proof of concept behind every chapter in this book.

I thank the readers who gave time and attention to earlier versions of this book. I am grateful to (in alphabetical order) Jack Chacko, former Vice President of Mergers & Acquisitions at Cisco Systems; Rob Foster, Professor at De Anza College (Cupertino, California); Jim Jeffries, Founder and CEO at the M&A Leadership Council; Saroj Koul, Ph.D., Professor at Jindal Global Business School (India); and Jack Prouty, President Emeritus at the M&A Leadership Council for their thoughtful feedback and care with the work.

The holistic framework at the center of my work stands on the shoulders of the United Research Company (URC circa 1988, the kernel of today's CapGemini), whose approach to business transformation I had the privilege of helping shape firsthand in the late 20th century. The discipline of treating strategy, process, people, systems, and change management as an integrated whole has shaped every engagement I have led since. I acknowledge my colleagues at URC for the experiences we shared in making a difference in our clients' businesses.

Further Reading

The books and articles below shaped the thinking behind this work. They are not the complete reading list of a forty-year career. They are the works I point to a CEO who wants to go more deeply into the questions this book raises.

On Alignment and the Rooms Where Decisions Get Made

Bob Frisch, *Who's in the Room? How Great Leaders Structure and Manage the Teams Around Them* (Hoboken, NJ: John Wiley & Sons, 2012). The single best treatment of the senior leadership team as a working institution rather than an org-chart artifact. Frisch makes the case that the team in the room is not the team on the chart, and that designing the actual decision-making group is one of the highest-leverage moves a CEO can make. Read it before any acquisition where alignment will matter, which is every acquisition.

Patrick M. Lencioni, *The Five Dysfunctions of a Team: A Leadership Fable* (San Francisco: Jossey-Bass, 2002). A short fable about why otherwise capable teams fail to commit. The diagnosis that the absence of trust at the bottom of the pyramid prevents commitment at the top explains much about why deal teams agree publicly and disagree privately.

On Acquisitions and Synergy

Mark L. Sirower and Jeffrey M. Weirens, *The Synergy Solution: How Companies Win the Mergers and Acquisitions Game* (Boston: Harvard Business Review Press, 2022). The most current rigorous treatment of acquisition performance. Sirower and Weirens carefully distinguish between deals that fail because the thesis was wrong and those that fail because the execution was wrong. They make the case that the latter is more common than the literature suggests. Their data discipline is also a model for how to argue honestly about failure rates.

Mark L. Sirower, *The Synergy Trap: How Companies Lose the Acquisition Game* (New York: Free Press, 1997). The foundational work behind the 2022 book is still the clearest statement of why most acquisitions destroy value. Sirower's central insight, that the acquisition premium is a hurdle the synergy must clear before any value is created for the buyer, is the discipline most deal teams skip.

On the Operating Disciplines That Shape Integration

Taiichi Ohno, *Toyota Production System: Beyond Large-Scale Production* (Cambridge, MA: Productivity Press, 1988). The originating text of the Toyota Production System, by the engineer who built it. Ohno's principles of jidoka and just-in-time production are usually read as manufacturing doctrines, but they are equally a doctrine for surfacing problems early and responding to them quickly. That is the same problem an acquisition team faces.

W. Edwards Deming, *Out of the Crisis* (Cambridge, MA: MIT Press, 1986). Deming's quality philosophy is the intellectual ancestor of most of what we now call operational excellence. His insistence that quality is built into the system, rather than inspected at the end, has direct implications for how integration teams should design feedback loops, rather than rely on heroic recovery.

On the Human-Machine Collaboration

Ethan Mollick, *Co-Intelligence: Living and Working with AI* (New York: Portfolio, 2024). The most useful single-volume introduction to working alongside large language models as a professional. Mollick treats the technology as a colleague with specific strengths and failure modes, a framing that Chapter 11 of this book extends to the deal team.

Erik Brynjolfsson and Andrew McAfee, *The Second Machine Age: Work, Progress, and Prosperity in a Time of Brilliant Technologies* (New York: W. W. Norton, 2014). Written before the current generation of generative AI, but still the clearest framing of why machine capability and human judgment are complements rather than substitutes. The book sets the stage for the human-machine deal team described in Chapter 11.

Figure Credits

Figure	Credit
Figure I.1	*Copilot* prompt: Find an image of the ancient Indian parable of the six blind men and the elephant. (2025)
Figure I.2	Data source: Dealogic (2025); image rendered by Rowland Chen (2025)
Figure I.3	Rowland Chen (2025)
Figure I.4	Rowland Chen (2015)
Figure 1.1	*OpenAI ChatGPT* prompt: Create a photorealistic image of two executives agreeing, one male, one female, one person of color. (2026)
Figure 1.2	Inspired by the United Research Company (c.1988); image rendered by Rowland Chen (2002)
Figure 1.3	Rowland Chen (2025)
Figure 2.1	*OpenAI ChatGPT* prompt: Create a photorealistic image of Deal Thesis Decomposition. (2026)
Figure 2.2	Rowland Chen (2010)
Figure 2.3	Rowland Chen (2015)
Figure 2.4	Rowland Chen (2017)
Figure 2.5	Rowland Chen (2017)
Figure 2.6	Rowland Chen (2018)
Figure 3.1	Rowland Chen (2026)
Figure 3.2	Rowland Chen (2016)
Figure 3.3	Rowland Chen (2022)
Figure 3.4	Rowland Chen (2022)
Figure 4.1	*OpenAI ChatGPT* prompt: Create a photorealistic image of a square peg in a round hole. (2026)
Figure 4.2	Rowland Chen (2005)
Figure 5.1	*OpenAI ChatGPT* prompt: Create a photorealistic image of a stopwatch. (2026)
Figure 5.2	Rowland Chen (2021)
Figure 5.3	Rowland Chen (2021)
Figure 5.4	Rowland Chen (2021)
Figure 5.5	Rowland Chen (2021)
Figure 6.1	Photo taken by Rowland Chen at Watkins Glen, New York (1974)
Figure 6.2	Rowland Chen (2007)
Figure 6.3	Rowland Chen (2007)
Figure 7.1	*OpenAI ChatGPT* prompt: Create a photorealistic image of two people arm wrestling. (2026)
Figure 7.2	Rowland Chen (2014)
Figure 8.1	*OpenAI ChatGPT* prompt: Create a photorealistic image of a coder sweating. (2026)
Figure 8.2	Rowland Chen (2012)

Figure 9.1	*OpenAI ChatGPT* prompt: Create a photorealistic image of a person with a tailor-made suit. (2026)
Figure 9.2	Rowland Chen (1998)
Figure 9.3	Rowland Chen (2007)
Figure 9.4	Rowland Chen (2018)
Figure 10.1	Inspired by Cisco Systems' acquisition integration playbook rendered by Rowland Chen (2018)
Figure 11.1	Rowland Chen (2025)
Figure 11.2	Rowland Chen (2026)
Figure 12.1	Illustration by John Tenniel, from *Alice's Adventures in Wonderland* (1865); public domain.

About the Author

Rowland Chen is the Founder of Framework Foundry. He builds thinking tools and competitive weapons for CEOs facing high-stakes strategic decisions. His career spans more than forty years, including roles at General Electric, Cisco Systems, and Yahoo!, and more than two hundred fifty consulting engagements with clients ranging from Global 1000 enterprises to solo-preneurs. His focus throughout has been mergers and acquisitions and business transformations that accelerate growth. Chen's work has appeared in Management Review Quarterly, the New York Times, the Boston Globe, and the proceedings of the 20th International Conference on Computational Creativity. He holds an MBA from the MIT Sloan School of Management. He was a Visiting Scientist at Carnegie Mellon University's School of Computer Science and currently teaches business and innovation at De Anza College in Cupertino, California. Based in Silicon Valley, he is a former Ironman triathlete and a practicing artist.

Learn more at www.frameworkfoundry.ai.

www.ingramcontent.com/pod-product-compliance
Lightning Source LLC
LaVergne TN
LVHW050811061126
851857LV00012B/758
* 9 7 9 8 9 9 6 8 1 6 2 0 0 *